BRITISH RAIL CLASS 60 LOCOMOTIVES

As part of the 125th anniversary celebrations held on 3 August 2014, 60001 *Steadfast* (originally named *Stedfast*) stands at its 'birthplace' at Brush Traction. A splendid 10¼in-gauge working model of 60001 stands alongside.

EDWARD GLEED

BRITISH RAIL CLASS 60 LOCOMOTIVES

EDWARD GLEED

THE CROWOOD PRESS

First published in 2016 by
The Crowood Press Ltd
Ramsbury, Marlborough
Wiltshire SN8 2HR

www.crowood.com

British Library Cataloguing-in-Publication Data
A catalogue record for this book is available from the British Library.

ISBN 978 1 78500 149 9

Typeset by Servis Filmsetting Ltd, Stockport, Cheshire

Printed and bound in Malaysia by Times Offset (M) Sdn Bhd

CONTENTS

DEDICATION   6

ACKNOWLEDGEMENTS   7

PREFACE   8

INTRODUCTION   10

CHAPTER 1   TENDERING AND CONTRACT   15

CHAPTER 2   CONSTRUCTION AND DELIVERY   27

CHAPTER 3   TECHNICAL DETAIL   51

CHAPTER 4   AREAS OF OPERATION OF THE CLASS 60   79

CHAPTER 5   LIVERIES, NUMBERS AND NAMES   112

CHAPTER 6   THE CLASS 60 REFURBISHMENT PROGRAMME   156

CHAPTER 7   THE COLAS CLASS 60s   168

APPENDIX: COMPONENTS, EQUIPMENT AND TOPS SCHEDULES   178

REFERENCES   190

FURTHER READING   190

ENGINEERING CONSULTANTS – TENDERING AND CONTRACT   190

INDEX   191

DEDICATION

For my Dad.

The peace and tranquillity of the countryside is momentarily shattered as DBS Class 60 No. 60092 thunders through Wollaston atop 6B13 Robeston–Westerleigh on a very hot 5 July 2013. EDWARD GLEED

ACKNOWLEDGEMENTS

Over the years the Class 60s have been much maligned, perhaps due to erroneous or misinterpreted information, and I hope this book will redress the balance. The rail industry now has a class of locomotives that is more than fit for purpose, and to quote a phrase from one of the British Rail Class 60 publicity videos, 'The power to move mountains' is certainly one that has resonance.

British Rail Class 60 Locomotives has taken a number of years to complete. It has been a very fulfilling project, but it would not have been possible without the valuable assistance of many individuals, family members, friends and organizations, to all of whom I owe a huge debt of gratitude. I would like to commence by thanking most sincerely all those who have contributed to this book in any way, either by their own personal stories and recollections of the Class 60, or through their provision of photographic material. The main contributors are listed below; I apologize for those I have left out, but it would be impossible to name every individual. These include the following:

Richard Tuplin, editor at the *Railway Herald* for disseminating my initial request for photographic images, for his advice, and for proofreading various chapters.

John Stretton, for his advice and for sharing his vast collection of Class 60 photographs, especially during the construction of the Class 60; also for enabling me to contact individuals retired from Brush Traction, and individuals working in various train operating companies.

Former employees of Brush Traction (a part of the Wabtec Rail Group) for their valuable assistance regarding the construction, manufacturing process and history of the Class 60.

Paul Johnson at the National Archive at Kew for granting permission to reproduce historical information surrounding the Class 60s.

I would also like to extend my sincere gratitude to the many individuals within the following companies:

DB Schenker Rail UK for supplying photographic material.

Colas Rail UK for supplying details of the 'Super 60' refurbishment programme, and for photographic material for use in this book.

Network Rail Infrastructure Ltd, for granting permission to reproduce TOPS material in this book.

Special thanks are also due to the signalling staff at Bristol Area Signalling Centre, for their endless assistance in indicating the whereabouts of the Class 60 fleet.

Leighton Prado for his dedication in offering advice for this book.

Last, but most importantly, I owe a huge debt of gratitude to my family, especially to my wife Sharon and my children Charlotte and Lauren, for their endless support, patience and understanding, and for maintaining family life at home when I was away obtaining material for this book, as well as countless hours of proofreading.

PREFACE

My interest in railways started from a very young age. I was born in Shropshire in the market town of Ludlow, which lies 28 miles (45km) south of Shrewsbury and 24 miles (38km) north of the city of Hereford, both of which are quite important railway centres. Ludlow is situated approximately midway along the Cardiff–Crewe main line, which today is very busy with both passenger services and a myriad of freight workings; these on occasions are served by Class 60s, notably 6M76 Margam–Dee Marsh and return working 6V75 Dee Marsh–Margam. This particular diagram conveys steel products.

It was most fortunate that my parents purchased a bungalow with a beautiful garden, behind which the Cardiff–Crewe main line runs, affording an almost 'grandstand' view of the railway. However, my sister and I were strictly forbidden to go over the boundary fence, or to cross the railway near our home using what is still known today as the '49 Steps Crossing', steeply graded steps leading up from the road on to the foot crossing. At the top of the steps it is virtually impossible to see trains coming up from Hereford, and users of the crossing have very little warning at all of any oncoming trains: when drivers sound their warning horn at the pre-set distance, the train is at the crossing within a matter of seconds. Trains coming from the Shrewsbury direction are not a great deal easier to see, either.

At the age of six I had my first electric train set, given to me by my parents as a Christmas present. I still own that beloved GWR 'Pannier' tank locomotive with two Great Western Mk1 chocolate and cream coaches, although alas the oval track has long gone; but this gift represented a pivotal moment in my interest in model railways. Then at the age of nine, I started what many schoolboys did at that time – trainspotting! There was much to see in those days on that line; the Class 33s were drafted in to replace the ailing Class 25s on the Cardiff–Crewe passenger services, as the 25s were not powerful enough to make up lost time in the event of delay. Class 37s, 40s, 45s and 47s reigned supreme on freight services, and these services were quite frequent; indeed in the summer months I would peer out of my bedroom window at bedtime to see the northbound Severn Tunnel Junction–Mossend (Glasgow) Freightliner service pass by. This train was usually headed by a Class 47, and on one occasion I remember No. 47 484 *Isambard Kingdom Brunel* hauling this working. Ironically this name would also be affixed to No. 60 081, described in Chapter 5. Single Class 117 postal DMUs could be seen in the early

DB Schenker Rail UK's 60100 passing through the station of my birthplace of Ludlow whilst working 6V75, 09:30 Dee Marsh–Margam steel on 29 September 2014. EDWARD GLEED

morning, and even the occasional Class 31 could put in an appearance.

My father was born in Bristol, and following his retirement, we returned there in the summer of 1983 when my interest in railways intensified. My secondary school was ideally situated to sustain my interest in railways, as it was in viewing distance of the main line from Bristol Temple Meads to Exeter. I was always interested in seeing which locomotive was hauling the lunchtime departure to Manchester Piccadilly, and more often than not it was a Class 50. I would also go on cycle rides with my friends to Winterbourne, Coalpit Heath, Bristol Parkway, and on occasions Bristol Temple Meads, which enabled me to see Classes 50 and 56, locomotives I had only seen in my railway books and magazines when I was living in Ludlow. HSTs (High Speed Trains) were never seen in the Ludlow area, though they continue to depart from Bristol St Philips Marsh HST depot and run empty stock to Hereford to form one of the Hereford–Paddington services. My first sighting of a HST was at Bristol Temple Meads, which was a truly momentous occasion.

My father, to whom I owe a huge debt of gratitude, wanted me to consider a career in the electronics industry, in which he had been involved for many years. However, my interest in electronics related solely to my model railway, and I decided to follow a career in the railway industry, something which suited me perfectly, having had a passion for trains from such a young age – and to this day I have never looked back.

My interest in trains not only encompasses my working career, it is also a major component of my hobbies. I have spent forty years honing my skills, creating my own railway layouts and also contributing to the creation of several layouts for a model railway club, which I regularly attend. All of these in some way replicate the first model railway I saw when I was just five years of age, albeit with the advantages of modern technology in the form of 'Digital Command Control', or DCC.

Alongside my railway modelling I have a strong interest in railway photography, taking every possible opportunity to photograph workings in various destinations around the United Kingdom. Some of my photographic work has been published in the acclaimed *Railway Herald* online magazine and other railway publications.

It has given me great pleasure to have been given the opportunity to write this book, and I hope that readers will enjoy reading it as much as I have enjoyed writing it.

A Note on the Images

A brief note should be made regarding the photographic images used in this book, which are based on my personal beliefs and not necessarily on those of others. Selecting the photographic material for this book has given me enormous pleasure, but although I have attempted to include as many locations as I can where the Class 60s have operated in the UK, it is impossible to include their every location and working.

Personally I am not a devotee of 'photographic manipulation'. Under certain circumstances I will enhance a particular shot to balance the lighting in relation to what the eye naturally sees. In particular this is more apparent where there are deep shadows, or in extreme cases where the shot is rare or never to be repeated and will be recording the event for posterity or historical value. I also firmly believe that one can only work with the moment that has been captured by the camera at any particular point in time; after all, photography is all about painting with light, and what is deemed right for one person is not necessarily right for another. Photography is very personal, and to some, manipulation under the right circumstances can be very creative and artistic.

Every effort has been made to credit the images used in this book to the copyright holder. Photographic images taken by myself will have been credited as 'Edward Gleed'.

In order to give a detailed and accurate account of the Class 60, much of the information has been sourced from the National Archives at Kew in West London. Certain parts of this book, notably Chapter 1, have utilized information that has hitherto not been made available for public viewing. Certain documents have been granted scrutiny under the 'Freedom of Information' request, although some information that might have been included in this book remains closed for access.

It should be understood that in places relating to current maintenance and overhaul work, especially regarding the 'Super 60' programme, it has not been possible to provide a detailed account of all the work being undertaken, as the majority of this information is deemed to be commercially sensitive and the companies involved have therefore declined to release some details of the project.

Edward Gleed
Bristol, July 2015

INTRODUCTION

The era of steam locomotives on Britain's main-line network spanned more than 120 years. During the 1950s, when the focus of attention was concentrated on how spiralling costs could be arrested, the railway network was made more cost effective, heralding the end of steam traction. The railways were a labour-intensive organization: the rising wages bill and the increasing cost of coal, in addition to the running costs and the amount of time it took to prepare, service, dispose of and maintain steam locomotives, resulted in major change within the railway industry. Steam traction was systematically reduced on the main lines across Britain during the 1960s, with the final workings coming to an end in the North West in August 1968 – although a number of steam locomotives continued to operate within industrial sites such as collieries well into the 1970s.

Before the general demise, British Railways commissioned locomotive manufacturers to produce a small number of diesel locomotives for evaluation, which would be suitable for handling main-line traffic. The first of these to appear under the British Railways modernization plan of 1955 was the English Electric Type 1 design in 1957, the pioneer being numbered D8000. It was the intention that these pilot-scheme locomotives would be fully assessed before any full-scale contracts were placed. However, some production orders were placed for locomotives that were deemed most suitable for the intended traffic flows, and in a number of cases, contracts were signed before a number of teething troubles had been discovered. Furthermore, second-generation locomotives appeared from 1962 onwards, resulting in a vast array of traction available to the railway industry by the end of steam traction.

With the exception of shunting locomotives, the traction was, and still is, ranked in 'Type' order ranging from one to five. The most powerful locomotives are ranked as Type 5, which today covers Classes 56, 57, 58, 59, 60, 66, 67, 68 and 70. Type 1s were the least powerful, being allocated to Classes 14, 15, 16, 17 and 20.

The Class 47s

Until the late 1970s, the ubiquitous Brush-designed Type 4 Class 47 diesel electric locomotive was employed on many of the long-distance passenger and freight trains across the country, earning itself the title 'jack of all trades, master of none' by many enthusiasts. In their defence, however, these locomotives were hugely versatile machines, which were, in many cases, rostered to work the heaviest of freight trains during the 1970s and 1980s. Being mixed-traffic locomotives they could never be expected to fulfil all demands at the extreme ends of the spectrum. From their earliest days of operation, they were most suited to operate lengthy Freightliner services on flows such as Thamesport (London)–Ditton (Liverpool) and Severn Tunnel Junction–Mossend (Glasgow), as well as many others. This was due to the fact that container trains, now familiarly known as intermodal services, could be timed to operate at 75mph (120km/h), and considering that the Class 47s could attain a top speed of 95mph (153km/h) this was well within their capabilities.

The Class 47s were constructed in significant numbers, with a total of 512 examples being built. In addition to containerized traffic, they could also be seen hauling the heavy oil trains such as those between Stanlow, near Ellesmere Port, and Jarrow in the North East. Indeed, this particular diagram was so heavy that pairs of 47s were used. However, operating the class in pairs was problematic to British Rail as they were not equipped for multiple working, which

A 'classic' view of Bristol Temple Meads is obtained as Colas Class 56, No. 56302, works 6V54 Chirk–Teigngrace timber on a beautiful 10 September 2014. EDWARD GLEED

required both 47s to be manned and was therefore a costly exercise.

However, during the mid-1980s, many of these locomotives were often relegated to more mundane duties such as engineering trains and trip workings, where short freight moves between marshalling yards involved depositing wagons en route. Their role as passenger locomotives on principal routes to and from the capital was reduced as a result of the introduction of the HSTs, which assumed express passenger duties, specifically on the East Coast and Great Western main lines, as well as some cross-country routes. As the HSTs were gradually introduced to high-speed diagrams, Classes 45, 46 and 50 were relegated to freight and engineering duties, or displaced to other routes.

The 47s were employed on MGR ('merry-go-round') trains utilizing the 32-tonne, HAA hopper wagons during their early years, with the introduction of a method of working that revolutionized the way coal trains were being operated. Loading characteristically took place from large overhead bunkers, with the train moving slowly beneath them. When the coal was being unloaded at the power station, the train was hauled at a slow and steady speed, normally around 3mph (5km/h), through the unloading hopper whilst the wagons were discharged. The entire operation was totally automated through the use of line-side apparatus known as 'daleks'. A number of 47s assigned to these diagrams were equipped with SSF ('sensor speed-fitted') equipment, which enabled the driver to control the movement at a precise speed. This operation instantly speeded up services, made more efficient use of both locomotives and wagons and substantially reduced operating costs.

Throughout this post-steam period, British Railways – and later the rebranded British Rail (BR) – had moved the concept of wagonload traffic away from the local station pick-up freight to one that concentrated more on the needs of industry. Marketed as 'Speedlink', the idea allowed businesses and industry to send products from their own premises or regional freight centres. Despite this, lower road-haulage costs led to an almost continual decline in wagonload traffic that would continue towards the end of the twentieth century, and result in its total cessation.

The Class 56s

During the 1980s, BR began to form itself into business units, or sectors, with each having charge of, among other things, locomotives, depots and staff. The underlying pressure for sectorization was political, applied by the government to encourage a more modern business-like approach to operating BR. During the early 1980s, BR felt there was a requirement for a more powerful freight locomotive. Authorization was given by the government to commence the tendering process for the construction of a more powerful Type 5 locomotive: this was to become known as the Class 56. Owing to time constraints, the end result was that this new design had a similar body shape to the Class 47, both having a monocoque construction. However, other associated equipment, such as the engine and generator, was very different.

The Class 56s were designed by Brush, and the first thirty machines were constructed by Electroputere of Craiova in Romania; construction of the remainder was divided between Crewe and Doncaster Works. However, once the locomotives built in Romania had arrived on UK shores, it was clear that all was not well with the quality of their construction. Issues surrounding wiring and incorrectly machined axles were soon brought to BR's attention, and the financial expense of rectifying the defects would almost certainly have been a costly process.

The Class 58s

To cope with further demand from the coal industry, BR sought approval for another further improved Type 5 freight locomotive. This new locomotive, to be known as the Class 58, was a very different machine from what had

A fine study of Seco Rail-liveried 58009 is seen at Toton Depot. Note the design of the bogie, which is similar to that in use on the Class 60. JOHN STRETTON

The first Class 59, No. 59001 *Yeoman Endeavour*, passes Fairwood Junction atop one of the many stone trains that emanate from the Whatley and Merehead quarries on the 4 August 2011. EDWARD GLEED

been operated by BR before. Efficiency was one of the key requirements, and furthermore, the Class 58 looked very different.

Following on from most of the older BR machines – with the exception of shunting locomotives and Type 1 locomotives, including the Class 20s – two cabs were provided. The main difference was the body shape, which was much narrower, thereby allowing maintenance staff to access parts of the engine via the solebar created by the narrow body. This in turn allowed a more efficient maintenance regime. Gone was the monocoque body, replaced by a return to bedplate construction. A new style of bogie with separately exited traction motors ('Sepex') was employed: it had been trialled on a member of the Class 56 fleet, 56042, with a positive response. The Class 58s were given the nickname 'Bones' by some rail enthusiasts due to their overall shape as viewed from above, this consisting of a full-width cab on each end of a narrow body.

With vast tonnages of aggregate being processed at the Mendip quarries, the customer required BR to run longer trains. Trains conveying aggregate could gross 4,000 tonnes, which was well beyond the limits of the 47s, although Class 56s would have no doubt been suitable; but 'pairs' of locomotives would have been needed, which would have been very costly – not due to manning levels, as the 56s were TDM fitted, but because of the cost of fuel and additional maintenance.

The Class 59s

By the mid-1980s, Foster Yeoman had become very discontented with the repeated poor performance of the Type

5 locomotives that BR had supplied to work the heavy aggregate trains from the Somerset quarries of Whatley and Merehead. However, they were impressed with the American shunting locomotives operating at their Merehead quarry, so they turned to the USA to provide main-line freight locomotives for their privately owned trains. In 1986, the first of what was to be known as the Class 59 touched down on UK shores.

The Class 59s were built by General Motors' Electro-Motive Division in the USA, and were based on the company's popular SD40-2 design, used extensively by US railroads – but here was yet another locomotive that was significantly different from other types of main-line traction in Britain. Although BR did not own the Class 59s, the locomotives were driven by BR drivers, and their use on the Mendip stone traffic was a huge success. Indeed one of them holds the European haulage record for a single locomotive, successfully moving a 5,415ft (1,650m) long train conveying 11,982 tonnes of aggregate in May 1991. In daily service the trains, which employed Foster Yeoman's own wagon fleet, were shorter and lighter, but regularly grossed 4,700 tonnes. The 59s were very successful, and their haulage capacity was far superior to that of the 56s and 58s.

It is worth noting that the success of the Class 59s was a factor in the development of the Class 66 fleet of locomotives. By the mid-1990s, the three privatized Trainload Freight companies – Loadhaul, Mainline Freight and Transrail Freight (which had been purchased by Wisconsin Central Transportation System) – had been merged and rebranded as English, Welsh and Scottish Railway (EW&S). With a fleet of ageing and uneconomic locomotives, the American company turned to GM for an updated Class 59, using a similar bodyshell and its JT42CWR engine.

EWS-liveried Class 66/0, No. 66055, rumbles through Bristol Temple Meads on a short engineers' working on 12 May 2012. EDWARD GLEED

The iron ore tippler house at Llanwern is the location for Corus-liveried 60006 *Scunthorpe Ironmaster*, at the helm of one of the many Port Talbot–Llanwern steel trains. December 2001. LEIGHTON PRADO

The outcome was an order from EW&S for 250 Class 66s Type 5 heavy-freight locomotives, and their design has subsequently become the mainstay of heavy freight motive power in the UK, with examples having been purchased by Direct Rail Services, Freightliner (for both its Heavy Haul and Intermodal divisions) and GB Railfreight. Subsequent changes in leasing have also resulted in the type now being used by Colas Rail.

The 59s were equipped with a two-stroke diesel engine, which has proved to be highly reliable in operation. The number of Class 59s in traffic totalled fifteen, with Foster Yeoman expanding its fleet to five, aggregate company ARC purchasing four and power generator National Power creating a fleet of six. The latter subsequently became part of EWS, and all now predominantly operate in the Westbury and West London areas on Mendip aggregate traffic. A downturn in the aggregate industry resulted in No. 59003 *Yeoman Highlander* being sold to Heavy Haul Power International and exported to Germany in the late 1990s. Recent negotiations have resulted in the locomotive returning to the UK in November 2014, and following extensive overhaul and modifications it entered revenue-earning traffic with GB Railfreight in mid-2015.

The Class 60s

During the mid-1980s, BR required another heavy freight locomotive, and having gained authorization from the Government, invited companies to tender. This locomotive would be constructed using lessons learned from the Classes 56 and 58. While six organizations were invited to tender, only three did so, the winner being Brush Electric Machines

(today, Brush Traction and part of the Wabtec Group) with a powerful 60mph (96km/h) Type 5 Co-Co design; this resulted in an order being placed for 100 locomotives.

With the technological advances that were available in the rail industry, the locomotives, designated Class 60, were a far more advanced product than the earlier Type 5 designs built by BR. Here was a locomotive that, at the planning stages, would afford superior haulage capacity and excellent fuel economy. The aim was to bring the new fleet more in line with the haulage capacity of the Foster Yeoman 59s than the BR-designed 56s and 58s. However, modern technology can also bring disadvantages, and the Class 60s experienced a multitude of technological problems, some of which related to cylinder-head blows and issues with the Deuta Health monitoring equipment, which constantly monitored the current state of the engine.

But with the technical problems sorted out, the Class 60s are widely regarded by drivers as the preferred choice to this day. These locomotives can develop phenomenal amounts of power, and in terms of capability for a single unit regarding performance and haulage ability, the Class 60s can afford superior traction with their 'creep control'. Despite all of this, however, the type are still second to the GM-built Class 59 in terms of horsepower. The latter-built Class 66 could not match the top-end performance or the creep control of the Class 60, which has a definite 'edge' over the Class 66 and almost certainly prevented the demise of the Class 60.

As will be described in Chapter 4, the Class 60s have been utilized on freight services across the UK, in many cases being reserved for the heaviest freight traffic where a single locomotive is required. Certain workings for the class, such as engineers' trains, require two locomotives, one at each

The first member of the Class 60 fleet passing through Barnetby atop 6T23 Immingham–Santon amidst a fine array of semaphore signals on 16 June 2014. EDWARD GLEED

end of the train, although this is more related to operating convenience than required tractive effort.

Over the years, the Class 60s have unfortunately been the subject of incorrect press reports. It was most unfortunate that from their earliest stages of construction, problem after problem arose. This culminated with BR almost cancelling the order from Brush Traction, a situation discussed in Chapter 2. Construction of the Class 60 commenced during 1989, but it was not until 1993 that all 100 members of the class had been accepted into traffic.

In the period that this book has been in preparation, DB Schenker Rail UK (the latest owner of what was English, Welsh & Scottish Railway) reduced the original 100-strong Class down to just a handful in service, although happily this situation has now improved, with over a quarter of the fleet currently in active service. In addition, twenty stored members of the DB Schenker Rail UK (DBS) fleet have

been sold to Colas Rail Freight, several of which have now progressed through the workshops at Toton for overhaul and have returned to traffic in the bright yellow and orange colour scheme of the latter company. DBS is also in the process of undertaking a 'life extension' programme on up to thirty-one members of the fleet, a move that is likely to support a further fifteen years' service for those members of the class. The project, which is labelled as the 'Super 60' programme, requires extensive work to all parts of the locomotive.

With a projected lifespan of forty years' service from new, and less than half the class currently in traffic, it seems a terrible waste of a fantastic piece of machinery that is fit for purpose in every respect. Thankfully, those selected for refurbishment should have a long future in supporting the rail freight industry, and enthusiasts will be able to enjoy them for years to come.

CHAPTER ONE

TENDERING AND CONTRACT

Why were the Class 60s required? During the 1980s, BR was faced with a major problem due to an upsurge in freight demand and heavier trainloads demanded by the customer. At that time the traction that BR could offer to haul the heavier demand was suffering from rising maintenance costs, and many locomotives had accrued twenty-five years of, in some cases, punishing service. The fact that many of the classes are still seen performing frontline operations on the main line today – notably Classes 20, 31, 37 and 47 (albeit in vastly reduced numbers from the original build) – is a credit to their designers and manufacturers.

But in the 1980s, BR could not meet the needs of the customer in terms of traction power. The oil crisis of the early 1970s caused BR to issue an urgent requirement for an 'intermediate freight locomotive' to be rated at 3,500hp for hauling coal traffic. During 1975 Brush had designed the Class 56, which was based on the Class 47 body; however, the Class 56 had a 3,500hp engine, which had been installed along with different bogies. The construction of the first thirty Class 56s had been undertaken by Electroputere in Craiova, Romania; these were considered to be a high power 'stop-gap' locomotive, though they suffered from quality problems, thought to include electrical wiring issues and poorly machined axles. The remaining 105 Class 56s were constructed by BREL (British Rail Engineering Limited) and were deemed to be of much better build quality, though by this time the engines had been de-rated to 3,250hp in order to afford greater reliability. Over the years, the Class 56's reliability improved to an adequate level and was considered by many to be a good second choice to the later Class 60; however, the tremendous tractive effort and hill start/all-weather performance capability of the Class 60 was (and still is) far superior to that of the Class 56.

In 1983 BR designed the radical-looking Class 58; it was constructed by BREL and was intended to be a general freight locomotive. However, in reality the Class 58s were used on heavy coal trains to which they were not best suited due to the mediocre wheelslip performance of their BR-designed bogies. Unfortunately the Class 58s were deemed to be as troublesome as the Class 56s, although during their careers the 58s settled down and, like the 56s, gave adequate performance – though not as good as even the 56s while hauling heavier freight.

In order for BR to satisfy their customers' requirements, a decision needed to be reached quickly, and so BR undertook a rigorous tendering process for a new Type 5 heavy freight locomotive. This would be a massive investment for BR, and so they required a contract that was not only robust, but one that could deliver the best value for money, even if it meant exploring the possibility of purchasing overseas. BR's preferred option would be to support British industry, but only if they could match or better the offer by overseas manufacturers. In the early 1980s, BR published their intent to purchase up to 200 new freight locomotives to replace the Class 37s, amongst others, which were to be nominally rated at 2,000hp. The freight locomotives were to utilize the Co-Co wheel arrangement, and to be uncomplicated in design in order to aid ease of maintenance and ensure high reliability. Low life-cycle expenditure was seen to be at least as important as the initial outlay.

An alternative solution would have been to carry out major overhauls of, and/or possibly to re-engine certain classes of locomotive to meet those requirements. This had been partially the case in the past, although not in any huge numbers. During the mid-1980s, six members of the Class 37 fleet (numbered 37901–37906 respectively) underwent extensive modification and alterations, and re-classification to 37/9. This involved the installation of new engines and other associated equipment, four of which were supplied by Mirrlees and two by Ruston. Following the installation of the engines in the Class 37/9s, BR then had to evaluate which of the two companies' engines would be the most cost effective, and best suited to hauling heavy loads up stiff gradients.

Was the Class 60 Needed?

The Railfreight sector of BR needed to be certain that the Class 60 was actually needed. Were there any advantages in ordering a less powerful locomotive such as a Class 38, for example, which could be used on certain traffic, or indeed in carrying out life extensions to other classes of locomotive? It was noted that certain classes, notably Class 33s and Class 47s, were deemed unsuitable for life extensions, citing the fact that such an extension would be prohibitively expensive. However, this theory relating to Class 47s was disproved during the late 1990s, as Brush Traction converted thirty-three Class 47s and rebuilt them as Class 57s. Interestingly, the Freightliner Class 57s (and 12-645-F3 at 2,750bhp for the ETS locomotives for Virgin Trains and First Great Western Class 57s) were equipped with a General Motors 12-645-E3 engine developing 2,500hp. As will be described later in this chapter, a General Motors engine was offered to BR to power the Class 60.

An appraisal was carried out in 1986 for a standard fleet replacement, to be known as the Class 38. However, in a memorandum to the Investment Committee for the Class 60 diesel electric locomotives, is was felt that the difference in cost between the Class 38 and Class 60 specification was not great, and it was preferred to invest in a fleet of locomotives that could haul heavier trains in the future should the need arise. Within the Investment Committee's memorandum, they had been asked to request authority for the issue of invitations to tender for 100 Class 60 diesel electric locomotives for the core trainload freight business.[4]

British Rail had gained experience from the private operator Foster Yeoman, who owned and operated an American 'Switcher' (shunting locomotive) – the General Motors EMD SW1001 No. 44 *Western Yeoman*, constructed in the USA, and which was put into use at their company quarry at Merehead in Somerset. Foster Yeoman, who had been impressed by this Switcher unit, went on to source the highly successful Class 59 diesel electric locomotives. This took place in 1985, and it was a significant event when the new Class 59 EMD locomotives arrived at Foster Yeoman.

The first batch of Class 59s was constructed between 1985 and 1989 by General Motors, Electro Motive Division, in La Grange, Chicago, USA. The Class 59's performance changed the thinking at BR, and the specification for the new freight locomotives was changed to 100 units at 3,100hp with adhesion enhancement: this would become the Class 60. The Class 59s had clearly shown that they were able to haul some of BR's heaviest trains, aided by technological advances in wheelslip control, known as 'Super Series' control. Moreover the Class 59's low running costs and high availability were sure to be in favour with BR.

In summary, BR laid down tough criteria: the new Type 5 locomotives had to be the most cost effective to build, test and commission. Furthermore, the locomotives had to have high availability coupled with low running costs; this

DBS 59202 powers one of the many aggregate workings that operate between the Somerset quarries and the south-east. This is *Crofton* on the Berks & Hants line on 14 August 2013.
EDWARD GLEED

would allow heavier trains to be hauled, negating the need for double heading. Although the GM Class 59 credentials certainly looked most favourable, the UK government was very keen to support British industry, which at that time was going through very difficult times. A substantial order such as the Class 60 would certainly go some way to alleviate the situation, and no doubt the government would have leant heavily on BR to select the British option. However, BR were keen to select a manufacturer that could supply the Class 60s within a short timeframe, and would also give the best value for money. The 100 Class 60 locomotives would allow 240 existing ageing locomotives to be withdrawn, in some cases en masse.[4]

Required Specifications for the Class 60

A business and operating specification for the Class 60 had been drawn up, which required following; a key selection of the operating specifications is described below.

Scope of the project:
The locomotive was required to haul specific heavy trains on a variety of routes throughout the country.

The fleet of 100 Class 60s were to be delivered within financial years ranging between 1989 and 1992.

The life expectancy was to be forty years, with half-life rebuilding.

Cost targets:
Maintenance costs: £45,000 per annum.

Fuel consumption: 400,000ltr (88,000gal) for an annual 96,000km (59,654 miles).

Performance:
Haulage capability: The locomotive had to be able to start a train of mixed stock 2,800 tonnes trailing load, and continuously haul a mixed train of 2,250 tonnes, both on a 1 in 100 rising gradient on relatively straight track. In addition, slow speed control was required at 0.8, 1.6 and 4.32km/h (0.5, 1.0 and 2.68mph).

General requirements:
Two driving cabs were to be provided, one at each end, and to be full width.

Ambient temperatures: −30° +40°.

The locomotive had to be able to negotiate snow left after the passage of snow ploughs, and to travel through wind-borne snow. Miniature snow-plough brackets were required.

The locomotive had to be able to negotiate 150mm (6in) floodwater above rail level.

Compatibility:
Track-circuit operation was to comply with signalling principles, No. 36.

AWS and Vigilance devices were to be fitted, together with NRN radio equipment.

The locomotive had to be able to work with all air-braked freight rolling stock, and be able to work in multiple with another Class 60 locomotive.

The 7 May 1988 proved to be an important day for the Class 60s. Having sought government approval for 100 Class 60 diesel electric locomotives, a letter was signed and sent from Paul Channon (Department of Transport) to Sir Robert Reid (British Railways Board), giving formal approval to the proposal for the purchase of 100 Class 60 diesel electric locomotives, at an estimated cost of £121.5m.[4]

The Tendering Process

On 23 July 1987, a memorandum to the British Railways Board Investment Committee was produced for the invitation to tender for the Class 60. The purpose of the memorandum was to seek authority to invite tenders for the Class 60 locomotives. The memorandum outlined the fact that the present fleet of diesel locomotives was in excess of twenty-five years' service, coupled with rising maintenance costs. It further mentioned that a proposal to acquire a quantity of Class 60 locomotives was being evaluated against a base case for the retention of a number of classes, namely Classes 20, 31 and 47.[4]

Hitherto, no life extension programme had been undertaken on these locomotives. Certain members of the Class 37 diesel electric locomotive fleet underwent extensive refurbishment, which commenced in the early 1980s. A realistic timetable had been written detailing the fastest possible timings between the authority to tender and the actual placement of the order, which was from 3 August 1987 to the end of March 1988. A number of key issues were highlighted in this memorandum, one of them being the timescale, which was thought to be extremely tight. This timetable mentioned the fact that in order to obtain the fastest delivery schedule for the locomotives, an order should be placed with General Motors for further Class 59s. If this were to be the case, then BR would expect delivery of an initial batch of twenty locomotives by early 1989. (At this juncture, it is worth noting that US firms were used to building locomotives continuously, whereas in the UK construction was sporadic.)

However, if BR placed an order with a UK-based company, it was felt that the timetable would need to be extended due to start-up times, with locomotives entering service during mid-1989. It was noted by BR that if the locomotives were sourced in the UK, the maximum feasible delivery would be approximately two years. In summarizing the realistic timetable, BR concluded that in order for new locomotives to be entering service during 1989, construction would have to be undertaken in the USA.[4]

The Tenderers

The British Railways Board (BRB) identified its various requirements and evaluation criteria. Having liaised with consultants Merz & McLellan, the BRB sent out letters inviting companies to tender for the Class 60 project. The companies who were invited to tender were: Brush Electrical Machines Traction Division (with parent company, Hawker Siddeley); GEC-Transportation Projects Limited; Metro Cammell Limited; General Electric; General Motors, Electro-Motive Division; and NEI Peebles Limited.[4]

A close-up photograph of the manufacturer's plate affixed to 60003. 11 December 1989. JOHN STRETTON

The tenderers who responded to the BRB were Metro Cammell Limited, GEC Transportation Projects Limited, General Motors USA and Brush Electrical Machines.

METRO CAMMELL LIMITED

Similar to the likes of Brush and GEC, Metro Cammell were long established in rolling stock construction. They supplied rolling stock to many parts of the world, including the Jamaican Railway Corporation, Peru and Hong Kong Mass Transit Railway Corporation. In the UK they were responsible for the construction of the highly acclaimed Class 101 Diesel Multiple Unit of 1956 and the plush Blue Pullman of 1962, and also the Class 156 'Sprinter' and certain rolling stock for the London Underground.[4]

On 6 November 1987, Mr B. S. Bonan (Managing Director of Metro Cammell Limited) formally submitted a booklet in support of their Class 60 tender to Mr J. K. Welsby of the BRB for their perusal. In the covering letter, Mr B. S. Bonan stated that he declined to send the booklet to the chairman Sir Robert Reid, as they thought it was up to Mr Welsby's discretion as to whether it would be of interest to him.[4]

Having given due consideration to the BRB's requirements, Metro Cammell felt that they could not meet the delivery start-up of a trial batch of twenty locomotives as the timescale was extremely tight. Metro Cammell requested that the BRB give consideration that a first batch five locomotives be supplied, and further asked for the last five since they could be supplied in a competitive timescale. Metro Cammell hoped that the opportunity to purchase the very best mix of locomotive technology would be of sufficient interest for the BRB to consider the offer. The booklet provided by Metro Cammell was most detailed, and they were keen to exhibit their credentials, some of which are detailed below.[4]

First, Metro Cammell had entered into an exclusive agreement with Brown Boveri (ASEA Brown Boveri Group) from 1 January 1988 to collaborate on the Class 60 project, and had also been in the international main contracting business for over 140 years. The company were also able to offer the BRB for the Class 60 absolute freedom of choice of technology, sub-system equipment and choices of supply, though Metro Cammell would retain total control and full responsibility for the performance of the locomotive. The BRB were also given the choice to select on the following:

- An alternative engine to Mirrlees
- An alternative bogie to Brush

■ A UK source of supply for the BBC three-phase equipment (BBC: Brown, Boveri & Cie. AG, Baden Switzerland (1891–1987))
■ A preferred UK source of supply for the locomotive body

It was further stipulated by Metro Cammell that any of the combinations should be under the main contractorship, responsibility and control of the company. Further to the aforementioned, Metro Cammell set out what they would deliver:

■ Proven BBC GTO (gate turn-off thyrystor) based three-phase technology
■ Flexibility and choice of key locomotive sub-components
■ Guarantees of performance of the locomotive of BR's choice
■ A main British contractor
■ An established and proven project management organization
■ An established and proven quality management organization
■ Substantial experience in international main contracting
■ An established and proven contracting and supplier management organization
■ The largest engineering and management base in the UK train industry, in addition to the combined resources of the ABB Group

Metro Cammell's selling points were a track record and consistency in the following:

■ Service
■ Quality
■ Sound engineering
■ Delivery
■ Performance

However, it is understood that Metro Cammell had not built a locomotive in twenty years, and their bid was discounted by BR who deemed it was not a viable proposition.[4]

GEC TRANSPORTATION PROJECTS LIMITED
Similar to the other contenders, GEC had a very long association with the railway industry, both in the UK and abroad.

For the UK market, GEC were the driving force behind the Class 91 project for the East Coast Main Line. Other locomotives that GEC had designed were locomotives for the African Class 9E Series 1.

A letter from GEC to Mr Blake (Chief Mechanical and Electrical Engineer to the BRB) indicated that their figures showed high availability and reliability with the Class 59 locomotives. Having been invited to tender for the Class 60 project, GEC were keen to emphasize that 'they would play a dominant role in assuring that our proposed Class 60 locomotive would be manufactured to the same standard as the British Railways would anticipate with locomotives wholly built by General Motors'. On 16 December 1987, a letter from Robert Hughes (House of Commons, London) to the chairman of the BRB Sir Robert Reid, stated that GEC might use the Class 59 engine made by General Motors of the USA, and wished to enquire what specification of engine was given to the Class 60.[4]

GENERAL MOTORS USA
General Motors have supplied locomotives on a global basis for many years, including to the UK. This has been in the form of the Class 59 locomotives, as has been mentioned earlier in this chapter, and continue to do so to the present day in the similar form of the Class 66 diesel electric locomotive.

Having been invited by the BRB to tender for the Class 60 locomotives, a letter dated 13 May 1988 from Mr C. J. Vaughan (Vice President of General Motors Corporation) had been sent to the BRB chairman indicating that they had been working with GEC to ensure that their locomotive 'would have a high degree of manufactured content'. The letter further explained that they had been working as a sub-contractor to GEC, and that such a move was not usual for them. Mr C. J. Vaughan also outlined that General Motors might have misunderstood the significance of the bid submission, and since then had undertaken significant improvements on their offer, in particular to comply with the requirements under the reliability section of the tender.[4]

BRUSH ELECTRICAL MACHINES
At the time of the tendering process for the Class 60, 'Brush' was actually known as 'Brush Electrical Machines Traction Division'. The BR tendering process had encouraged a dual source of engine, therefore the Brush bid included a Ruston 8-cylinder in-line engine – though this could only develop up

to 2,800hp as opposed to the chosen Mirrlees Blackstone 8MB275RT engine that could develop up to 3,100hp. Brush Traction were also aware that the Class 59s that were already in service were proving their worth, and their company, Electro-Motive Division, could supply a Class 59 within the timeframe. In order for Brush to remain competitive, they had to commit to their submitted tender to the BRB. However, in hindsight it is further understood that a minimum of thirty months would have been realistic.

The main selling points for Brush were as follows:[4]

- They were a UK-based industry supplier and manufacturer with many years of experience in the railway industry
- They could meet the timeframe and technical compliance specification as requested by BR

The Appointment of Engineering Consultants

The British Railways Board sent out invitations to tender for the Class 60 project, and the government was keen for an outside view on the viability of each tender. Therefore the services of engineering consultants were sourced in order for an impartial assessment to be made in terms of the evaluation process. In a correspondence from Mr P. S. Higham (Director of Supply of the British Railways Board), letters were sent out to four consulting engineering companies, dated 16 November 1987. They were: Merz & McLellan (Consulting Engineers); Kennedy Henderson Limited (Consulting Engineers and Economists); Rendel, Palmer & Tritton (Consulting and Design Engineers); and Bechtel Limited.[4] (For contact details, see page 190.)

The letter advised that the British Railways Board had decided to employ the services of consultants to obtain an impartial assessment of the objectivity and competence of tender appraisal. The companies were formally asked if they wished to be considered for the consulting assignment, and stated that their response was required quickly. In a letter dated 10 November 1987, Mr Colin Driver (Director of Railfreight) wrote to Mr J. K. Welsby (Managing Director Procurement and Specialist Projects) indicating his support of the idea to use an independent adviser regarding the responses to the Class 60 tender. In the opinion of Mr M. V. Casey (Director of Mechanical and Electrical Engineering), Merz & McLellan, Rendel, Palmer and Tritton, and Kennedy Henderson should receive consideration on the grounds

that these three companies had undertaken similar work with suitably trained staff. Mr M. V. Casey further added that the first two companies had capabilities in the type of evaluation that BR were seeking.[4]

In a letter dated 16 November 1988 from Mr Higham (Director of Supply of the BRB) to Rendel, Palmer & Tritton, the company were formally invited to indicate whether they wished to be considered to the assignment of an impartial assessment of the objectivity and competence of the process of tender appraisal of the construction of the Class 60s. The letter also indicated that bids had been received by three firms. The letter set out the requirements of the process in advising the BRB on what information was needed in order to advise the Board of the credentials of the aforementioned tenders. In order for the consultants to reach a recommendation, a scoring method had been employed. The scoring method, derived from the tender evaluation, had to be undertaken by specialist engineers of the DM&EE (Director of Mechanical and Electrical Engineering) staff at the Railway Technical Centre based in Derby. The method of evaluation was spilt into three headings: operating/technical, safety and health legislation. Each category was most specific, calling for items ranging from locomotive performance to locomotive fire protection to be scrutinized.[4]

Hawker Siddeley Engine Trials

In order to ensure a prime position when bidding commenced for the Class 60s, Hawker Siddeley decided to trial their highly fuel-efficient MB275 engine in a locomotive. The Class 37 fleet was undergoing a 'heavy general repair' at Crewe at the time, where Brush alternators were replacing the DC generators; therefore it was a prime opportunity to install the MB275 in a locomotive similar to the planned new units. In the event, four Class 37s were repowered with 6-cylinder MB275 engines rated at 1,800hp at 1,000rpm: these were 37901, 37902, 37903 and 37904, while GEC repowered two Class 37s with their RK270 engine: 37905 and 37906.

Work commenced in 1984 with Brush designing the new engine installation, Mirrlees building the engines, and Crewe undertaking the assembly and static testing. Hawker Siddeley decided that the MB275 engine would continue to be offered for the Class 60, but in 8-cylinder form. The new rating would be 3,100hp at 1,000rpm. For the Class 37 installation, the engine was producing 300hp per cylinder; for the Class 60 it would have to be nearly 400hp per cylinder, a very significant uprate. The uprate drove some fundamental changes, a notable one being a change to the cylinder-head construction. The Class 37 engine utilized the proven three-deck cylinder heads, but the flame face was not strong enough to resist the higher firing pressures of the increased rating, and a change was made to bore-cooled heads.[5] In the interests of simplification, the cooling system was changed from the twin-circuit system used on the Class 37 (separate jacket water and charge air cooling) to a single-circuit system. The combination of the power per cylinder uprate and the changes to the engine design meant that the reliability and durability demonstrated on the Class 37 repower project was of limited value. It is worth noting that although these modified units were intended to run for only a couple of years to gain experience on the engine, they ran until withdrawal in the late 1990s.[5]

The conversions were also undertaken for possible use in a new class of locomotive, the Class 38, which never materialized. Certainly, hitherto, the vast majority of locomotives from the 1955 British Transport Commission Modernization plan* had in many cases given sterling performance, notably Classes 20, 31, 37 and 47, all of which are still in use today, though since railway privatization under different ownership. In some cases, major rebuilds or modifications have been carried out to bring them up to today's required standard.

In similarity with Brush, Mirrlees Blackstone at Stockport has had a long association with the railway industry over the years – though it has to be said there were issues concerning the K. Major engines that were fitted to the Class 31 diesel electric locomotive. In the end, BR removed the Mirrlees engines and re-engined the entire fleet with English Electric engines.

Evaluation of the Tenders

A meeting was held in Euston House to discuss the latest position of bids for the Class 60s. In the meeting Mr J. K. Welsby stated that its purpose was to establish the current position regarding the evaluation of tenders for the Class 60 diesel electric locomotive, which had been invited from Brush, GEC and Metro Cammell. The evaluation of the tenders looked at the strengths and weaknesses of each tender, which fell into four categories: locomotive equipment, locomotive performance, track forces/noise levels and contract performance. The strengths and weaknesses were measured on a scale ranging from zero to ten, where a figure of ten would indicate that total compliance was achieved, while a score of zero in any area would indicate non-compliance and render disqualification of that tender. In the event of any uncertainties with the evaluations, the tenderer would be called in for the Board to seek clarification.

Of the companies that tendered, under the following criteria it was found that in the technical assessment in terms of quality assurance GEC was found to be superior, but in all other areas Brush was superior. When comparing Metro Cammell with GEC it was found that technically, Metro Cammell was superior, though the consultants' views were 'that Metro Cammell's response was unacceptable because the basis of the tender was not clear and they had not met the delivery times'. Further to this, the consultants were of the opinion that Brush had produced a better offer than GEC, though Dr Hore of Merz & McLellan consultants was concerned that the assessment had looked at the detail rather than the whole, and wished to undertake some further evaluation of the locomotives as an entity and report back. It was agreed by all present that this should happen.[4]

On the commercial side, a financial assessment found that the bids had produced the following ranking: 1: Brush, 2: GEC, 3: Metro Cammell, though Metro Cammell had been ruled out on financial grounds. It was then stated that both Brush and GEC met the delivery terms, although Brush was found to be marginally better in that area. However, it was decided that further evaluation of unit prices was required. From the above, the next requirement was to put together a draft contract document including both technical and commercial terms and conditions. It was planned to discuss the aforementioned at a meeting on Thursday 31 March 1988. A further requirement was to send draft contracts to Brush and GEC seeking the best and final offers for award of the contract, and for such a contract to be placed by the end of March. Mr J. K. Welsby was most explicit, instructing that it was strictly forbidden for anyone to engage in further discussions with the bidders other than through Director of Supply.[4]

*The aforementioned 1955 British Transport Commission plan was implemented to afford companies an opportunity to construct a small batch of locomotives of varying capabilities in order for BR to trial them under mainstream conditions. Should a particular class of locomotive be deemed to be successful and meet with the British Railway Board's requirements, then further locomotive orders of that class would be placed.[6]

Following the meeting, the timetable set out below was compiled:[4]

9 March: Letters and draft contracts issued
25 March: Replies to be received by 12 noon
31 March: Technical evaluation to be completed
7 April: Papers to supply committee issued
14 April: Supply committee
25 April: Placement of contract

The Involvement of the National Union of Railwaymen (NUR)

As with any item of rolling stock that was presented to BR Operations, the trade union needed to be consulted on matters of safety and operational use. In addition, the unions were keen to support their workforce on matters concerning job security. To support this matter, Mr J. Knapp (General Secretary of the National Union of Railwaymen) wrote a letter to Mr T. Toolan (Managing Director, Personnel of the British Railways Board) on 20 August 1987 airing his concerns, having learned from the Press that BR had decided to invite both General Motors and GEC to bid for an order to supply 100 Class 60 diesel electric locomotives.

Mr J. Knapp also mentioned in his letter that the decision was fundamental to the future of BRB's subsidiary BREL (British Rail Engineering Limited), and that as a matter of courtesy, the trade union could have been informed in advance of the press. Mr J. Knapp was further concerned that BR was contemplating purchasing equipment from abroad that could jeopardize the future of railway manufacturing in the UK. According to Mr J. Knapp, Press reports had suggested that BREL had hoped to participate in the tendering process as sub-contractors. Mr J. Knapp also asked BR to confirm whether BREL would not be prevented from becoming subcontractors.

It is clear in a letter dated 19 September 1987 from Mr Eastham MP of the House of Commons, that although at that time the USA had produced locomotives with an excellent track record, the Class 60 project was seen as a major opportunity for UK manufacturers. BR was keen to give assurance that they would try to support the UK engineering industry and manufacturing.[4]

The Relative Performance of GEC and Brush Tenders

Dr Hore had compiled an overview on behalf of Merz & McLellan of the relative performance of tenders of both GEC and Brush. In Dr Hore's report, it mentioned that the Brush tender was 'one of the most comprehensive'[4] that the BRB had received since the introduction of competitive tendering, and further demonstrated a very high degree of compliance. Brush had produced a technical design for BR that was almost entirely specification compliant. Electro-Motive Division (EMD) offered a version of the Class 59 and were not particularly interested in undertaking many modifications in order to be more compliant for such a small order to them. Their bid had raised roughly 600 questions, as it was deemed to be largely non-spec compliant, as opposed to the Brush tender, which acquired far fewer questions, this being due to the fact that its specification was deemed to be highly compliant. In addition, EMD's Crewe-built locomotive would have required an imperial to metric conversion process, and this was a concern with regard to quality. Even the 74-volt (rather than the BR 110-volt) equipment meant that the spares would be 'unique', which caused great concern to BR.

From a commercial point of view, EMD's Crewe-built locomotive was more expensive by £100,000 per locomotive due to BREL's levy. It is interesting to note that the EMD at no time supplied a four-year warranty, which is what BR required. One thing that is certain is that BR would not consider a deal without a warranty.[11] However, in the case of GEC, Dr Hore was of the opinion that the process with GEC was 'long and tortuous',[4] and further thought that their tender responses were 'patchy'.

From the delivery point of view the report mentioned that Brush Electrical Machines had offered a more 'compact' delivery timeframe, and that it had offered 100 Class 60s by 20 December 1990, whilst GEC offered their delivery by 14 March 1992. The report mentioned that GEC had a much more reliable profile than Brush, citing the fact that GEC had been awarded the Class 91 contract, though technical problems with GEC software had affected the Class 319 25kV EMUs, and both Class 90 and 91 25kV electric locomotives, further citing weaknesses in their project management capability.

The report also felt that the GEC project management of the Class 60 tender submission had been very poor. However, it was felt that the Brush Traction equipment was more reliable than the corresponding GEC equipment. As far as the Class 60 was concerned, GEC stated that their bid would comprise traction equipment from General Motors Electro-Motive Division, this being built under licence by GEC, though the report clearly stated that this did not reduce risk.

The report also mentioned the fact that the Class 59s constructed by General Motors were perceived to be more reliable than the Class 58s, which had been constructed in the UK. This was purely fallacious, and was not to influence which way the decision would be made. In a further correspondence by Merz & McLellan to the Board, it was therefore recommended that it would be in the Board's interest to place an order for 100 Class 60 diesel electric locomotives with Brush Electrical Machines.

Having received and scrutinized the submitted tenders for the Class 60 contract, and further sought the advice from the engineering consultants, the BRB (therein known as the 'Board') of '24 Eversholt Street, London, NW1 1DZ, did on 14 December 1988 set out an agreement for the design, development, manufacture, supply and commissioning of 100 Class 60 diesel electric locomotives for Trainload Freight with Brush Electrical Machines Limited and parent company Hawker Siddeley (to be known as the Contractor) at PO Box 18, Falcon Works, Loughborough, Leicestershire, LE11 1HJ.'[4]

On 29 February 1988 the Investment Committee authorized the purchase of 100 Class 60 freight locomotives. Further to this, a letter signed by the Secretary of State for Transport, Paul Channon, on 7 May 1988, gave formal approval to the BRB for the proposal of 100 Class 60 diesel electric locomotives for the freight sector, at an estimated cost of £121.5m. It is most likely that Brush Traction supported this, and the fact that they had a long association in the construction of railway locomotives for many years would almost certainly have been one of the deciding factors in appointing Brush Traction to supply the Class 60s, though as described later in the book, much work was put out to other companies and manufacturers.[4]

The Contract is Awarded

Having advised the BRB on the best course of action, Merz & McLellan wrote to Mr J. K. Welsby on 29 April 1988 indicating that the Board had been most thorough in assessing whether there were any advantages in placing an order for the Class 60s with GEC/General Motors. Mr Welsby had clearly faced a dilemma and was thus possibly undecided as to the best course of action to take, hence the dates for the decision being delayed. However, Brush had not been granted more time to deliver the locomotive, and furthermore was required to adhere to the thirteen months, with the delivery date not being moved. It was further pointed out to Mr Welsby that GEC had been allowed more time to modify their offer in order to meet the Board's requirements.

In the same letter, Merz & McLellan advised the Board that there were no advantages in splitting the contract, citing the following reasons. The offer from GEC was deemed to be non-compliant on the technical specification from BR and therefore unacceptable, and the fact that although GEC had been given extended time to revise their offer, they had failed to do so. Therefore, the contract to design, develop, manufacture, supply and commission 100 Class 60 diesel electric locomotives was awarded to Brush Electrical Machines.[4]

For many years Brush Electrical Machines had supplied locomotives for the railway industry, both in the UK and overseas, which would suggest that their skill and expertise almost certainly had influence as one of the deciding factors for BR to award the contract to this well regarded company. Indeed, it is a widely known fact amongst railwaymen that the Class 60 was the last 'proper' diesel locomotive to be constructed in the UK under what was British Rail, though the Class 60s were actually procured under the latter-day Railfreight sectorized Trainload Freight administration.

Another factor for this decision was that the country was going through an economic downturn, and the government was keen to press BR into awarding the contract to Brush in order to generate new manufacturing within the UK, which would in turn help to boost morale and support economic growth.[4]

On 23 May 1988, having awarded the contract to Brush Electrical Machines, Sir Robert Reid (Chairman of the British Rail Board) wrote to the Vice President of the General Motors Corporation Mr C. J. Vaughan indicating the appointment of Brush to design, construct, test and commission the Class 60 diesel electric locomotives. Undoubtedly this would have been a disappointment for General Motors who, having already supplied the Class 59 fleet, had hoped that they would have been awarded this new contract from BR. Sir Robert Reid thanked Mr C. J. Vaughan for the work that had been put into bidding for the contract to supply the Class 60s. Sir Robert went on to say that it was likely that there would be further requirements for new locomotives in the next few years, and looked forward to inviting Mr C. J. Vaughan to tender for any such contracts.[4]

The Contract

The authority details were broken down as follows:

Locomotives	£112.00m
Main spares	£8.00m
Commissioning	£1.50m

The agreement was most explicit in its requirements, and extracts of the said agreement are as follows:

Whereas:
1) The Board have a requirement for a quantity of 100 Class 60 Diesel Electric locomotives for use within the Freight Sector.
2) In order to introduce the Locomotives into service in accordance with the Board's time-table, all such Locomotives are required to be delivered between 30 June 1989 and 17 January 1992.
3) The Contractor has agreed with the Board to design, develop, manufacture, supply and com-mission the said Locomotives in accordance with the terms and conditions of this agreement.[4]

In the agreement, clauses were set out, some of which are detailed below.

Definition and Objectives

This clearly defined who was responsible for the construc-tion of the locomotives, and the costs and timescale of delivery. At a little over £1 million per locomotive at 1988's prices, this presented a significant order for Brush.

At this juncture it is worth noting that some employees at Brush thought that the order timescale was too short and the task too daunting, therefore morale in some areas worsened. To fulfil the contract within the timescales – 30 June 1989 and 17 January 1992 – was certainly a tough criterion.

The contract was very clear in its objectives. It required that Brush undertook to fully comply with the require-ments of the agreements, and that it was incumbent on

the manufacturer to design, develop, manufacture, supply and commission 100 Class 60 diesel electric locomotives. A clause stated that there was a requirement for an initial build of forty Class 60s, and as long as the first ten of these locomotives proved to be reliable and met with the Board's approval, a further sixty locomotives were to be constructed.

The Contractor was also to ensure that the locomo-tives were constructed and tested in accordance, and met the requirements within the specification in all respects. If the build of the first ten locomotives did not meet the Board's standards, they were required to inform the Contractor. The closing date for making any notification was 30 March 1990, after which the Contractor could continue to construct and supply the outstanding sixty Class 60 locomotives. If the first ten locomotives failed to meet the rigours of the testing and reliability trials, the Board had the right to cancel the remainder of the order, without liability.[4]

Delivery of the Locomotives

The Contractor was required to deliver the locomotives to the Board on an agreed date, which would have allowed enough time for all the necessary elements of the contract to have been fulfilled, as set out in a project time plan.

Under the terms of the contract, the Contractor was also required to design the locomotive with detailed drawings in accordance with the specification, which also included production drawings, and to order key components, such as bogies and necessary power equipment, along with other associated materials.

It was also incumbent on the Contractor to undertake the following measures, namely to fabricate each important element, and to put down the underframe for the locomo-tives; in addition they were to supply dates for when the locomotive structure, bogies and electrical equipment for individual locomotives might be completed.

The contract also required the Contractor to supply dates for fitting out each locomotive, which also included the inspection and testing of the locomotives at the Contractor's works.

With regard to the first locomotive, the Contractor was required to undertake routine on-track and performance 'type tests', and further to this, subsequent locomotives were required to undergo a series of routine tests, namely '1,000 trouble-free miles' for each locomotive with a

A very fine model built by Bassett Lowke. This photograph depicts 60001 wearing 'General' subsector logos; none of the class was allocated to this sector.
ROUNDEL DESIGNS GROUP/
BRITISH RAIL

view to commissioning following successful results of the aforementioned tests. These tests were in order for the Contractor to meet the delivery dates set out in the terms of the contract, and in addition, the drawings had to be scrutinized by the engineer. It was also permissible for the project time plan to be adjusted as deemed necessary, providing that any alterations were put in writing and that the agreed contractual dates remained unaffected.[4]

Payment and Price Variation

As with many contracts, interim payments were drawn up in the terms of the contract. Under the terms of the contract for the Class 60, the BRB was required to make interim payments to the Contractor during various stages of construction. These interim payments were made in stages, some of which are detailed below:

- The project time plan   £60,000
- Drawings and diagrams   £967,140
- Maintenance documentation/operating
  manuals and wearing parts. The contract
  required that these were presented no later
  than three months before the delivery of the
  locomotive   £60,000
- A 1:20 scale model of the Class 60**   £6,000
- A 'mock-up' of the locomotive   £110,000
- Tooling costs and jigs   £492,150

As regards payment for the actual construction of the locomotive, this was carried out in percentages as various stages of the construction categories were completed. In addition, the prices were subject to Value Added Tax. It was mentioned that the price of each locomotive would be adjusted if the construction or procurement costs differed from those stated in the contract. The Board also required the Contractor to provide a cash flow schedule indicating the dates when the Contractor was due to be paid. It was also noted that until 6 November 1987, in the event of fluctuations in costs for labour and materials, the payments would be adjusted accordingly, provided the Contractor was not deemed to be found at fault. In the latter case, the Contractor would be liable, and any rise in costs would be at their expense. The contract required that both the Board and the Contractor reach a clear understanding of what was expected of them by the terms of the contract.[4]

**As part of the contract, two Class 60 models were constructed: one was by Bassett Lowke of the proposed design and numbered 60 001, finished in 'two-tone grey' livery with 'General User' logos. ('General User' logos were not used on any of the production Class 60s: Chapter 5 of this book amplifies this further.) A second model was built for Brush by the renowned model manufacturer Bassett Lowke, who numbered it 60 001. It, too, was finished in 'two-tone grey' but wore the 'Construction' logos as applied to certain members of the Class 60; both models were unnamed.[4]

Contract Implementation

The contract required the Contractor to comply with its obligations in accordance with both the Project Management System and procedures having been approved by the Board. This was contained in the Contract Implementation Plan. This plan called for the appointment of an experienced and qualified project engineer. The Board required that progress meetings be undertaken at monthly intervals.

LIABILITY FOR FAILURE TO MAINTAIN LEVEL OF SERVICE

The Board had stressed the importance of successful commissioning of the locomotive, and made it clear that loss of revenue due to unsuccessful commissioning would be shouldered by the Board. The Board deemed it fair to impose a liability for liquidated damages should levels of service fail to satisfy the Board.

PARENT BODY GUARANTEE

It was stated that the agreement should be conditional upon the Contractor providing the Board with a parent body guarantee. This was to be undertaken at the Contractor's expense, and in addition completed and sealed by Hawker Siddeley Group PLC within fourteen days after signing this agreement.

CONFIDENTIALITY

The Board's stance was that this agreement was to remain confidential to the parties concerned; however, it was accepted that the names of companies might be disclosed to suppliers or sub-contractors if the government or law required them to do so.[4]

CHAPTER TWO

CONSTRUCTION AND DELIVERY

Two principal differences lie between Brush and General Motors: Brush were (and still are) bespoke locomotive builders, while General Motors are not. Although Brush had in the past designed and manufactured locomotives for both freight and passenger traffic use, in the main, their components were bespoke. This was clearly demonstrated in the design and manufacture of the Class 60. General Motors were quite different. Their prime role was to supply locomotives for freight applications, often employing components that were utilized on their previous locomotives. EMD had a large back catalogue of locomotive 'building blocks' to draw on, ranging from engines, bogies and control systems.

Design

Following the decision by the BRB to award the contract to Brush, an artist's impression of the Class 60 was created. This illustration is most interesting because at the time it clearly showed how the Class 60 might appear. Although the illustration depicts the Class 60 more or less as it appears today, there are detail differences, as outlined below, which are worthy of mention.

One area of the locomotive that clearly differs from the production fleet concerns the warning horns. The horn area is illustrated with an overall cover with louvres, and is very

An artist's impression of the proposed Class 60 3,100hp diesel electric locomotive. BRUSH TRACTION

similar to the horn housing fitted to the Class 47 and the unique Class 53 *Falcon* built by Brush during the 1960s. The louvres were installed to prevent snow ingress, which can prove troublesome with uncovered horns.

The cab side windows differ from the production locomotives in that the illustration depicts the windows as rectangular with a single vertical bar. Interestingly, a black-painted triangle in front of the cab side window has been painted to afford a neater appearance; however, the production Class 60s cab side windows are very different. All four sets of cab side window frames have a raked-back forward edge that is most neat in appearance, as it follows the contour of the upper front cab. This negates the need for the black-painted triangle as it is depicted in the artist's illustration.

The driver's cab side window is divided into three sections, the middle window being moveable to allow the driver to communicate to outside staff. This is a modification that was carried out following complaints from drivers who had difficulty in looking backwards with the original 'two-piece' unit. The latter driver's window was retro-fitted after about six months from delivery. From new, the driver's cab side window was the same as the secondman's window, which had been approved by ASLEF representatives who viewed the mock-up at Brush. The secondman's cab side window differs from the driver's window in that it is a two-piece unit.

The snowplough also differs from the illustration because at that stage, notches to the lower corners had not been included, as initially none were asked for by BR. Clearly this was not the case, as notches were retro-introduced at a later post-production stage, having taken into account the third rail clearance and height adjustment methods.

Another interesting feature is the inclusion of the overall wraparound black band at solebar level. Although this was not included in the original trainload liveries, DB Schenker Rail UK has adopted a similar variation to this, though it is only applied to the lower bodysides and is coloured light grey and does not extend along the cab fronts.

The depicted livery is also interesting on a number of counts. The most obvious is the overall yellow wraparound cab. This method had been applied to many earlier classes during the 'large logo' era, though as will be seen later in the book, this design was very different from what is shown on the illustration. The new Trainload livery is clearly evident, though, as mentioned earlier in this chapter, the General User subsector element was not applied to any of the production Class 60s, as none was allocated to this particular subsector.

Further to the artist's illustration of the Class 60, a development model of the Class 60 was also produced. Similar to the illustration, the model differed from the production locomotives. The development model Class 60 is depicted with a grille arrangement that differs from both the artist's illustration and the production locomotive. Three small grilles, equal in size, are present towards the rear of the locomotive, while at the front (as defined in the accompanying photograph), two large vertical grilles are present, both with horizontal vanes. The production locomotives are equipped with square mesh.

An early development Class 60 model, in this instance 60001. Note the further use of the 'General' subsector logos.
ROUNDEL DESIGN GROUP/BRITISH RAIL

The buffer beam area also differs, as the model sports a wrap-round cowl, from which both upper and lower recesses are cut out for the fitment of the 'WIPAC' lights and buffers, coupling and pipe arrangements. Although the placement of running numbers is described in Chapter 5, it is worth mentioning that on the development model, the running number sits conveniently between the light clusters. The warning horn box remains the same as the artist's illustration.

Finally it is clear to see that the bogie is more or less the same shape as the production locomotive, minus the many detail differences.

The Specification

British Rail were very clear in their requirements for the construction of the Class 60 locomotive, and further presented Brush with a highly detailed specification plan, which called for full compliance with their exacting standards. To afford an example, if the BRB had requested the Class 60 to have a particular style of bolt fitted, which had been called for in the original specification, and subsequently the style of bolt was changed, this became a further specification, which generated a 'works variation order'. This also meant that the entire Class 60 fleet was required to undergo the alteration to meet the new specification.

This put tremendous pressure on Brush, as BR refused to allow more time to undertake this additional work, requiring that the thirteen-month deadline was still met. This had an overall effect on BR in accepting locomotives into traffic.

Regarding the detail in the livery elements, described in Chapter 5, the BRB laid down strict guidelines appertaining to the overall appearance of the Class 60, down to the very last detail, something that was always a high priority for BR. The specification was so detailed, even the cab handrail shape and finish were detailed, as further described in Chapter 3.[11]

A number of varied specifications and requirements are detailed below, in an attempt to indicate to the reader just how stringent the specifications were.

WARNING HORN
The warning horn had to emit two different notes, these being independently operated as the driver required. Each warning note had to produce a sound rich in harmonics.

The note had to sound continuously at the discretion of the driver, and operate normally over the full range of meteorological conditions in which the locomotive was required to operate, including falling snow. The horns had to be mounted in such a manner that rain and snow were not able to accumulate in the horns, thereby impeding their operation.[11]

CAB HEATING AND VENTILATION
The cab design had to preclude the ingress of draughts, and not present cold surfaces in close proximity of the driver. The heating and ventilation system within each cab had to be manually controlled by means of a single switch to select the desired mode of operation. The air distribution had to be sufficient to ensure no direct air jets impinged on the driver in the seated position. Furthermore, fans had to be robust and resiliently mounted, if significant structure-borne noise was likely to be induced, with consequent annoyance to the driver.[11]

FASTENINGS
All nuts, bolts and hexagonal screw heads were to be accessible to all sockets capable of applying the required torque. Nuts and set screws that required specific torque loadings had to be clearly identified on the drawings.[11]

The Construction Process

During the early part of the Class 60 programme, Brush Traction was a division of Brush Electrical Machines Ltd, but due to organizational changes it became a subsidiary company in its own right. Initially little had changed, but in later years it resulted in parts of the supply chain being divorced from each other.

Having scrutinized the highly detailed specification laid down by BR, Brush Traction called upon various departments within their company to work out how best to construct the Class 60. The Locomotive Design Department had a high proportion of the total build, and was responsible for bodies, bogies, engine installation and all other associated equipment and cabs. The Control Gear Design Department undertook to create a power and control system. The control equipment is situated in cubicles and effectively gives the locomotive its control ability and ultimately its performance. The Electrical Machines Department was responsible for manufacturing the traction motors, alternators and other electrical rotating machines, including the radiator fan motors. Other items such as blower motors were procured externally from Brush. As with all new designs, it cost millions to design the Class 60 before the actual construction had even begun.[11]

For the construction of the Class 60 it had become quite clear that in order to meet the BRB specification, many of the items would have to be designed and constructed from new. Unlike the Class 56 locomotives whose bodyshell bore a resemblance to the earlier Class 47 locomotives, the Class 60 bodyshells were a completely new design. As mentioned earlier, the bodyshells were fabricated by Procor at their factory in Wakefield, and were transported by road to the Falcon works at Loughborough for fitting out. The new bogies that had been designed for the Class 60 were similar to those employed on the Class 89 25kV electric locomotive.[11]

The 100 fleet of Class 60s was purchased by BR for one purpose only: to haul freight traffic. This made it somewhat easier for Brush as they could design a locomotive specifically for that purpose: a true freight locomotive. Indeed it could be asked, did BR really need to purchase so many? It could be further speculated that because of all the aforementioned issues that afflicted the Class 60 at an early stage, BR might have been better off to have purchased a small number of Class 60s and to have fully tested them in every respect in order to be sure they met the specification, with a follow-on order if the first five proved successful. This would almost certainly have reduced the pressure on Brush to modify so many Class 60s, thereby enabling them to deliver all the locomotives on time and also in a fit state for traffic, without all the difficulties that had been encountered.[11]

With so many Class 60s in traffic, it was quite common to see members of the class hauling trains of only one or two wagons, which is not something that the Class 60s were originally designed to do. Indeed one engineer was heard to say 'a Class 60 doesn't really get out of bed for anything less than 2,000 tonnes' – which is, of course, the purpose for which it was designed.

Brush Electrical Machines Ltd (BEM) were given full control over the production and testing of electrical machines and control gear, with all the associated equipment and staff needed to design, build and test such equipment before fitting it to a locomotive. Workshops devoted to these ends had existed since the 1940s and were well prepared for this type of production.

Brush Electrical Machines Traction Division had manufactured locomotives for many years, and not just for the BR market. Prior to the construction of the Class 60, full size wooden mock-ups had been constructed in order to evaluate the overall shape of the body as required in the specification. The mock-ups included driving desks in order to evaluate the driving positions.

A number of mock-ups were made, one of which went on display as one of the exhibits at the NS150

A wooden mock-up of the Class 60, the engine block being most prominent. BRUSH TRACTION

A Class 60 wooden mock-up looking towards the cab. Note the cab door and the framework for the cover of the traction motor blower. BRUSH TRACTION

A cab mock-up of 60001 on display as one of the exhibits at the NS150 (Nederlandse Spoorwegen) celebrations marking the 150th anniversary of the Dutch Railways at Utrecht during the summer of 1989. DAVE COXON

(Nederlandse Spoorwegen) celebrations that marked the 150th anniversary of the Dutch Railways, to which BR had been invited to show an example of their latest example of rolling stock. This particular mock-up showed the cab fully painted, and interestingly, it was depicted wearing three BR cast arrows, one of which was affixed to the cab front, though this was not included on the production locomotives.

Unlike locomotives that had been constructed in previous years, where the locomotive was painted at its last stage of construction, part of the subcontract required Procor to fully paint the bodyshells throughout. This was unusual

because the procedure with many locomotive manufacturers is that locomotives are generally constructed on a 'rolling' process, and it is not necessarily just one type of locomotive that is being constructed at the same time in the same workshops.[11]

As will be described further in this chapter and Chapter 3, many components were manufactured 'off site', which was the case with the Class 60 where components such as the engine (from Mirrlees at Stockport) and the braking systems (from Westinghouse at Chippenham) were delivered to Brush for installation in the bodyshell. The completed bodyshells were then transported by road to the Falcon Works at Brush in Loughborough. Even with outsourcing, the Class 60 was roughly 95 per cent UK built.

Construction of the Bodyshell

The Class 60 bodyshell was constructed utilizing the mono-coque design (similar to an aircraft fuselage): this design comprises the bodysides, which are connected by cross stretchers, the deck plate, bulkheads and roof sections, terminated at each end by drag boxes and end trusses, all of which are load bearing. The integral underframe affords tremendous strength: placed on stands, the underframes are fabricated from rolled steel sections to which the bodysides are welded, hence creating the monocoque body.

The outer skin is stressed in order for the shell to with-stand the heavy load of the engine and other items of associated equipment. However, the opening roof hatches above the power unit are not. Each of the eight roof hatches are pivoted at their base and can be opened by the assistance of gas-filled struts, which also restrain the hatches whilst in the open position.

The four roof-mounted hatches are longer in length on the 'B' side of the locomotive, and overlap the 'A' side hatches in order to reduce the ingress of water. The overall construction utilized jigs to assemble and weld the component parts. Traction and vertical loads are transferred from bogie pivots and power unit mountings to the bodyside by sizeable cross-members. Reinforced bracing is added to areas such as body access doors and air intakes, in order to add rigidity to the main body. [11]

British Rail had specified that under no circumstances should any leaked fluids from the locomotive be permitted to fall on to the Permanent Way. Therefore retention tanks were also fabricated to contain leakages, and continuously

The steel framework of the Class 60 showing four elevations. BRUSH TRACTION

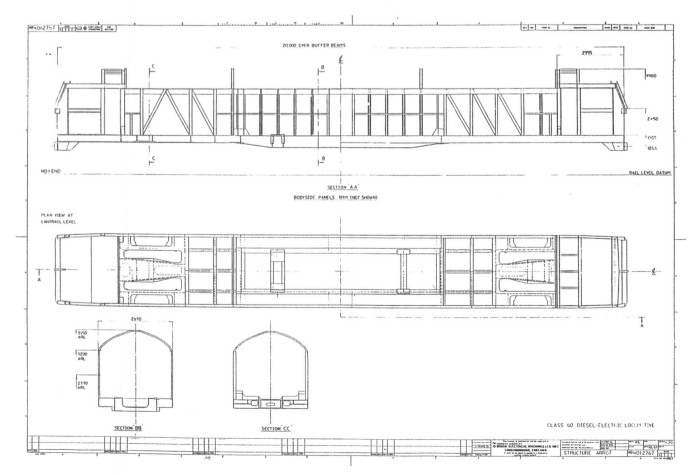

The Class 60 underframe during construction at Procor. Another Class 60 is viewed in the distance with the cabs in place. BRUSH TRACTION

An overhead view of the Class 60 at Procor, depicting both sides and cabs in situ. The cooler group will be situated in the void in the front of the image. BRUSH TRACTION

A view of the Class 60 underframe at Procor, with one of the body sides welded in place. BRUSH TRACTION

in the process of producing detailed drawings to facilitate the construction of buckeye couplings enabling the Class 60 to be coupled to wagon sets with compatible coupling arrangements.[11]

The cab structures are connected from the cantrail sections of the main body to the solebar, which provides the correct distribution of end and buffing loads.

A missile plate is welded to the inner cab roof, affording greater protection to the driver in the event of an impact. The outer cab roof is manufactured from GRP (glass reinforced plastic), or 'fibreglass', which is permanently affixed to the roof and is attached to the main locomotive body roof and secured by weather strips. The accompanying photographs depict both the existing solution and proposal: these are drawings that were undertaken by Jones Garrard

welded floor plates were installed to assist with this requirement. Conventional draw gear and buffing arrangements were also utilized; however, it is understood that DBS are

A general view inside the Procor Works on 25 April 1989: the bodyshells of 60005 and 60006 can be seen in the advanced stages of construction. BRIAN MORRISON

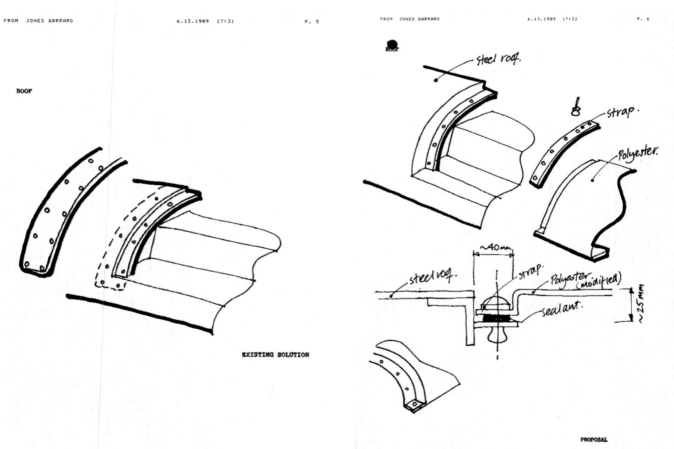

An existing solution shows how the cab roof is fixed to the main body. The step that can be seen is the missile plate, directly above the cab. THE NATIONAL ARCHIVES

An arrangement proposed by Jones Garrard of affixing the cab roof, a procedure that had proved troublesome on the original design. THE NATIONAL ARCHIVES

A completed Class 60 bodyshell in the latter stages of painting at Procor. Note the position of the lifting jacks, whose apertures are plated over in service.
BRUSH TRACTION

in response to BR's query from Brush Traction regarding the method of joining the GRP cab roof to the main body.

The missile plate also has the necessary aperture for fitting the warning horns. Design consultants Jones Garrard mooted the 'truck look' for the cab, incorporating chrome-plated horns; however, the styling was not chosen by BR.[11]

Having been constructed and painted at Procor, the completed bodyshell would arrive at the Falcon Works by low loader, which was taken inside the workshops. In the first instance it was taken to the Locomotive Erecting Shop. The bodyshells would be lifted from the low loader on to stands by way of an overhead travelling crane with stands that

afforded roughly 5ft of clearance from the concrete floor. Initial acceptance followed inspection, as long as the inspection proved satisfactory.

A huge amount of preparation was required to equip a bodyshell, which was done via the agreed specification that had been laid down well in advance by BR, along with associated drawings. Brush Traction had commenced with both the designing and prototype before the contract award, but nothing was actually made until a contract was signed. [11]

An interesting aspect surrounding the bodyshell was the style of the lamp brackets. There had clearly been issues, as Jones Garrard had been asked to provide three possible solutions of lamp bracket, which are detailed in the following five photographs.

The Class 60 bodyshell arriving at Brush Traction, having been transported by road from Procor at Wakefield. ROY HUTCHINSON

The completed bodyshell of 60001 inside **No. 25 Shop** at **Brush Traction. The Class 60 wooden mock-up is just visible in the background.** BRUSH TRACTION

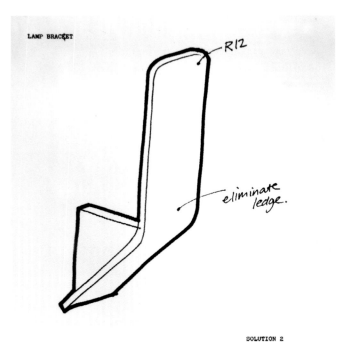

The Class 60 lamp bracket, solution No. 2.
THE NATIONAL ARCHIVES

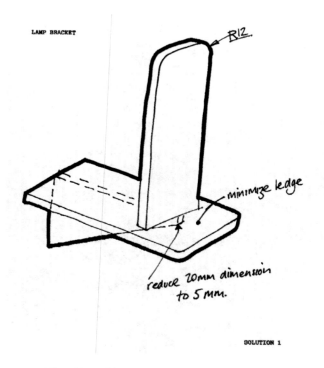

The Class 60 lamp bracket, solution No. 1.
THE NATIONAL ARCHIVES

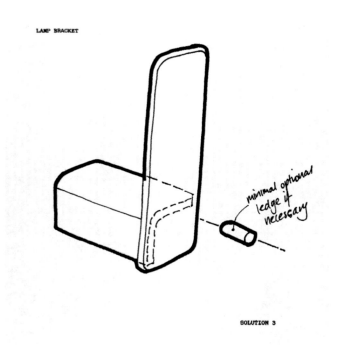

The Class 60 lamp bracket, solution No. 3.
THE NATIONAL ARCHIVES

Class 60 with solution No. 1 lamp bracket.
EDWARD GLEED

Class 60 with solution No. 2 lamp bracket.
EDWARD GLEED

The completed bodyshell of 60001 awaits fitting out at Brush Traction on 3 March 1989. JOHN STRETTON

Fitting Out

Equipping the bodyshell required the locomotive pipe runs – which could be either fixed or flexible, though electrical cables required ducting and conduit for added protection – to be fixed and secured to prevent unnecessary movement. The basic pipe and cable runs were fitted first wherever possible. As the system components were fitted, they were inspected and tested for leakages and other faults that may have occurred. It is worth noting that with electrical circuits, it is important that the wiring fitted at these early stages is not faulty, either in continuity or through insulation damage, as this would allow earth faults to the bodyshell and/or its fittings. Much of the wiring was therefore pre-tested before the looms/harnesses were installed.[11]

As the construction of the locomotive progressed, various items of equipment were lowered into the body-shell, ranging from cubicles to air compressors. Some of these were inspected and tested prior to fitting, whilst other components required testing and inspecting when connected to previously installed parts.[11]

Engines were provided for the Class 60 by Mirrlees, another sister constituent company of the Hawker Siddeley Group, therefore design, production and testing of the engines as an individual unit ensured that each engine was functioning prior to despatch to Loughborough, having been coupled to its associated Brush alternator. The power unit was one of the later fittings to be installed, and it was often the case that the engine representatives were present to undertake or oversee this installation and testing.[11]

60030 and 60032 during the fitting-out process at Brush Traction on 30 May 1990. JOHN STRETTON

Large items such as bogies were manufactured separately in the Brush works. The Brush-built traction motors were fitted during the process, along with gearboxes. When completed, the bogies were placed in the erecting shop in a position ready to receive the locomotive. Once the bogies were fitted, the various air and electrical systems were linked to the locomotive, compressed air for brakes and sanding, and the traction motor cables for linking with the main electrical power transmission. Some items required strict sequences of operation, and these were continually monitored during the testing processes.

When the interior of the locomotive was reasonably complete, with all the systems linked, inspected and tested, the locomotive was manoeuvred into the locomotive test

yard to receive its fluids of diesel fuel, coolant water, hydraulic oil and lubricating oil. At this stage it was essential to have the engine in running condition with its controls in place for scheduled testing. Initially, each run, starting from just a few seconds to longer periods, was punctuated with visual inspections of the engine and possible re-setting of the governor, which would increase until the output of the alternator could be set up and coordinated with the control systems and the engine.

Once the power unit and its associated systems had been test run, the locomotive was towed to the load bank and the alternator/rectifier output connected to it. The engines were run for specified times and loads, to test the loading on both the engines and alternators, to ensure that the systems

Fitting out continues with 60048 and 60054 at Brush Traction. The two gentlemen are John Gent on the right, and Paddy O'Connell on the left. JOHN STRETTON

60016 is viewed during the final stages of construction at Brush Traction. The original two-piece driver's window is clearly seen. 30 May 1990. JOHN STRETTON

A completed Class 60 bogie is viewed in the workshops at Brush Traction. BRUSH TRACTION

worked properly and within specification, and to run in the engine fully. Brush electrical equipment was tested as far as was practical at the workshop stage and upon delivery to the main erecting shops: these items would still have to interact with other items as the locomotive progressed towards completion.

As production continued, various pre-agreed stages were completed, which triggered payments; these payments were forthcoming when production was deemed satisfactory, and the received income further enabled the construction programme to keep running. [11]

Another important aspect of locomotive construction and testing is weighing it, and its weight must strictly comply with the specification.

It was also important that the loading of the locomotive was evenly distributed around each wheel. If the weight was found to be unbalanced, the suspension was inspected and a short run was undertaken in the works' complex to ensure that any adjustments met the loading requirements. The movements were undertaken immediately before the locomotive passed through the loading gauge, enabling the Brush inspector to check clearances along the entire length of the body, including its bogie fittings, to ensure that the locomotive was within the BR loading gauge.

At this stage of the construction process the locomotive was almost complete. The paint-shop team was fairly mobile and available to apply the locomotive running numbers

Two brand new Class 60s, 60040 *Brecon Beacons* and 60066 *John Logie Baird*, prepare to depart from Brush Traction, 30 June 1991. JOHN STRETTON

The first Class 60 off the production line was 60001 *Steadfast*, photographed at Brush Traction on 25 June 1989. Note the grey snowplough. BRIAN MORRISON

and other livery requirements, though the BR cast arrows would already have been affixed to the body while it was at Procor. Although this was not deemed to be important to the functioning of the locomotive, it was a requirement that it was fully decorated prior to despatch. Furthermore, in order for the locomotive to be despatched from works, it would receive a 'fitness to run' certificate, which required an inspection by the customer's representatives. These were BR inspectors who had an office on the works' site, enabling them to undertake the witness inspections of both components and the locomotive as a complete entity.

Once the locomotives had met the necessary criteria, they would always leave the works under their own power with a BR crew and Brush personnel on board. On occasions, the Class 60s would leave works in pairs for onward despatch to their commissioning locations, Leicester Depot being the most common.[11]

Class 60 Delivery

The Official Handover of 60001

Following thirteen months of challenges, 30 June 1989 was a momentous occasion for all who had been concerned with the Class 60 project. A letter dated 2 June 1989 was sent from Mr W. M. M. Petrie (Managing Director of Brush Electrical Machines) to Mr J. Tidmarsh (Project Director Major Railway Projects), inviting him to attend the formal handover ceremony of the first Class 60 locomotive.

The letter sent by Mr W. M. M. Petrie to Mr J. D. Tidmarsh, inviting him to attend the official handover ceremony of 60001. THE NATIONAL ARCHIVES

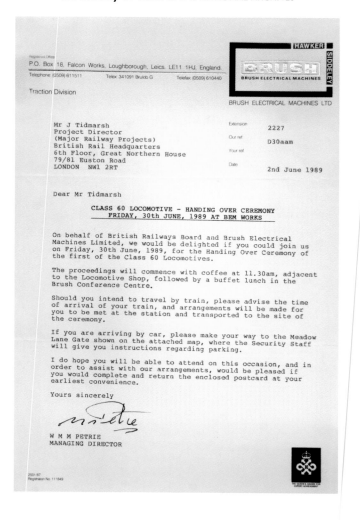

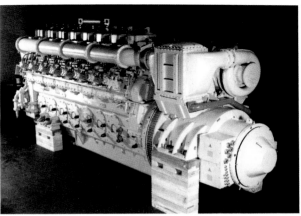

Mirrlees 8 MB 275T 8 cylinder engine with Brush built alternator as installed in Class 60 Locomotive.

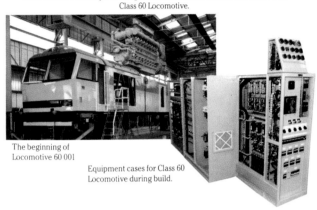

The beginning of Locomotive 60 001

Equipment cases for Class 60 Locomotive during build.

CLASS 60
LOCOMOTIVE
HANDING OVER
AND NAMING OF

60 001

BRUSH ELECTRICAL
MACHINES LTD.
LOUGHBOROUGH

30th June 1989

Cover view of the locomotive handover and naming ceremony brochure of 60001 *Steadfast* on 30 June 1989. Note the use of the 'General User' subsector symbol.
BRUSH TRACTION

The programme of events detailing the official Class 60 handover ceremony, held on 30 June 1989.
BRUSH TRACTION

Inside view of the brochure for the Class 60 handover ceremony; it details the engine and other internal components. 30 June 1989. BRUSH TRACTION

Rear cover view of the brochure detailing the locomotive handover and naming ceremony of 60001 *Steadfast* on 30 June 1989. BRUSH TRACTION

BRUSH ELECTRICAL MACHINES this year celebrates 100 years of design and manufacture of transport vehicles, rotating electrical machines and control equipment and has been a major supplier of traction equipment to the world's railway systems for many years.

In 1889 the Brush Electrical Engineering Company was formed. This brought together the Anglo-American Brush Electric Light Corporation and the Falcon Engine and Car Works; the latter company had been producing horse drawn tram cars, rail coaches, wagons and steam locomotives on the Loughborough site since 1865.

We are delighted that our guests, and representatives of the company, are able to join us in handing over the first of the Class 60 Locomotives to British Rail. The locomotive, the first of one hundred on the contract, has been completed in just 13 months from contract award, this notable performance has been aided by the very close co-operation between BEM personnel, British Rail staff, and equipment suppliers.

PROGRAMME

11.15 a.m.	Reception and Coffee
11.45 a.m.	Handing over of Locomotive 60 001 by Mr. W. M. M. Petrie, Managing Director Brush Electrical Machines Ltd.
	Mr. C. J. Driver, Director, Freight B.R.B. will receive and name the locomotive.
12.30 p.m.	Buffet lunch in Brush Conference Centre for invited guests.
	Transport to Railway Station available.

Brush Electrical Machines Ltd.,
P.O. Box 18, Falcon Works,
Loughborough,
Leics. LE11 1HJ, England.

It is quite clear that this ceremony had been planned for some time, because in addition to the above, a letter had been sent by Suzanne Knight on behalf of Mr J. Tidmarsh to Mr C. J. Driver (Director of Freight at BR) to enquire who from Railfreight would like to be invited to the ceremony. This letter was also sent in order to support Brush in the handover ceremony of 60001.[11]

There was a gathering of invited guests and a formal handover ceremony in a marquee adjacent to the erecting shop at Brush. Mr Colin Driver and other BR staff inspected the locomotive, and then it was handed over to the two traction inspectors and two driver instructors, who took it to Toton that evening, along with two Brush traction engineers and also a BR field support engineer.[4]

Testing and Analysis

Following the official handover ceremony at the Falcon works in Loughborough, the locomotive went firstly to Toton Traction Maintenance Depot and then on to the Railway Technical Centre in Derby, to undergo detailed testing and analysis. However, there were problems, with technical issues arising mainly related to the control software and bogie suspension. These issues were time-consuming, and work continued right through the commissioning period; as a result the BR on-track performance testing was not completed until June 1990.

Following essential and critical modifications, the first locomotives to be accepted into traffic were actually 60017, 60018 and 60019: these were allocated to Thornaby Depot on 11 September 1990 – sixty-three weeks after the contractual delivery date for 60001. As Roger Ford remarked: 'It took two and a half years for Electro Motive Division to deliver a locomotive built from assembled catalogued parts, and Brush took thirteen months to produce a higher specification locomotive, half a mile thick.'[5] Even after delivery of the 100 Class 60 locomotives, there was much outstanding work to be done, and an extensive modification programme was implemented.

Faults and Modifications

Over the years it has been widely misunderstood and wrongly publicized that each Class 60 suffered well in excess of 100 major faults. This is not true, because many of the faults were actually not faults at all but merely modifications, and in some cases very small ones. Many of these 'faults/

modifications' were due to software issues, including false indications, which were more or less rectified within a year. Other components that had given trouble and required rebuilding were the bogies and the main rectifier; extensive software development work was also required.

After 1991 when all the Class 60s had been delivered, there were issues including radiator elements splitting and intercooler fractures; however, these did not by any means constitute an avalanche of troubles, and were rectified in conjunction with suppliers along with other modifications.

By 1992/93 the capable Mirrlees engine was starting to give significant trouble. These problems crept in with usage, and ranged from cylinder-head blows to cracks, though these were rectified by Mirrlees.

By this time there were 100 Class 60s, and a tremendous amount of work had to be undertaken by Mirrlees on the engines to remedy the faults. Even so, the modifications never stopped the fleet, as only three or four locomotives would be out of service for remedial work at any one time. March Depot in Cambridgeshire was used to undertake these modifications, and it was usual to have two Class 60s at March, with Mirrlees spending about a week working on each engine, whilst Brush attended to other modifications. Upon completion, the locomotives would return to their depots, and would be replaced at March by another two locomotives. This rolling programme continued for about three years.[11]

The Mirrlees engine develops 3,100hp, which is less than the Classes 56 and 59; the Class 60 therefore looked a less powerful locomotive. However, 'power is speed on hills'[11] and the Class 60 maintained its speed on gradients and was therefore deemed to be satisfactory. At this point it must be also be remembered that over time, the Mirrlees 8MB275RT established itself to be about the best four-stroke engine that BR was ever to purchase.

Significant engine faults manifested themselves after about three years of operational service. Often the causes of service troubles were attributable to control and software issues and were rectified promptly. On the suspension, the 'rolling rubber ring' had to be replaced by 'guide post', but this work was carried out during the first year. Two groups had been set up in order to rectify the engine defects. The engine problems management had been assigned to an upper management group, whilst a lower action group – known as the 'task force' – consisting of Brush, Mirrlees and BR specialist engineers, dealt with the following issues:

Fractured cylinder liners

Cylinder-head gas joint leaks

Cylinder-head valve-gear failures

Cam-follower roller and camshaft failures

Failed fuel-injector pumps

Heat-exchanger and bracket failures

Overspeed trip units

Lubricating oil leaking from the alternator outlet casing

Fuel-pressure relief valve

Fuel-pump rack

Coolant filling valve

Lubricating oil flow filter

Cracks in the silencer inlet bellows

Air-intake duct fractures

Exhaust heat shields and manifold joints

Intercooler failures

Governor failures

Fuel-filter blockages (a Brush part, but too small a filter)

High-pressure fuel-pipe failures[11]

From an environmental point of view, the Class 60 was deemed to comply fully with the noise specification – indeed it was found to be significantly quieter than other classes of traction under the operation of BR. British Rail had a very specific testing procedure to measure noise levels, which involved placing microphones at strategically defined distances and heights at the track side.

The Class 60s met the specification for tractive effort, braking performance, structural strength and ride performance. Following modifications, this also applied to ride performance and bogie suspension. Complaints had been received from drivers regarding the cab side window, in that it was awkward for the driver to look back at the ground staff or train whilst at the same time grasping the power handle in his right hand. Hitherto all four cab side windows were of a two-piece design, with the rear pane able to slide to the open position. In a modification carried out in the first year, the driver's cab window was replaced with a three-piece unit, with the centre pane able to slide but the two outer panes fixed in position.

A completed Class 60 bodyshell was sent to the BR Research Structures Department in order for proof testing to be undertaken, in which no gross deformation was found and no failure occurred. The Deuta-Werke (Germany) Health Monitoring system that had been installed on the Class 60 had also given trouble, with instances of system 'lock-up' being reported with loss and/or corruption of

data. This was the last piece of software/electronics to be fully working, and as such became a completion milestone. The Class 60s were the first locomotives to have this health monitoring system installed on locomotives in the UK, now mandatory as the OTMR ('on-train monitor recorder').

Although there were improvements in further delivery timings, Brush Traction never fully recovered their contractual schedule of delivering the modified Class 60s without faults, the earliest rectified locomotive being delivered ten weeks late. A number of Class 60s were used for artisan driver training and familiarization purposes as they were not in an acceptable modified state to haul trains in revenue-earning service. The Class 60s involved were 60003 to 60016, which hauled numerous trains during driver training.

As mentioned earlier, all BR traction units had to undergo an exhaustive commissioning and testing programme, which also required each locomotive to accumulate 1,000 trouble-free miles before acceptance into traffic by BR. Each locomotive was subjected to a light engine 'shake-down' run, and then a long-distance run with load on revenue-earning trains, with all traction units undergoing an exhaustive commissioning and testing programme. It was further stipulated by BR that before being accepted into service, each locomotive was to undergo 1,000 consecutive fault-free miles, which excludes delivery from the Contractor's works. The mileage would be in freight service or whilst undergoing crew training, which would be timetabled at the Board's discretion.[4]

Testing and Commissioning

Before any item of rolling stock was permitted to move on the mainline railway it had to undergo the most stringent and exhaustive testing. Indeed, many components were tested in order to make sure that they and certain materials used for projects such as the Class 60 were able to withstand many hours of intense use and in the harshest of environments. For example, brake block material would have been tested far beyond the design limitations required under extreme conditions. These tests were run at the Railway Technical Centre (RTC) based at Derby, and also the Mickleover test track on the former section of the Great Northern cross-country route from Grantham to Nottingham and Stafford. The actual test track ran between Mickleover itself for just over 5.6 miles (9km) to Egginton Junction, situated along the Derby to Stoke line.

As well as the two listed sites, the Old Dalby test track was another test facility that ran between Melton Junction and Edwalton, a distance of just over 13 miles (21km). On 6 March 1990, 60001 had been recorded on the Old Dalby test track coupled to Mk 2 test car 6, No. QXA ADB975290. The test vehicle was fitted with a diesel generator and equipped with B4 bogies, permitting speeds of up to 100mph (160km/h).[11]

Testing of the Class 60s was extensive, with trials being undertaken initially on the BR Research Mickleover test track. On 13 July 1989 the first member of the Class, 60001, was the subject of trials, with further tests being made on the main line. In one of the tests 60001 *Steadfast* worked 6Z25 from Tees Yard to Inverness. The working involved the Railway Technical Centre's test car 6 being coupled to a lengthy train of Redland PCA two-axle stone-hopper wagons. 60001 and test car 6 worked the Inverness PCAs, whilst 60002 hauled another rake the following day. They were then combined and a number of runs were made over the route.

The primary purpose of the test was to check the wheelset thermal performance whilst braking. This downhill run to Inverness is the longest downhill braking requirement in the UK. Further workings required members of the Class 60 fleet to venture into Scotland, notably 60001 *Steadfast* and 60002 *Capability Brown*, with the RTC's test car 6 marshalled between the locomotives. The working also consisted of the Redland two-axle PGA stone-hopper wagons.

Several locations in Scotland were used for the testing, one of which was the Highland mainline between Aviemore and Inverness. Another was the ascent of Slochd summit, which is 1,315ft (400m); this was a real test for the locomotives because it is 6 miles (10km) long and the gradient is as much as 1 in 60 in places, though the overall gradient is much longer.

The Settle and Carlisle line was used for mainline driver training; in one instance 60006 *Great Gable* was reported to have been used for trials during August 1992 with a lengthy train of HEA coal wagons in tow. Crew training is, of course, a very important part of any locomotive testing, and as such it is understood that 60006 *Great Gable* spent time at several depots, including Old Oak Common, March, Hither Green and Leicester.[11]

Part of the testing required 60001 to undertake BR type tests at the Old Dalby test track between Edwalton and Melton Mowbray. On this occasion 60001 was coupled to the Railway Technical Centre's test car 6 and a formation of

During the Class 60 testing, 60001 *Steadfast* is photographed as it propels test car 6 near Stanton tunnel. Note the test cabling leading from the rear cab.
ANON

tank wagons totalling 1,000 tonnes, with 60002 attached to the rear of the formation.

The tests required the following: slow speed control on both dry and wet rails, normal control at low speed on both wet and dry rails, and normal control at high speed on both wet and dry rails. In order for low adhesion to take place, a soap solution was sprayed on to the rail ahead of 60001's leading wheelset. The tests revealed that at 0.5mph (0.8km/h) on a dry rail and with no load changes, speed remained at a steady 0.5mph. The load was then changed by applying 0.5 bar of straight air brake on 60002: this caused the speed on 60001 to drop to zero, it then recovered to 1.5mph (2.4km/h) and finally settled back to 0.5mph.

Upon review by the electrical equipment engineer, it was felt that the response of the slow speed control was not up to standard and that further improvements should be carried out before the locomotive was permitted to work MGR (Merry-Go-Round) trains.

Every detail of the locomotive performance was scrutinized by the Trainload Freight engineers, having been measured by BR's Test and Performance Department (test car 6). This is, of course, most important, as the speed of the entire train of this type must be regulated and maintained so as not to impede the movement, as this could upset the precise timing of loading and unloading commodities passing through the silos. As part of the acceptance 'type test programme'

Thirteen Class 60s are seen at Brush awaiting modification/rectification. Six are identifiable, from left to right: 60030, 60025, 60029, 60018, 60022 and 60021. 5 August 1990. JOHN STRETTON

60084 SADDLEBACK is photographed at Brush Traction awaiting a new alternator and modifications. Channel Tunnel locomotive 92018 *Stendhal* is also seen, on 18 October 1994. JOHN STRETTON

a test run was made between Syston and Corby to test the braking system under normal operating conditions; this proved successful and met the required stopping distances.[11]

It was noted in the review that the current software did not have what would be the final method of wheelslip control, now known as 'creep control'. It is understood that conventional wheelslip control would be operative at all speeds until creep control was developed.[11]

The review further highlighted that whilst the locomotive was under slow speed control, a curious effect was observed: when wheelslip occurred at a speed of 0.5mph (0.8km/h), the primary suspension started to oscillate at approximately 5Hz. It was noted that the oscillation occurred on all axles, and was sustained for several tens of seconds, depending on the adhesion conditions. Brush was not clear if this was due to mechanical resonance initiated by the mechanical drive.

This effect was noted by Mr Roe of Brush Traction, who was concerned about the reported longitudinal movement of the wheelset and its possible detrimental effect on the bogie. He was of the opinion that BR would expect a statement from Brush before the locomotives were committed to hauling heavy trains.

The review also noted an unconnected concern relating to the accuracy and calibration of the speedometer. It was pointed out that the present system drove the speedometer off the radar signal, though its accuracy had been called into question. This was the traction type test first evaluation. Subsequently the shortlisted issues were also addressed, and a second traction type test conducted some weeks later

was successful in satisfying the Board of the locomotive's capabilities.[11]

Due to the many modifications needed to bring the Class 60 into service, the Brush Falcon works was struggling to find enough space in their complex to accommodate all the Class 60s awaiting modification and or rectification. Part of the way through the construction of the Class 60 programme, No. 25 shop was extended to almost double its size to enable the construction of further Class 60s and the modification of Class 60s that had already been constructed.

In order for the Class 60s to be accepted by the Board, 'works release' and 'fitness to run' certificates were required, and it is important to note that until the BRB accepted the design, Brush Traction would not receive payment, and could not supply any locomotive: hence the stockpiled locomotives.

Liquidated Damages Dispute

At the very end of Class 60 production a claim for liquidated damages was put forward by the BRB, as a result of which locomotives 60097, 60098, and 60099 were 'unofficially' impounded by Brush Traction until the dispute was resolved.

Unfortunately, commercial matters for Brush Traction had gone from bad to worse in the course of the acceptance and delivery of the Class 60s. Not only had they failed to deliver the locomotives within the agreed timeframe as set out in the contract, but other major issues had forced the BRB to put forward a claim for liquidated damages in accordance with condition 20 of the contract agreement with Brush Electrical Machines, 'Damages for Delay in Completion'.[4]

This condition stipulated that Brush Traction paid liquidated damages to the BRB, which was tantamount to 0.75 per cent of the price per locomotive for each week between the contractual delivery date and delivery. This was deemed to be on signing by the engineer of the Works Acceptance and Test Certificate, BR 8107/2. Also if the actual delivery date was later, then up to a maximum of 10 per cent of the locomotive price was to be paid. This was equal to a little over thirteen weeks, which prevailed for most of the locomotives.

The reasoning behind the BRB's decision to bring such claims was due in the main to the following issues:

■ Refusal by Brush Traction to pay fees incurred in respect of the reliability contract. This was non-payment of periods 1 to 8 inclusive (a single period being twelve weeks' duration)
■ A dispute with Brush Traction regarding the contractual definition of delivery, taken by the BRB to be the signing of the BR 8107/2 after light and loaded runs
■ Problems with the Mirrlees 8MB275RT engine
■ The Deuta Health Monitoring system not functioning correctly
■ Resources provided by Brush Traction to resolve technical issues and expedite the modification programme
■ Dispute over the cost of providing Brush Traction site service engineers on BR main depots at five locations
■ Dispute over the need to provide a *Workshop Overhaul Manual*, as specified in MT/123

This liquidated damages claim lasted well over a year, commencing in October 1991 and lasting until an agreement was reached on 1 April 1993. This agreement took the form of a 'Class 60 Locomotive Settlement Agreement', signed jointly on that particular date by representatives from Trainload Freight and Brush Traction.

Class 60 Locomotive Contract, Lessons Learned

As the Class 60s had been delivered late to BR for a variety of reasons, as explained earlier in this chapter, in a facsimile from Mr M. Frampton (Class 60 Project Manager) to Mr J.

D. Tidmarsh, Mr Frampton was of the opinion that lessons could be learned from the delays. The first point pertained to the timeframe, namely that the duration of the process from design to delivery needed to be extended from thirteen months to a more achievable timeframe of two and a half years. Mr M. Frampton recommended that time had to be built into the schedule to enable tests and on-track development to be carried out between the first and second locomotive.

He also made recommendations regarding: contractual details; payment and its link with the production and completion of manuals; training and test equipment; and materials in terms of the price and accountability of resources, suggesting that materials required for the warranty were purchased and re-ordered at the same price, whether for the contractor or BR, in order to ensure that there was nothing surplus that was not fully accounted for.[4]

The Class 60 Timelines

Class 60 No. 60001 *Steadfast* Timeline

Following the official handover ceremony from Brush Electrical Machines to the British Railways Board, No. 60001 was driven light engine to Toton on 30 June 1989, arriving there at 20:30.

02/07/1989	60001 ran light engine to EDU Derby Railway Technical Centre; it weighed in at 126.4 tonnes (as new).
08/07/1989	Returned to Toton as a light engine move.
09/07/1989	Running in sidings.
10/07/1989	Ran light engine to the Mickleover test facility.
23/07/1989	Returned to Brush for traction motor change (wheel skated on axle 4).
27/07/1989	Returned to Mickleover test track.
08/08/1989	At Railway Technical Centre at Derby.
09/08/1989	Returned to Brush coupled to RTC's test car 6.*
11/08/1989	Attended Old Dalby test track.
12/08/1989	Attended Mickleover test track.
18/08/1989– 21/08/1989	Derby–Cricklewood ride undertook tests with RTC's test car 6.
25/09/1989– 26/09/1989	Derby RTC–Corby: undertook brake tests with test car 6.

27/09/1989   Attended Mickleover test track with test car 6.

28/10/1989   Commissioning starts at Old Dalby.

08/10/1989   Attended Derby EDU.

The Director of Mechanical & Electrical Engineering (DM&EE) converted a MK2 FII, S13396 coach into test car 6, ADB 975290, which had been fitted out with test instruments.

Detailed testing was carried out on the Class 60s, which required every aspect of the locomotive's performance to be scrutinized. Computers were plugged into the locomotive in order for data to be analysed.

A fine portrait of 60002 *Capability Brown* outside the test facility at Brush Traction. Note the absence of both snowplough and orange cant-rail stripe. 12 August 1989. JOHN STRETTON

Computers were used extensively during the rigorous testing of the Class 60s, as depicted in this view.
ANON

60001 *Steadfast* with 60002 *Capability Brown* at Mickleover with test car 6. Note also the abundance of test cabling at solebar level. ANON

No. 60001 *Steadfast* and No. 60002 *Capability Brown* Timelines

08/10/1989   No. 60002 *Capability Brown* ran from Brush to Derby RTC.

09/10/1989   Attended Mickleover test track.

26/10/1989   Both 60001 and 60002 attended the Mickleover test track for brake tests.

27/10/1989   Traction motor seriously damaged.

28/10/1989   60001 and 60002, coupled with RTC test car 6, undertook a test run to the Old Dalby test track hauling twenty-two TTAs.

30/10/1989	60001 coupled to test car 6 to Derby (repairs to test car 6 cabling).
31/10/1989	60002 was returned to Toton for tyre turning.
01/11/1989	60002 returned to Old Dalby.
02/02/1990	Rolling ring rubber suspension units on 60001 and 60002 found to be defective.
26/02/1990	First unsuccessful type test begins.
26/04/1990	Guide post bogie on 60001 at Mickleover.
30/04/1990	Successful type test begins at Mickleover.
16/05/1990	60001 hauls 3,700 tonne train 'Supatrain' between Mountsorrel and Cricklewood.

Class 60 General Timeline Testing and Notable Events

18/12/1989	60005 was coupled to 56061 hauling 42 PGAs, which was the first main line freight run, Mountsorrel~Radlett. By 18/01/1990 at Old Dalby, trainloads of 50 HEAs plus 19 TTAs had been tested, which was 3,600 tonnes.
08/02/1990	60011 was taken to Old Dalby for test use.
12/02/1990	60001 plus test car 6 and 60011 undertook testing between Calverton–Ratcliffe. It returned to Old Dalby on 13/03/1990. On 20/04/1990 this returned to Mickleover with rebuilt bogie-axle box suspension.
30/04/1990	Type testing at Mickleover, continued at Bentick.
16 & 17/05/1990	'Supertrain' comprised 60001 and 60002 hauling a trailing load totalling 3,590 tonnes, which ran between Mountsorrel and Cricklewood.
07/06/1990	Brake tests undertaken on the Inverness route.
04/07/1990	60001 and 60002 returned to Old Dalby for final acceptance tests.
17/08/1990	60024 was the first Class 60 to have modified engine-room extractor fans. This was tested between Mountsorrel and Radlett.
04/09/1990	Concentration on Deuta Health Monitoring testing on various Class 60s, 60023 with 60016, 60015, 60029, 60017 and 60028.

24/10/1990	60010 with 60023 undertook a hauled working between Mountsorrel and Radlett with a trailing load of 3,700 tonnes.
11/1990	Deuta Health monitor accepted.
11/1990	60017 becomes the first Class 60 to have completed 1,000 trouble-free miles into service at Thornaby (Lackenby–Corby coil train).
26/05/1991	60032 and 60057 operated the Coalville Swansong (St Pancras–Coalville and return).
05/07/1991	60041 hauled seventy-two PGAs totalling 3,800 tonnes between Mountsorrel and Radlett.
05/11/1991	60041 hauled a load totalling 3,757 tonnes between Mountsorrel and March.
30/11/1992	60097, 60098, 60099 and 60100 become the last four new Class 60s to leave Brush.
18/02/1993	Commencement of Mod. 17 engine temperature control on 60033 at Brush. Two Class 60s, 60033 and 60055, ran to Radlett.
Mid-1995	Software Version '1' operational.
17/10/2007	Work on control gear/electrical reliability undertaken for the Class 60 overhaul programme, now known as 'Super 60' refurbishment programme.

The following are the senior individuals who were involved in the construction of the Class 60 project as mentioned in the text and records:

John Tidmarsh	Project Director	BR
Mike Frampton	Project Manager	BR
Colin Driver	M.D. Trainload Freight	BR
Ken Dunn	Power equipment	BR
Tony Coles	Commissioning Engineer	BR
David Russell	Freight Engineer	BR
Bruce Sephton	Director, Traction Division	Brush
Mick Roe	Bogie and suspension	Brush
Jim Buchannan	Power equipment	Brush

Class 60 Delivery Dates

A table is set out below detailing the differences between the contractual dates and the actual delivery dates. A locomotive could not be accepted by the board unless a 'Fitness to run' certificate has been issued.

Differences between Contractual and Actual Delivery Dates

Locomotive number	Contractual delivery date	Actual delivery date
60001	30/06/89	28/08/91 * After modification upgrades
60002	04/08/89	02/12/92 * After modification upgrades
60003	25/08/89	21/01/92 #
60004	15/09/89	17/05/91 #
60005	29/09/89	12/04/91 #
60006	20/10/89	12/04/91 #
60007	03/11/89	18/12/92 #
60008	24/11/89	03/12/92 #
60009	01/12/89	29/01/93 #
60010	08/12/89	13/11/90 #
60011	15/12/89	23/09/91 #
60012	22/12/89	29/10/91 #
60013	05/01/90	07/01/93 #
60014	15/01/90	16/12/92 #
60015	19/01/90	24/03/93 #
60016	26/01/90	03/12/92 #
60017	09/02/90	03/10/90
60018	16/02/90	19/10/90
60019	23/02/90	19/10/90
60020	02/03/90	14/01/91
60021	09/03/90	13/11/90
60022	16/03/90	07/12/90
60023**	23/03/90	11/09/90
60024	30/03/90	13/12/90
60025	13/04/90	07/12/90
60026	20/04/90	07/12/90
60027	27/04/90	20/12/90
60028	04/05/90	30/10/90

Locomotive number	Contractual delivery date	Actual delivery date
60029	11/05/90	02/11/90
60030	25/05/90	13/11/90
60031	01/06/90	16/04/91
60032	08/06/90	26/11/90
60033	15/06/90	28/01/91
60034	22/06/90	27/11/90
60035	29/06/90	04/04/91
60036	20/07/90	17/06/91
60037	27/07/90	31/01/91
60038	03/08/90	21/02/91
60039	10/08/90	03/05/91
60040	17/08/90	03/09/90
60041	24/08/90	08/05/91
60042	07/09/90	30/05/91
60043	14/09/90	18/06/91
60044	21/09/90	26/06/91
60045	28/09/90	07/03/91
60046	05/10/90	04/03/91
60047	19/10/90	04/03/91
60048	26/10/90	24/04/91
60049	02/11/90	26/04/91
60050	09/11/90	25/02/91
60051	23/11/90	22/03/91
60052	30/11/90	24/04/91
60053	07/12/90	10/04/91
60054	14/12/90	15/04/91
60055	21/12/90	15/05/91
60056	04/01/91	09/05/91
60057	11/01/91	29/05/91
60058	18/01/90	30/05/91
60059	25/01/90	29/05/91
60060	08/02/91	20/06/91

Locomotive number	Contractual delivery date	Actual delivery date
60061	15/02/91	29/05/91
60062	22/02/91	12/06/91
60063	01/03/91	06/06/91
60064	08/03/91	28/06/91
60065	15/03/91	01/07/91
60066	22/03/91	14/08/91
60067	29/03/91	20/08/91
60068	12/04/91	29/08/91
60069	16/08/91	20/11/91
60070	26/04/91	07/10/91
60071	03/05/91	29/08/91
60072	10/05/91	27/09/91
60073	24/05/91	21/10/91
60074	31/05/91	29/??/91
60075	07/06/91	30/10/91
60077	21/06/91	31/10/91
60078	28/06/91	20/??/91
60079	19/07/91	05/12/91
60080	26/07/91	05/11/91
60081	02/08/91	14/11/91
60082	09/08/91	15/11/91
60083	16/08/91	20/11/91
60084	23/08/91	03/12/92 ^
60085	06/09/91	04/12/91
60086	13/09/91	13/12/91

Locomotive number	Contractual delivery date	Actual delivery date
60087	20/09/91	06/12/91
60088	27/07/91	11/01/92
60089	04/10/91	12/12/91
60090	18/10/90	17/01/92
60091	25/10/91	20/01/92
60092	01/11/91	23/01/92
60093	08/11/91	13/02/92
60094	22/11/91	13/02/92
60095	29/11/91	26/02/92
60096	06/12/91	18/03/92
60097	13/12/91	16/12/92 ^
60098	20/12/91	01/12/92 ^
60099	01/01/92	15/12/92 ^
60100	17/01/92	01/12/92 ^

*	Locomotives used for driver training prior to delivery
**	60023 was the first Class 60 to accumulate 1,000 trouble-free miles
^	Locomotives retained at Brush during the LD dispute
#	Locomotive used for artisan staff training

60003–60016 show later dates because they were returned to Brush for final modification upgrades after the other Class 60s had been modified.

60024 was the first Class 60 to undergo new engine-room extractor fan testing.

CHAPTER THREE

TECHNICAL DETAIL

The Class 60 diesel electric locomotives were constructed for the Trainload Freight sector of British Rail as a mainline Type 5 heavy freight locomotive. Unlike many earlier classes of locomotive, namely the Classes 37 and 47, the 100 Class 60s have undergone very few visible external modifications, other than of course the many livery changes that have taken place over the years to reflect changes in ownership. Minor roof alterations have been necessary due to issues surrounding excessive build-up of heat in the engine room, requiring extra grilles and vents to be fitted. Some of the vents are still present, though others that are no longer required have been sealed up. A detailed outline of the locomotives is given in this chapter.

Full power is required of 'Super 60' refurbished 60092, as it powers the diverted 6B13 Robeston–Westerleigh tanks at Pilning with 66194 dead-in-tow on the rear. 17 October 2013. EDWARD GLEED

Later on the Class 60s were refurbished under the 'Super 60' refurbishment programme, which required the engine to be overhauled, together with bogies and brake equipment, in addition to various reliability modifications regarding both software and hardware. This included the following:

- Traction motor overheat protection
- Improved engine governor reliability and optimized control
- Overhauled and simulator-tested control electronics and power electronics
- Improved Doppler radar located at the No. 2 end of the locomotive
- Various electronic and electrical upgrades on radiator fan control

General Details of the Class 60 Locomotive[11]

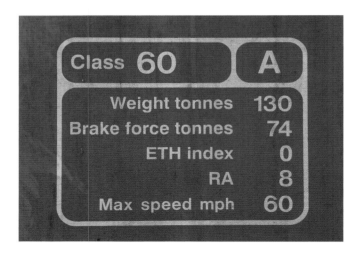

The Class 60 data label, which is affixed to the bodyside behind the driver's cab door. EDWARD GLEED

Locomotive design code:	60 AA (built to lot No. 1520)
Class code:	60/0
Wheel arrangement:	Co-Co
Track gauge:	1,435mm (565in)
Engine model:	Mirrlees Blackstone Type 8MB275RT, inline 8 cylinder of 145ltr (32gal) capacity
Engine rating:	3,100hp at 1,000rpm

Main generator:	Type BA1006A three-phase, salient pole, single-bearing, self-ventilated (slip-ring alternator), twelve-pole
Continuous rating:	2,015kW, 2,042kVA, 0.98PF, 796V, 1,480A
One-hour rating:	1,996kW, 423V, 4,620A (DC), through rectifier 1,000rpm
Auxiliary generator:	Type: BAA702A dual wound, eight-pole slip-ring alternator (two windings: three-phase and six-phase)
Continuous rating three-phase:	142.8kW, 168kVA, 0.85PF, 553V, 175A
Continuous rating six-phase:	92.04kW, 354kVA, 0.26PF, 236V, 250A (66.6Hz, 1,000rpm)
One-hour rating three-phase:	157.25kW, 185kVA, 0.85PF, 553V, 192A
One-hour rating six-phase:	101.40kW, 389kVA, 0.26PF, 236V, 275A (66.6Hz, 1,000rpm)
Traction motors:	Each type: TM 2161A, four-pole, separately excited ('Sepex'), force-ventilated, and axle-hung
Continuous rating:	304kW, 478V, 700A, 480rpm
One-hour rating:	298kW, 432V, 770A, 426rpm
Length over buffers:	21,340mm (840in)
Overall width:	2,720mm (107in)
Overall height:	3,950mm (155in)
Wheel diameter:	1,120mm (44in) from new (minimum is 1,080mm (42.5in))
Bogie wheelbase:	4,130mm (163in)
Wheelbase:	17,220mm (678in)
Distance between bogie pivots:	14,180mm (558in)
Minimum curve negotiable:	80m (263ft) radius
Maximum speed:	60mph (design specification 62mph, 100km/h)
Maximum starting tractive effort:	535kN (design specification 500kN (112,400lb ft))
Continuous tractive effort:	336kN (75,600lb ft) at 18.7 or 19.2km/h (11.6 or 11.9mph)
Fuel capacity:	4,500ltr (990gal) (6,000ltr/1,320gal) for Class

60s fitted with extended long-range fuel tanks)

Weight in working order:	129 tonnes nominal (131 tonnes for Class 60s equipped with a long-range fuel tank holding an additional 1,500ltr (330gal)
Axle load:	21 tonnes nominal
Brake type:	Air, PBL Westinghouse
Gear ratio:	97:19
Route availability:	9
Electric train heating index:	Not fitted, no requirement

Engine Data

View of the 8MB275RT engine looking towards the No. 2 end of the locomotive.
EDWARD GLEED

View of the 8MB275RT engine looking towards the No. 1 end of the locomotive. The cooler group is situated beyond the access door. EDWARD GLEED

As previously mentioned in this chapter, the engine installed in the Class 60 is a Mirrlees Blackstone Type 8MB275RT, in-line 8-cylinder, of 145 litre capacity developing 3,100hp. The engine block was manufactured from cast iron, as were the cylinder heads.

The engine identification number is derived according to the following code:

8 (cylinder) **MB** (Mirrlees Blackstone) **RT** (Rail Traction)

Mirrlees Blackstone is now part of the MAN B&W Group. The Class 60 engine is a larger version of the Mirrlees Blackstone 6MB275RT in-line 6-cylinder engine (developing 1,800hp), which had been installed in four members of the Class 37/9 fleet, 37901-37904.'

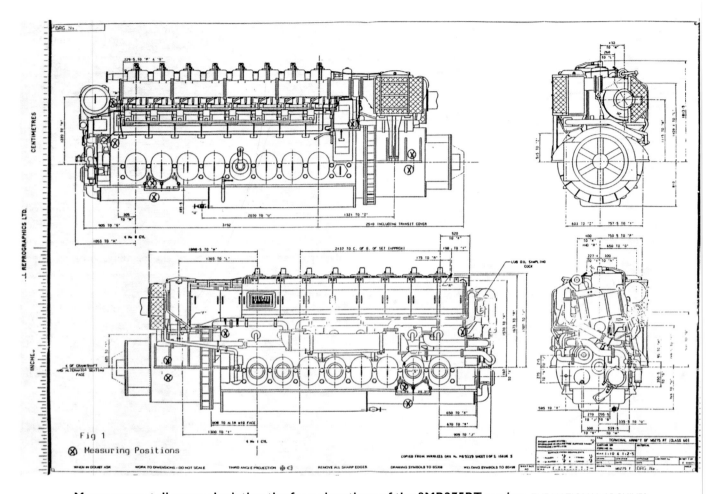

Measurement diagram depicting the four elevations of the 8MB275RT engine. THE NATIONAL ARCHIVES

Firing order of the cylinders:	1, 3, 2, 5, 8, 6, 7, 4
Piston crown diameter:	27.5cm (10in)
Piston stroke:	30.5cm (13in)
Piston rings:	Compression rings and oil control rings
Lubricating oil capacity:	1,000ltr (220gal)
Coolant capacity:	567ltr (124gal)

A number of Class 60s have been equipped with long-range fuel tanks with an additional 1,500ltr (330gal) capacity. These locomotives have been allocated under the WCBT pool, while Class 60 locomotives equipped with standard-range fuel tanks are allocated to the WCAT pool.[11]

The Lubricating Oil System

The Class 60 lubricating oil system is a full-flow type with coarse and fine filtration, pressure regulation, temperature control and oil low-level shut-down features. An electrically powered priming pump is provided in order to circulate oil prior to engine start-up; following start-up, the mechanical engine pump takes over and maintains pressure at what used to be 60psi but is now 70psi.

Oil is drawn from the sump via a coarse filter to the oil pump. On leaving the oil pump, oil flows to the pressure relief valve, which protects the thermostatic valve, heat exchanger and pressure check valve, which guards against excessive pressure on cold starts. Oil in excess of 5bar will return to the sump. After the pressure relief valve,

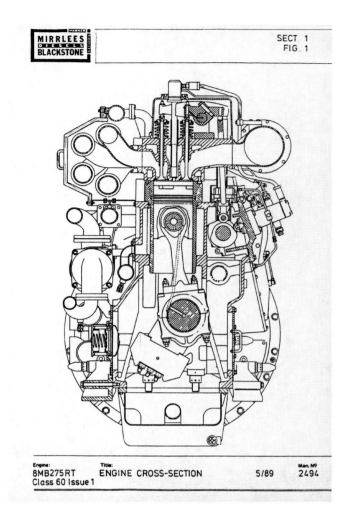

MIRRLEES
DIESELS
BLACKSTONE

SECT. 1
FIG. 1

Engine:
8MB275RT
Class 60 Issue 1

Title:
ENGINE CROSS-SECTION

5/89

Man. No
2494

Cross-section drawing of the 8MB275RT engine.
THE NATIONAL ARCHIVES

the lubricating oil passes through the heat exchanger or bypasses it, subject to an oil temperature controlled valve. The oil is then passed through a full flow type filter, with a filter blocked/restricted visual indicator. Oil passes from the filter to the regulating valve, which limits the pressure in the main oil gallery to 4.2bar, the excess being returned to the sump. The oil is passed throughout the engine via internally drilled ports, and then returns to the sump from a hole in the centre of the underside of the piston.

Oil is also supplied to the over-speed trip governor, turbocharger and engine governor. Inside the engine governor, the lubricating oil performs two functions: first it lubricates the governor driveshaft, and second it supplies a pressure indication to the low lubricating oil pressure shut-down

system. In the event of low pressure, this protection system returns the governor to the 'no fuel' position, causing the engine to shut down before damage can occur.

On the Class 60, the engine shut-down is either via the running oil pressure switch or the engine governor. In either case, the engine will stop when oil pressure falls to 1bar. Normal pressure is approximately 4.2bar. The governor will detect falling pressure and reduce engine speed (below 3.1bar) towards idle (1.38bar). At 1bar pressure, after twenty seconds delay it will return the fuel rack to the 'no fuel'/'shut-down' position.

An electrically (battery-) driven priming pump draws oil from the sump via a coarse strainer and then around the engine via the same route as mentioned above. A non-return valve is fitted on the outside of the priming pump to keep the system primed and to protect the priming pump against excessive pressure. The lubricating oil priming pump runs for thirty seconds prior to the engine sequence commencing. This permits the lubricating oil to circulate throughout the engine in order to minimize metal-to-metal contact taking place on start-up, thereby causing less wear and tear on vital components.

Ventilation of the crankcase is afforded by an electric motor-driven fan. Oil is separated out and returns by gravity to the sump. The air and gases are discharged out of the engine roof via a small grille.[8]

The Engine Governor

A Woodward PGE electro-mechanical governor is fitted to the engine, mounted on top of the engine block adjacent to the main alternator. The role of the governor is to control the fuel racks that regulate the amount of fuel delivered by the fuel injectors to the cylinders. The governor is controlled by a micro-processor. The idle speed of the governor is set to produce 4,500rpm, and the maximum speed to produce 1,000rpm. Although the driver's power handle is 'notchless', the actual engine speed is in eight steps.[8]

Fuel Delivery

Like many other classes of locomotive, an underslung fuel tank is fitted to the Class 60, though certain members of the class have an additional long-range fuel tank fitted between the air compressors. The main fuel tank is equipped with a fuel gauge operated by a mechanical float. The fuel gauge is

A photograph of the Woodward governor, fitted to the Class 60. ANON

The 8MB275RT engine installed in the Class 60 fleet is provided with both a high performance charge air-cooling system and exhaust system. On this particular engine more attention has been given to providing good fuel economy and low noise levels. In a climate where noise levels are under constant scrutiny, the Class 60 is very quiet, in stark contrast to the Class 37s, which are capable of producing a very loud exhaust. While this will doubtless appeal to many, I feel certain that many individuals who are not railway enthusiasts would rather the locomotive were seen and not heard.

The Class 60 employs a single unit, high-performance turbocharger, as was widely used in earlier classes of motive power. Air enters the locomotive via primary centrifugal inertia filters located in the bodyside. It is passed into the clean air compartment for combustion, and is then taken to the secondary filter box by ducting to the turbocharger. Compressed combustion air is passed through the intercooler to the air manifold and then to the cylinders. Exhaust gases pass from the cylinders via the outlet manifold to the turbocharger, and are then expelled to the atmosphere through the large roof-mounted silencer, this being mounted at the No. 2 end of the locomotive. The spin-tube air filters are of the 'self-cleaning' type, and any dirt that has accumulated in the filters is discharged through the bottom of the locomotive and on to the track. [8]

The Braking System

The compressed air system employed on the Class 60 was designed by Westinghouse, based at the time in Chippenham, Wiltshire. Like Brush, Westinghouse has held a long association with the railway industry in supplying the industry with braking systems. On the Class 60, the compressed air system is split into three different working pressures:

Main air, 10bar
Main reservoir supply and pipe, 7bar
Air-brake pipe, 5bar

The locomotive is equipped with two three-phase, AC-motored compressors, each being equipped with an air after-cooler. Air is drawn into each compressor through its associated air-intake filter and flexible hose. This air is then delivered into the main reservoir via a pressure flexible hose and check valve. The check valve prevents air loss in the event of a burst delivery hose or failed compressor.

indicated in increments, with lettered quarter increments labelled. Fuel filters are fitted between the tank and the fuel pump. The fuel system is a high flow type, with the rate of flow being three times the amount required at maximum load. Fuel is drawn from the main underslung fuel tank via a strainer by an electrically driven fuel transfer pump; it is then fed through a fine filter to the supply manifold, and finally on to the injector pumps.

Fuel is supplied to the cylinders by an injector fitted to each of the cylinders. The injectors are 700mm (28in) and have their own camshaft-operated fuel pump, which delivers fuel to the injectors at 5,570psi (380bar). Excess fuel flows to the return manifold and then back to the fuel transfer pump. The injector pumps have fuel flowing through them at all times the engine is running. [8]

The governor pressures are nominally set to 8.5bar to start the compressors, and 10bar to stop them. Should the governor fail, it can be isolated by operating the governor isolating cock, and the system will then be regulated at 12bar by a safety valve. A Salem air dryer is located in the main reservoir supply line, which ensures that only dry air reaches all air-operated equipment by removing moisture condensate from the compressed air supply. In addition, further air filtration takes place before the air enters the main reservoirs, which have auto-drain valves to clear moisture.

The Class 60 is equipped with air brakes only. Two pairs of pipes are fitted at buffer-beam level at either end of the locomotive, and are identified as follows:

Red brake pipe: 5bar controlling pipe for the train air-brake equipment.

Yellow brake pipe: this pipe is connected to the main air reservoir and is used when coupled to a train or locomotive. This is the preferred air supply for modern 'two pipe' systems.[11]

Design of the Class 60 Locomotive

The Class 60 locomotive is divided into various compartments: the radiator compartment located at the No. 1 end, the engine compartment in the centre portion of the locomotive, and the clean air compartment located at the No. 2 end.

The radiator compartment: this compartment contains the following:

Diesel engine cooler group
Crankcase extractor fan
Traction motor air filter
Air dryer
Auxiliary engine equipment
Air reservoirs
Fuel lift pump
Lubricating oil priming pump
Traction motor blower for No. 1 bogie

The Class 60 identification chart. THE NATIONAL ARCHIVES

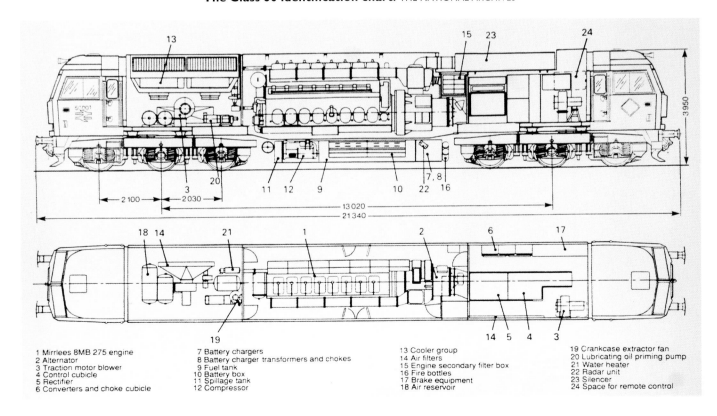

1 Mirrlees 8MB 275 engine	7 Battery chargers
2 Alternator	8 Battery charger transformers and chokes
3 Traction motor blower	9 Fuel tank
4 Control cubicle	10 Battery box
5 Rectifier	11 Spillage tank
6 Converters and choke cubicle	12 Compressor

13 Cooler group	19 Crankcase extractor fan
14 Air filters	20 Lubricating oil priming pump
15 Engine secondary filter box	21 Water heater
16 Fire bottles	22 Radar unit
17 Brake equipment	23 Silencer
18 Air reservoir	24 Space for remote control

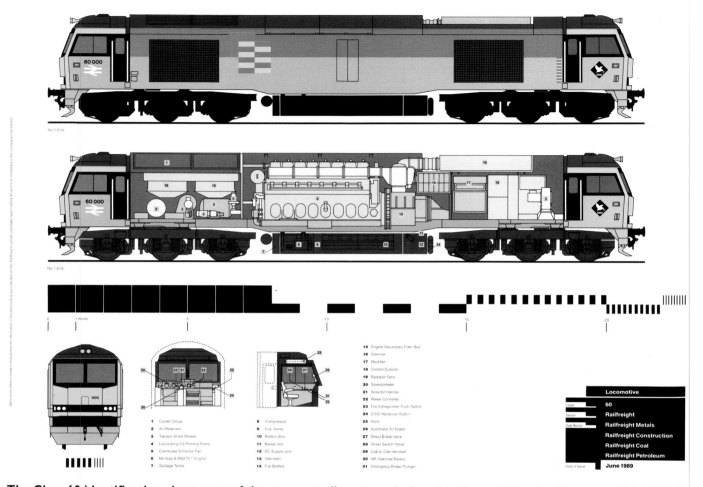

	Locomotive
Class	60
Sector	Railfreight
Sub-Sector	Railfreight Metals
	Railfreight Construction
	Railfreight Coal
	Railfreight Petroleum
Date of Issue	June 1989

1 Cooler Group
2 Air Reservoir
3 Traction Motor Blower
4 Lubricating Oil Priming Pump
5 Crankcase Extractor Fan
6 Mirrlees 8 MB275-T Engine
7 Spillage Tanks
8 Compressor
9 Fuel Tanks
10 Battery Box
11 Radar Unit
12 DC Supply Unit
13 Alternator
14 Fire Bottles
15 Engine Secondary Filter Box
16 Silencer
17 Rectifier
18 Control Cubicle
19 Radiator Fans
20 Speedometer
21 Selector Handle
22 Power Controller
23 Fire Extinguisher Push Button
24 D.S.D Holdover Button
25 Horn
26 Automatic Air Brake
27 Direct Brake Valve
28 Driver Switch Panel
29 Cab to Cab Handset
30 NR (National Radio)
31 Emergency Brake Plunger

The Class 60 identification chart, part of the corporate literature designed by Roundel Design Group for British Rail (Railfreight) in June 1989. ROUNDEL DESIGN GROUP/BRITISH RAIL

The radiator and fan compartment on 60059
Swinden Dalesman **at Westerleigh, 30 October 2012.**
EDWARD GLEED

The engine compartment: this compartment contains the following:

Mirrlees diesel engine, type 8MB275RT
Engine secondary filter box
Main and auxiliary alternators
Engine compartment extractor fans

The clean air compartment: this compartment contains the following:[11]

Silencer (externally roof-mounted)
Control cubicle
Diagnostic panel
Dump blower

The traction motor blower for No. 2 bogie, situated in the clean air compartment at the No. 2 end of the locomotive. EDWARD GLEED

Brake frame incorporating the air-brake system isolating cocks and hydraulic parking brake-control unit
Converters/choke cubicle
Main rectifier
Air filters
Traction motor blower for No. 2 bogie
Primary 'Donaldson' spin tube filter for engine combustion air and associated extractor filler blower

The diagnostic panel: one unique feature of the Class 60 is the diagnostic panel located in the clean air compartment. Should a fault occur, the diagnostic panel will self-diagnose and indicate to the driver the type of fault, and in many cases the driver can reset certain functions that might permit the locomotive to remain in service rather than be deemed a failure. From a commercial point of view, this piece of equipment has potentially saved vast amounts of money in terms of delays to both the train-operating companies and of course the freight customer.

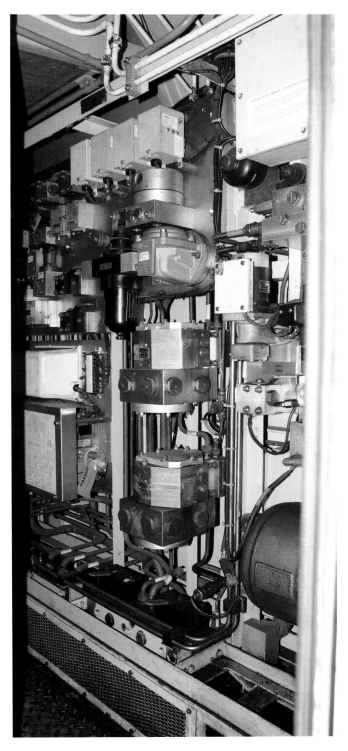

The brake frame, situated in the clean air compartment at the No. 2 end of the locomotive.
EDWARD GLEED

A further view of the brake frame, in the clean air compartment at the No. 2 end. EDWARD GLEED

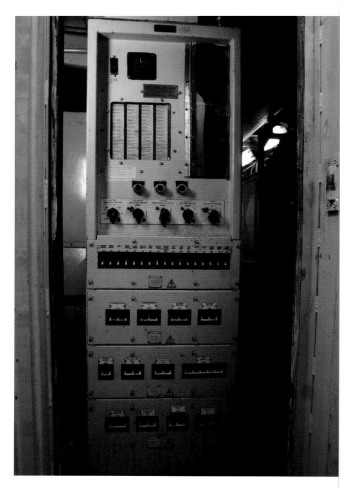

The diagnostic panel, located in the clean air compartment at the No. 2 end of the locomotive.
EDWARD GLEED

Circuit breakers and switches: directly below the diagnostic panel a series of circuit breakers and switches is provided. These include rotary isolating switches, DC circuit breakers and AC circuit breakers.

Rotary isolating switches: these are for the following:

Traction motor isolation
Vigilance isolate
Engine maintenance
Cut-out
AWS isolate

DC circuit breakers: these are for the following:

Function	Rating
Control circuit	20A
Brake control	10A
AWS	5A
Parking brake	10A
Electronic	15A
Deuta Health Monitor*	5A (*Now OTMR)
Fuel pump	10A
Lubrication oil pump	70A
Screen heater	30A
Hotplate	30A
Cab heat	50A

Lights 1 and 2	10A each
Start circuit	20A
Communications equipment	5A
Fire protection	15A

AC circuit breakers: these are for the following:

Compressor No. 1	40A
Compressor No. 2	40A
Traction motor blower No. 1	30A
Traction motor blower No. 2	30A
Extractor fan No. 1	15A
Extractor fan No. 2	15A
DC supply	100A
Filter blower	15A
Scavenge pump	15A
Radiator fan No. 1	100A
Radiator fan No. 2	100A

In addition to the three compartments and in common with most mainline locomotives in use on the UK rail network (excluding most shunting locomotives and the Class 20 diesel electric locomotive), two 'full width' driving cabs are provided, No. 1 end cab and No. 2 end cab. Longitudinally the locomotive is divided into two sections, the 'A' side and the 'B' side.[11]

Electrical Equipment[11]

The following components make up the Class 60 electrical equipment.

Main alternator: a salient pole machine, fitted with slip rings; it is self-ventilated and flange-mounted with a single bearing arrangement. It is type BA 1006A dual-wound.

Auxiliary alternator: an eight-pole, dual-wound machine with three-phase and six-phase outputs. The AVR-controlled three-phase windings supply the auxiliary machines; the six-phase windings provide excitation for the main and auxiliary alternators, together with the six field converters for the separately excited traction motors and the DC supply unit (battery chargers).

Traction motors: The six traction motors are connected in an 'all parallel' arrangement and are of the four-pole,

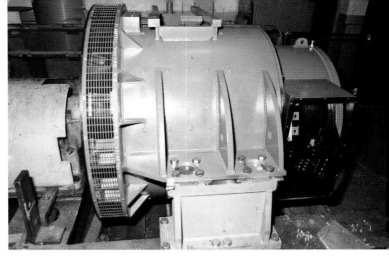

The Class 60 alternator on the test rig at Brush.
BRUSH TRACTION

force-ventilated, axle-hung type. All six traction motors face 'inboard'.

Continuous rating: 300kW.

Access to the Locomotive

Access into the locomotive is via bogie-mounted steps with grab handles fitted on each side. The steps have four rungs that are chequer-plated for added grip. Four inward-opening cab doors are provided, hinged on the inner side, facing towards the middle of the locomotive. Miniature rain gutters extend from between the door and over the cab side window. Polished metal handrails are recessed into the bodywork. An additional polished metal handrail is fitted directly below the two front cab windows on both cabs. The British Rail specification required the handrails to be oval in design, and without intermediate fixings; they also had to be sufficiently robust to support a bodyweight of at least 200kg (440lb) and to provide at least 50mm (2in) of space around each handrail to accommodate a gloved hand.[11]

In similar fashion to other locomotives, two door handles are provided for each door and are interlinked; the lower handle has a keyhole, positioned so that the cab doors may be locked at trackside level. Directly below the inner grab handle there is a small rectangular cover plate on the body-side below each cab door, with arrows indicating the lifting point. When the plate is removed, the attachments for lifting apparatus such as a jack or crane may be inserted into the pocket.

Twin engine-room doors are also provided on both sides of the locomotive body. These doors open inwards, and can only be opened from the inside of the engine room; they

The cab steps on 60074 with additional grab handles fitted to their sides. The four steps are chequer-plated for added grip. 30 January 2014. EDWARD GLEED

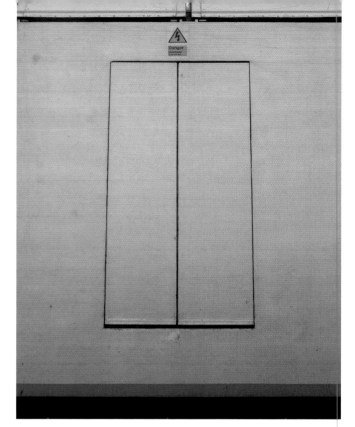

The engine-room access doors on 60099. They are inward opening, and can only be opened from the inside. Note the small lip at their base, preventing water ingress. 4 January 2013. EDWARD GLEED

allow maintenance staff direct access to the engine itself, and also pre-empt staff walking oily items through the rest of the engine room, clean air compartment and vestibule or cabs.

Design of the Driving Cab

Each cab is accessed through a vestibule that separates it from the body. The vestibule has four doors: two inward-opening external doors with non-opening windows (which are rounded at their corners), an inward-opening cab door and the engine-room door. The vestibule forms two vital roles: it affords better sound protection for the train crew, and should a fire occur in the engine room the fumes, smoke and heat will be concentrated in that area, making it safer for the train crew to alight.

Side view of the cab of 60047 at Bristol illustrating the cab steps, dual interlinked door handles, inset grab handles and side air-intake grille. Note the revised 'tilted' Colas Rail logo. 10 December 2015. EDWARD GLEED

Much effort has gone into the design of driving cabs in relation to ergonomics, crashworthiness and aesthetics. In the past British Rail employed Wilkes & Ashmore, the British Transport Commission's design consultants, to design a cab with the controls arranged in a neat and orderly fashion. Much attention was also given to the cab interior from an aesthetic point of view.

In the case of the Class 60, cab design has changed quite considerably, though it is still similar to that of the Class 58. On earlier classes of locomotive, cab interior colours were cream, grey and in some cases light green and even a vivid blue; the Class 58s, however, were quite different, with a reddish-orange colour used on the lower panels, and this has also been used for the lower panels and main cab entry door of the Class 60, though the colour is more red than orange. The upper cab wall and sides are light grey, with the front corner cab pillars and internal cab window frames tastefully finished off with aluminium trim. The cab bulkhead is light grey, while the cab roof is grey and soundproofed.

Directly above the cab entry/exit door is the fire alarm bell, aptly coloured red. The fire bell will only be heard in the event of a fire. An electric shock/resuscitation notice is fixed to the cab door. Directly behind the driver's seat an instruction is provided to help identify whether any outbreak of fire is major or minor, and the different procedures required to fight it. (There is a coat-hanger behind the secondman's seat.) At just behind cab roof level behind the secondman's seat there is a box containing a two-way fibre-optic link for a computer to be plugged in to test the control equipment. This apparatus is only fitted in cab No. 2.

View depicting the location of the fire bell. On the left, a box contains a two-way fibre-optic link for the Brush engineers' computers that test the control equipment.
EDWARD GLEED

CAB 2

ELECTRIC SHOCK
RESCUE AND TREATMENT

As in the driving cab of other modes of transport, the driver must have a clear view of the controls and instrumentation, and they must be within easy reach. More importantly, his view of the line ahead must be unhindered. The Class 60 cab is spacious, unlike that of the Class 59s and 66s, where the main driving controls are mounted on a tower pedestal. Unlike some members of the Class 66 fleet, hitherto the Class 60s have not been equipped with wing mirrors. The driver's seat is fully adjustable, and there is also a seat for the secondman; both are padded and covered in grey textured cloth.

Visibility from the cab is excellent, with unrestricted views of the line ahead for both driver and secondman. On the outside the front cab windows have conventional windscreen wipers, fixed at the top.

The cab side windows on the driver's side differ in style from those on the secondman's side: on the driver's side the window is a three-piece unit, and only the middle glazed unit may be opened; as already mentioned, this window arrangement was altered from the two-piece unit installed during the original construction. The secondman's cab side window remained unaltered and is a two-piece unit, and only the rear pane may be opened. All other cab windows are fixed. The exterior window frames were painted satin black during the Trainload livery era, though since then they are in most cases painted to suit the livery of the locomotive.

Window blinds are coloured black and are non-reflective; they are also fitted to both front cab windows. In earlier classes of traction the sun visors were fabricated from tinted perspex, with or without aluminium trim; the Class 60s, however, were equipped with roller blinds for both driver and secondman. In each case the visor is pulled down to suit the lighting conditions. The window blinds are tensioned, and are fitted with protruding lugs at their base, which slot into guide rails: this allows the blind to remain in situ without flapping about. The guide rails terminate at just over half-way down the cab window, so if the blind gets stuck in the fully lowered position, visibility is maintained. Both front cab windows are equipped with window demisters.

Cab Instrumentation and Controls

Many of the driving controls of the Class 60 are standard equipment as utilized in other BR classes – for example the

General interior view of the cab depicting the driver's main desk and other associated equipment. Note the red lower panels. EDWARD GLEED

speedometer and brake gauges. This includes some of the following items, which are shown clearly in the photographs.

Light Switches

Directly above the driver's head is a panel of illuminated rocker switches, which allow the driver to select head-and/or tail-lights; he can also select between day and night running modes, as follows:

Day mode: right-hand headlight and left-hand marker light

Night mode: left-hand headlight and right-hand marker light

View of the switches controlling the head- and tail-lamps. EDWARD GLEED

Yard working: two marker lights and two red tail-lights at both ends

Adjacent to the switches is a small panel, which indicates to the driver whether the exterior driving lights are illuminated or not, in the following manner:

Marker lights, left and right
Headlight
Tail-lights, left and right

Being able to select right and left on the marker and tail-lamps is of great importance. In normal running mode, both marker and tail-lamps must be illuminated (if the locomotive is hauling a train, then the tail-lamps on the locomotive must be extinguished). In addition, a rotary switch is provided for the driver to select the marker-light combinations indicating yard work in night- and day-running mode.

There is also a brake continuity rotary switch with three positions: service, isolate, test. On the same panel, an inspection lamp socket is provided.

Other Switches and Control Sticks

To the left of the driver's seat are the following items of equipment:

■ Clipboard
■ Warning horn joystick

View of the direct brake, auto-brake controller and emergency brake plunger. The train-length and hazard warning buttons can also be seen. The warning horn control is just out of view.
EDWARD GLEED

■ Auto airbrake (push forwards to apply, pull back to release) – also known as a 'wig-wag' stick
■ Straight airbrake (push forwards to apply, pull back to release)

Brake Controls

One item of equipment that has changed in recent locomotive construction for the UK is the brake controller: instead of it being designed like the power handle, two vertical control sticks with black rounded caps are provided: one is the straight airbrake controller and the other is the auto airbrake controller. Both have rubber gaiters fitted at their base to prevent dust and debris falling through the facia. To apply the brakes, the stick is pushed forwards; to release them, the stick is pulled back; braking is activated by electrical impulses from the auto airbrake controller. The straight airbrake is an air valve and is non-electrical in operation.

As with all traction units, there must always be an overriding control, and in an emergency situation, a red plunger is provided that, when struck in a downward movement, vents the brake pipe, which applies the brake. The direct brake controller is for stopping the locomotive, whilst the auto brake is used when hauling a train. The auto brake will exert a proportional amount of brake force in relation to the train and locomotive. Conventional brake cast-iron

blocks that bear directly on the tyre tread are fitted to the Class 60.

Train-Length Button

A rather novel system is the train-length button, which was fitted in the late 1990s with the Q-Tron system. As already mentioned, train lengths have risen dramatically over the years, to such an extent that some goods loops are not long enough to accommodate them or they are a very tight fit. The signalman will be able to see if the train is 'clear' of the line by looking at the panel or box track circuit diagram, but for the driver it has hitherto sometimes been difficult to gauge whether the entire train has fitted into the loop and is therefore clear of the line. To assist in this matter the driver can input the train-length data and depress a yellow train-length button, which will 'count down' the length of the train. The system will identify and indicate to the driver when the train is not fouling the main line, while an alarm will be heard confirming if it is.

Hazard Warning Buttons

A yellow hazard push button is provided, which the driver can actuate in the event of an emergency. This causes the marker lights to flash to oncoming drivers or trackside staff. This system was installed at the same time as the Q-Tron system.

The Main Driver's Desk

The overall facia of the main driver's desk is very neat in appearance. It is a prefabricated, glassfibre, moulded unit, mid-grey in colour, with the controls and instruments arranged in an orderly manner mounted on a prefabricated metal plate that is secured to the main desk. The desk is hinged throughout its entire bottom length to allow maintenance staff easy access. The layout of the driver's desk is described below.

Subsidiary Controls and Switches

The upper left row of buttons are for the following purpose:

■ Parking brake button: coloured black indicates ON, with an illuminated indicator situated to the right

View of the instruments and controls of the main driving desk. EDWARD GLEED

- Parking brake button: coloured red indicates OFF
- Brake overcharge button: coloured black
- Three indicators consisting of two colours, one red *or* two yellow. The red indicator is situated in between the two yellow indicators. The red and the yellow indicators are never illuminated at the same time, but are used as follows:

  Brake test: double yellow

  AWS: in, double yellow; out, red

  Engine stop: running, double yellow; stop, red

  Wheelslip: normal conditions, double yellow; wheelslip indication is red. Creep control operates when it is needed most, for example from a standstill, when there is the least momentum and the greatest need for traction

  General fault: normal conditions, double yellow; fault, red

  Auto-sanding: normal conditions, double yellow; sanding occurrence, red

Windscreen wiper controls: the front cab windows are manufactured of toughened triplex glass with demisting elements fitted. There is an arrowed rotary switch for slow speed, one, two and three; a silver plunger commences wiping, and if pushed will eject screen wash.

Other switches and controls:

- The three recessed buttons are for the following purpose:

  Green: engine start

  Red: engine stop

  Clear: fire alarm test

- Single indicator: this is the crew communication buzzer between both cabs
- Top rotary switch: this is for the hotplate, and has the following increments: off, low, medium and high. The hotplate has a metal guard with slats, on which there are two horizontal bars that can be adjusted so that different-sized cooking receptacles can be held securely. It has a closable cover when it is not in use
- A further set of windscreen wiper controls is provided for the secondman, or other train crew
- Directly below this is the covered fire-system plunger. To actuate this, the ring-pull is used to remove the cover and the accompanying red label reads: 'Shut down diesel engine and push button'
- The cable between the driver's desk and the lower facia panel is an earthing bond

The Seven Dials

The seven dials and AWS 'sunflower' indicator are all illuminated for night-time operation. The dials themselves are painted matt black with white numerals and white needles. Class 60s have illumination by conventional incandescent lamp. The seven dials are as follows (left to right):

- Main air reservoir gauge measured in 'bar'
- Brake-pressure gauge for both bogies
- Main brake-pipe pressure gauge
- Speedometer, measured in 5mph (8km/h) increments
- Slow speed speedometer, measured in 0.1mph (0.16km/h) increments (*see* Note below)
- Ammeter, measured in 100amp numerical increments with 10.0amp increments; maximum current is 6,800amp
- Airflow indicator: this indicates to the driver the amount of air flowing into the train from the locomotive. It assists to indicate when the brakes at

the rear of the train are released when used with the brake-pipe gauge

Note: Unlike traction units, which are specifically designed for passenger operation such as the high speed train, freight locomotives have a second speedometer. Unlike the main speedometer that is calibrated in 5mph (8km/h) increments, the secondary speedometer is calibrated in 0.1mph (0,16km/h) increments. This secondary speedometer is used when the 'slow speed control' function is in use. This is an important feature in that it allows more accurate automatic control of the locomotive at very low speeds, and when in use at loading/unloading facilities. Due to the fact that the commodities are bulk loaded/unloaded from each wagon, these facilities require that the movement be maintained at a given slow speed.

AWS Alarm and 'Sunflower' Indicator

Between the speedometer and main brake-pipe gauge is the AWS alarm and accompanying 'sunflower' indicator. Should the driver receive a clear signal, the indicator changes to all black and the AWS will emit a 'ping' sound. If the driver receives a cautionary or red signal, a permanent speed restriction (PSR) or temporary speed restriction (TSR), the indicator will change to both yellow and black segments (hence the term 'sunflower indicator') and a horn will be heard. This alarm must be acknowledged by the driver, who must strike the AWS reset button. If he fails to do this, an emergency brake will be applied, which cannot be overridden by the driver until the train has been brought to a standstill.

SSF (Speed Sensor Fitted) System

Directly above the two cab windows is a notice denoting that the SSF (Speed Sensor Fitted) system is fitted to the locomotive. This system was introduced by BR. It is activated by applying the locomotive brakes if the locomotive had rolled away while placed in 'engine only' mode.

TPWS (Train Protection Warning System)

At the top of the front cab windscreen pillar is the TPWS ('Train Protection Warning System') equipment. This system was not installed during the construction of the Class 60s, but was fitted retrospectively by the end of 2002 to the entire fleet, indeed to all driving cabs throughout the UK.

Train Protection Warning System (TPWS) module.
EDWARD GLEED

This is associated with the signalling equipment, and consists of the following:

Brake demand red indicator: this is extinguished under normal conditions; however, should the driver fail to reduce the speed of the train in sufficient time, this indicator will light up and the braking will intervene, bringing the movement to a standstill.

Temporary isolation/fault: this indicator is extinguished under normal conditions; however, should a fault with the system occur, it will illuminate to inform the driver.

Train stop override: should it be necessary for the driver to pass a signal at danger on the authority of the signalman, the driver will press this button to override the brake demand. In this instance, the brake demand will not intervene when that signal* has been passed at danger (*only that signal during normal operations).

The Q-Tron equipment. EDWARD GLEED

Q-Tron Equipment

Below the TPWS equipment is the 'Datacord' or Q-Tron equipment: this was introduced during the 1990s and records every action by the driver. Should an alarm be present with the system, this will be displayed. The driver is also required to enter a PIN number before the locomotive is operated.

Below the Q-Tron equipment are twin air vents, which the train crew can adjust to their liking. Further to this, a fan has been installed on the 'Super 60' overhaul to augment airflow of the cab interior. Earlier air vents had two, and then three vents in a staggered manner, all three directed to the driver.

The Secondman's Controls

A hotplate is provided with slats to arrest the movement of cooking utensils for use by both the driver and secondman. The secondman has a joystick for the horn, allowing a high or low sound to be emitted as desired.

The secondman's side of the cab showing the hotplate. A hinged cover is lowered when this is not in use.
EDWARD GLEED

DSD and Vigilance Equipment

A DSD ('driver's safety device') holdover joystick lever is also provided for the driver. This duplicates the action of the DSD pedal when the holdover switch is operated.

All the lower panels are removable by maintenance staff; they are fastened by a series of quarter-turn screws.

There is a sounder that contains the driver's vigilance alarm. This works alongside the DSD, which must be operated when the sound is heard. If the driver has placed a foot on the pedal and the alarm is triggered, he must remove his foot from the pedal. Failure to do so will initiate a full emergency brake application, which is non-recoverable until the train has been brought to a standstill. Both the DSD and vigilance equipment are suspended when the locomotive is stationary and the selector handle is set to 'Engine only'.

Directly below the sounder is the DSD pedal. As with all modern traction units, this pedal must be depressed. In the event of the driver being incapacitated, the DSD apparatus will intervene and bring the locomotive to a stand, whether the pedal has been depressed or not.

The Cab Heater

To the right of the sounder a rotary switch is provided for the cab heater. The driver can control the fan heater at the level he wants under the following settings, the off position being top centre: low vent, high vent, low heat and high heat.

Directly to the right of the controls is a dual grille.

The Front and the Rear Pedestals

Directly to the right of the driver's seat are twin pedestals, the front and the rear pedestals. The front pedestal contains the following items:

- **The power handle**: this has four controls of operation, three traction and one sanding. The fourth control is a sanding push button, which is positioned in the power handle knob. This permits drivers to apply sand at their discretion.

The power handle has one notch, this being between OFF (engine only) and ON.

OFF, engine running but with no power being supplied to the traction motors.

ON, power supplied to the traction motors.

MAX, full power is delivered to the traction motors. Between the ON and MAX positions, the power handle is notchless though the engine has eight speed steps.

Fuel conservation arm: directly below the power handle is a small metal arm. This has been fitted to a number of Class 60s in an attempt to conserve fuel. It is so positioned to prevent the driver from selecting the fully 'open' position of the power handle, and is set to the maximum fuel economy setting. It must be pushed aside in order to select 'true' full power.

Selector handle: to the right of the power handle is the selector handle. This has three positions:

- Engine only, auxiliaries only
- Forwards, where the traction motor contactors are closed and power is available to the traction motors
- Reverse, where the traction motor contactors are closed and power is available to the traction motors

Other features:

- To the right of the selector handle is the barrel for the driver's master key
- Behind the power handle is the AWS re-set button
- To the right of the AWS re-set button is a recessed cup holder

View of the front and rear pedestals. EDWARD GLEED

The rear pedestal contains telecommunications equipment for use between signalboxes, and under certain conditions, operations control. Two pieces of equipment are provided: the NRN (national radio network) telephone apparatus and the GSM-R equipment.

The upper piece of equipment contains the NRN telephone apparatus, a two-part system between driver and signalman. The operating console has a liquid crystal display detailing telephone calls and other operating menus. There is a series of coloured buttons, one of them being red: if this button is pressed because of an emergency, any other calls that are in progress in the area concerned are suspended during this emergency call. This NRN system, described in detail below, is now being phased out in favour of a more advanced system known as 'GSM-R' (Global Satellite Mobile-Railway).

GSM-R EQUIPMENT

The lower piece of equipment contains the GSM-R equipment. This is also a 'two-part' system between the driver and signalman. The GSM-R handset is mounted directly above the NRN equipment. Unlike the NRN handset, the GSM-R system is a 'two-way' conversation that does not require the 'push to talk' button that is fitted to the NRN handset. The GSM-R console is mounted below the NRN system and comprises an illuminated blue dot matrix screen detailing the calls and operating menus. It also has an illuminated alpha/numerical keypad along with buttons for menu navigation and general communication to signalmen.

The GSM-R console is equipped with two large, coloured buttons that are illuminated and shrouded to prevent accidental activation. The upper red button is round, and when pressed, immediately sends a railway emergency call to the controlling signalbox. Should the signaller not be able to take the call due to, for example, another emergency, this call will be diverted to operations control who will answer the call on the signalman's behalf. As in the NRN system, the red emergency button will take priority over other calls. The signalman is equipped with a larger base station that details every train and traction unit under their control. He is able to contact the driver via two methods, either using the train reporting headcode, for example 6B13, or the displayed locomotive number, for example 60066.

The lower yellow button is square, and when pressed sends an urgent priority call (which is not deemed to be an emergency) to the signalman.

The SG button is used by the driver to send a 'railway text message' to the controlling signalbox. The text consists of the locomotive running number and signal identification plate – for example '60066 at Signal B115'. On receipt of this text the controlling signalman must respond either by sending a 'wait' instruction telling the driver to remain at that signal, or by telephoning the driver directly. All railway text messages are pre-set.

Should it be necessary for the driver to communicate with the signalman or other operational staff, there are several ways in which this may be done. Traditionally, signalmen requiring communication with a driver will place or maintain a stop signal to danger. The driver is then required to bring the train to a standstill and leave the cab to speak to the signalman via the signal post telephone (SPT). At certain locations where it is deemed to be limited clearance, the use of SPTs is prohibited, therefore communication must be made by alternative authorized methods.

The GSM-R communications system is designed to operate in all areas including tunnels (regardless of length) and deep cuttings, so drivers never need leave their cab to speak to the signalman.

THE NRN (NATIONAL RADIO NETWORK) SYSTEM

The NRN system is now being phased out. It was fitted to all driving cabs and enabled the driver to communicate with the signalman whilst remaining at the driving controls.

However, there were drawbacks, as the NRN system was built up of cells, which, unlike the far superior GSM-R system, did not overlap, causing black spots in communication. Also, the system would not operate within the confines of most tunnels or deep cuttings. Further to this, the conversation between driver and signalman was 'one-way', requiring each party to use the words 'over' or 'out'. This system required the driver to input area codes throughout the duration of the journey via a numerical panel; for example, the NRN area code for Bristol was '072'.

The NRN system has been gradually phased out in favour of the more advanced GSM-R that is being introduced across the UK rail network.

Directly below both pieces of equipment is a loudspeaker so that incoming emergency calls can be heard without the driver having to lift the telephone handset.

The Locomotive Exterior

The locomotive body is of the monocoque design whereby the bodyshell is a load-bearing structure, unlike the Class 66s and Class 70s, which have heavyweight chassis and the body sections just cover these structures (hence the name 'shed' given to the Class 66 by some enthusiasts).

There are four lifting points on the locomotive, which are identified in the accompanying photograph. They are situated below the right-hand side of the driver's door and the left-hand side of the secondman's door, all at solebar level. Should it be necessary for the locomotive to be lifted, each cover plate is removed and lifting bars are inserted, and a crane or hoist is then attached to these bars.

Underframe Components

The following underframe components can be identified in the Class 60 exterior structure:[11]

- Fuel tank (some models are fitted with a long-range fuel tank: this is mounted between the compressors and contains a further 200gal (909ltr))
- Battery boxes
- DC supply unit, containing a battery charger, transformer and chokes
- Battery isolation switch
- Two air compressors
- Fire bottles associated with firefighting equipment

View of the lifting point cover with four Allen key bolts.
EDWARD GLEED

- Various colour-coordinated filler caps
- Spillage tank
- Two Doppler radars for the wheelslip/creep control system

The main fuel tank, its filling point and fuel drain. The battery isolating switch can be seen, with the fire apparatus bottles on the left. 30 October 2012.
EDWARD GLEED

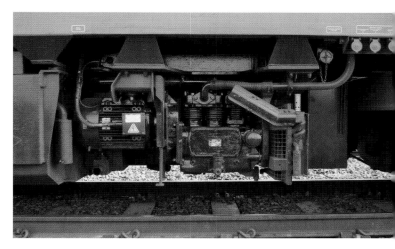

The air compressors. EDWARD GLEED

A detailed photograph of the fire bottles. EDWARD GLEED

The battery box on the 'B' side of the locomotive.
EDWARD GLEED

At Solebar Level

At solebar level there are ports/caps for various liquids and test points. These may be identified as follows:

Cooling water filler and air test points. EDWARD GLEED

- Cooling water filler: blue cap
- Three air-test points:

    Brake cylinder pressure at No. 2 end

    Brake cylinder pressure at No. 1 end

    Main air reservoir

- Lubrication oil filler and drain point: pink
- Fuel-tank filler: brown
- Fuel-tank sight glass: full is 4,546ltr; capacity is measured in eighth and quarter increments from full to empty; quarter increments are lettered
- Spill drain pipe

Lubricating oil filler and drain point, with the fuel-tank filler below. EDWARD GLEED

Fuel-tank sight glass. EDWARD GLEED

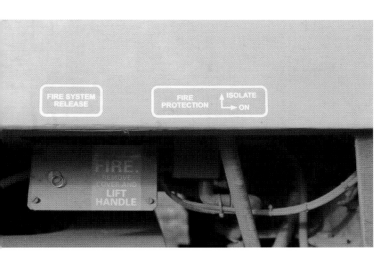

Fire-system handle, operate and isolate. EDWARD GLEED

- Cooling water drain
- Cooling water fill-valve failed overflow
- Fire system operate (remove cover and lift handle); fire protection: isolate or 'on'

Other Switches and Attachments

Other switches, sockets and attachments that can be seen are as follows:

- External battery isolation switch: there are two battery isolation switches located one on each side of the locomotive, mounted beneath the solebar. Each is a long double-ended handle with a knob at each end; the centre point of the switch is arrowed. The switch can be moved to the following three positions:

    Isolate: the locomotive is to be completely shut down

    Off: the lights, telecommunications equipment and fire-fighting system remain operative

    On: all systems are available for normal running

- MU socket: this permits multiple working with other Class 60s (only)
- Conventional screw coupling
- Height-adjustable snowploughs (*see* the construction section in Chapter 1)
- Brake-pipe air hose: this is at both ends and has red couplers

Second battery switch. EDWARD GLEED

Multiple working socket. EDWARD GLEED

One of eight sandboxes installed at the corners of each bogie.
EDWARD GLEED

■ Air hose from the main reservoir: this is at both ends of the locomotive and has yellow couplers
■ Sandboxes: there are eight sandboxes fitted on each corner of each bogie with each pipe angled towards the wheel and rail interface
■ The white-coloured pipes are for the air-brake cylinders and are on one side of each bogie
■ The brown pipework on one side of each bogie is the pressure pipework for actuating the centre-axle parking-brake cylinders, which are hydraulically operated
■ Bodyside grilles and vents: the grilles are bolted to the vent apertures

Bogie Arrangement

The bogie is of a low weight transfer design, with all motors mounted facing inboard of the locomotive. Rolling rubber-ring axle-box guides were superseded by the guide-post type during commissioning. Rubber-stack secondary suspension is incorporated. Brake actuators are direct acting, which eliminates the need for brake rigging.[11]

The building of the Class 60 diesel electric locomotive benefited from many years of experience gleaned from a variety of sources. The 'CP' design of bogie was constructed at BREL (British Rail Engineering Limited) of Doncaster, and

was used for the Class 58 locomotive several years earlier – indeed one member of the Class 56 fleet used these bogies, namely 56042. Another locomotive equipped to use this

Class 60 bogie during construction at Brush Traction, 27 November 1990. JOHN STRETTON

type of bogie is the unique Class 89 electric locomotive, 89001.

Locomotive manufacturers have always strived to afford the best possible traction control, thereby permitting heavier trains to be hauled whilst at the same time being the most cost effective. With vast tonnages being moved, there is a greater demand for longer and heavier trains, and this will obviously have an effect on the traction being used.

THE SEPEX SYSTEM

The traction motor control utilized on the Class 60 is known as 'Sepex' ('separately excited') and is unique. This excitation is afforded by each traction motor having independent traction-motor field converters: this excites the individual motor fields, which are fully variable and reversible, and are electronically controlled. The Sepex system is a very clever piece of equipment: its prime role is to control wheelslip and therefore afford a greater tractive effort, and it does this by automatically detecting wheelslip and adjusting the current to each traction motor.[11]

Classes such as the 59 and 66 utilize a different system, called the 'Super Series' control system. However, this system does not operate below 4mph (6km/h), and British Rail's requirement was for optimum traction control from standstill.[11] This was important for BR, as starting a heavy load on a wet rail and rising gradient is always going to be challenging. The Sepex system affords excellent control at low speeds where situations require a train to be drawn, for example through loading and unloading facilities at coal terminals. In a further attempt to minimize wheelslip, the bogie traction centres are very low. The reasoning behind this is that when full tractive effort is applied when hauling a heavy load, wheelset offloading occurs, and this also induces wheelslip.

On locomotive classes that were not equipped with Sepex, wheelslip was a serious problem and in some cases very costly. On heavy diagrams, notably some of the heavy oil and steel workings, wheels could sometimes slip, especially on a damp or wet rail, requiring sanding equipment to activate and/or shut off power, and to reapply it when traction had been regained. The driver is always made aware that wheelslip is occurring by a warning indication in the cab, which invites him to correct it manually by operating the sanding equipment or by shutting off power. Prolonged wheelslip could cause severe rail burn, identifiable as scorch marks on the railhead.

Snowploughs

A single 'one-piece' plough is fitted at each end of the locomotive, though these differ from ploughs that have been fitted to other classes. Snowploughs fitted to older classes were of a three-piece design and were painted bright yellow. The snowplough is height-adjustable by way of six bolts, and has an equal number of vertical slots to permit vertical movement – though it is understood that in practice, adjustment is seldom used.

The ploughs fitted to the Class 60 also have notches cut out at the bottom end of the corners to give greater clearance while operating over third rail territory, notably the former British Rail Southern region. These snowploughs were all painted black, with the exception of 60001 *Steadfast*, which was outshopped with light grey and was not notched; the notches were included later.

Detail of the snowplough with the notch cut in so as to afford greater height clearance when operating in third rail territory. EDWARD GLEED

Couplings

The Class 60s are equipped with conventional drawgear by way of conventional screw couplings. At present, buckeye couplers are not fitted to any members of the Class 60, though these could possibly be fitted in the future. Should it be necessary for two Class 60s to work in multiple, a thirty-six-way MU socket is provided, enabling one driver to assume control over both locomotives; however, the Class 60s are not compatible with other types of traction. The socket is hidden behind a closed cover on the front of the locomotive, below the front cab windows. In the event that a Class 60 requires assistance from a different class of locomotive that is attached to it, and as long as both locomotives are still providing traction, two drivers will be required. This will not be the case if the Class 60 is 'dead' and within a consist of rolling stock. Traditional spring oval buffers, which are bolted at each corner, are fitted to the buffer beam.

Coupling arrangement between locomotive and rolling stock. In this instance 60054 _Charles Babbage_ is coupled to an engineering train at Bristol on 12 February 2006.
EDWARD GLEED

Roof Components

Warning horns are fitted on the cab roof; they are generally painted in the same livery as the cab roof, and are operated by compressed air. The trumpet stems are of differing lengths, which offers the familiar 'two-tone' sound. The horns are covered by grilles, which offer a certain amount of protection from potential damage caused by frost or foreign objects. At the No. 2 end of the locomotive, both trumpet stems are covered by a fabricated metal cover plate, to the top section of which an antenna is fixed. This antenna is a GPS tracking device, and was fixed to a certain number of Class 60s a few years ago.

The Locomotive Body

The locomotive body is divided into three sections, as already described, but it is also 'handed', as defined by the following standard methods: side 'A', side 'B', No. 1 end and No. 2 end.

Looking at the locomotive from the 'A' side elevation and from left to right, the following is seen: No. 2 end cab with a large bodyside air-intake mesh, engine side access doors, and No. 1 end cab.

Looking at the locomotive from the 'B' side elevation and from left to right, the following is seen: No. 1 end cab with a large bodyside air-intake mesh, engine side access doors, a large bodyside air-intake mesh for the clean air compartment, a cover with two flush-mounted handrails affording access to the traction motor blower, and No. 2 end cab.

The exhaust silencer is mounted on the roof at the No. 2 end of the locomotive. It is very neat in its appearance as it follows the contour of the overall roof line. The silencer is fixed to the recessed section of the roof by a series of flexible mounts.

There are eight roof hatches: these are described in detail in the construction section.

At the No. 1 end, two large roof-mounted air vents are fitted as part of the engine-room ventilation. Two large electrically driven fans draw large volumes of air through two large bodyside grilles on either side of the locomotive. This air is blown through the cooling radiators mounted in the roof section. The internal mesh situated behind the main bodyside grilles at No. 1 end is the Donaldson spin-tube air filter, which provides filtered air to the traction motor blower.

The main silencer, shown on 60039 at Tees Yard on 17 June 2014. EDWARD GLEED

There are eight roof hatches fitted to the Class 60, four on each side. Struts support the hatches in the open position. EDWARD GLEED

A large mesh mounted below the exhaust silencer at the No. 2 end of the locomotive covers the Donaldson spin-tube filter that provides filtered clean air for the engine, No. 2 traction motor blower and the electrical cubicle.[11]

The small roof-mounted vertical grilles directly behind the exhaust silencers are exits for the scavenger fans that are present on both sides of the locomotive. They are offset one from the other, and were installed as a later addition. When the locomotive was subjected to hard working conditions, it caused high engine-room air temperatures and the scavenger fans were installed to remove hot air from the engine room. When the first Class 60 was tested, British Rail withheld payment until this situation had been fixed, causing Brush's yard to be full of locomotives. The first locomotive to be fitted with the fans was No. 60024.[11]

The three stepped roof ports on either side of the locomotive are crankcase 'breathers'. These are redundant vents from the Mark 1 air-management scheme, and although they are left in situ, they have been blocked off.[11]

The Mirrlees Engine 8MB275RT

During the tendering process, the British Railways Board were offered various engine models, and it was mooted that General Motors Electro Motive Division (EMD) were interested in providing an engine for the Class 60. Having already supplied the UK market with one of the company's engines – namely two-stroke 16-645E3C developing 3,300hp, as used in the highly successful Class 59 in 1985 – this proposal could have been seen as a viable option.[2]

Hitherto, diesel propulsion in the UK had been afforded by four-stroke units in varying forms: some were in V form, 12- and 16-cylinder, while others, such as the Class 47, were double in-line 6 configuration. Some highly complex engines have been used in the past, notably the triangular form 'Napier' Deltic engine installed in the BR Class 55 'Deltic' locomotive. The 'Deltic' engine – which had also been used in the marine industry – was so called because of the triple crank, arranged in the form of a delta; it was of a two-stroke design. In similar vein, the engines installed in the highly acclaimed HST Class 253/4 power cars were in the form of a V12, which had been supplied from Paxman. The Paxman V engines that were employed in the HST Power Cars were a development from the Ventura engine, and were known as the Valenta; both had been used in the marine industry.

Having looked at several engine options, Mirrlees of Stockport were chosen to provide an engine for the Class 60. There was already experience of Mirrlees Blackstone engines, as their 6MB275RT 1,000hp 6-cylinder engines had been installed in four members of the Class 37 fleet – though this was a 6-cylinder engine as opposed to the 8-cylinder engine installed in the Class 60.

In service, the Mirrlees 8MB275RT engine in fact presented several major problems, with cylinder liners cracking and cylinder head blows. In his memorandum to Sir Bob Reid (Chairman of British Rail), Dr Stuart Hill (Director of Technical Strategy) stated that despite efforts to rectify the problem with cracking, it continued without a definitive resolution. He believed this was due to deficiencies in the approach used by the manufacturers, and to parts that failed to provide evidence of sufficient longevity in terms of robustness, in order to cope with the demands of service as required by the initial contract.

'In BR's opinion only, the work carried out by the manufacturers lacked structure and was not focused on providing components which would demonstrably last the twenty years called for in the contract.'[2]

In an attempt to find a solution to the cracking issue, a reliability task force was founded using resources provided by Mirrlees Blackstone Limited, Brush Traction (a division of Brush Electrical Machines) and British Rail. They undertook detailed programmes ranging from development testing, field trials and fleet implementation. In addition, a Reliability Steering Committee was established in partnership with British Rail to supervise the work. According to Dr Stuart Hill, the impact of these groups was a more strategic approach to resolving the problem, which was caused by gas blows, and finding out why some engines with relatively minor blows failed through cracking, whilst others with more significant blows did not, and were still in operation.

Hill's report commented that improvements had been made in the research of the metals used in the construction of the liner, and no deficiencies were found in the materials. One of the findings was regarding the critical importance of managing variations in engine water temperatures, and that lowering the cooling water temperature variations from 18°C to 6°C would improve the longevity of the joints and liners.

The manufacturers believed that in order to achieve greater joint durability, wider joints with higher stud leads were required. They decided to bring out a trial batch of ten locomotives ('Mod State 17') with wider joints and 21,000psi stud loads.

Hill concluded that progress was 'disappointing', and cited its ponderous rate of progress; this was because of inadequate resourcing, higher priorities elsewhere and failure of the test rig. Hill was also of the opinion that if 'Mod State 17' did not prove its capability to resolve the issues, more robust design options would have to be identified.[2]

CHAPTER FOUR

AREAS OF OPERATION OF THE CLASS 60

From the very beginning, the areas of operation and the use of Class 60 locomotives have been extensive, covering the length and breadth of the country, ranging from the harsh gradients of Schlod in the Scottish Highlands to Kent, and from Cornwall to Northumbria. Following their construction under what was then British Rail, the Class 60s were all required to complete 1,000 fault-free miles before being accepted into BR stock (see Chapter 1). The Class 60 was constructed as a Type 5 heavy freight locomotive, with the ability to haul much heavier trains than many other classes of locomotive. This chapter is designed to afford readers a brief insight into the many commodities and workings for which the Class 60s have been used – though as one might imagine, it would be impossible to include every area, working and destination.

Although the Class 60 was constructed for use in the freight sector due to its phenomenal haulage capabilities, it has also found a place within the rail–tour market, as described later in this chapter. A detailed list of some of the notable workings of the Class 60 is provided in the appendices, giving actual timing points, along with details of one railtour that took place in August 2014, namely 'TaffyTug ii'.

The Automotive Industry

The automotive industry has used rail for the transportation of motor vehicles for many years. The car transporter wagons that have conveyed this type of traffic have varied enormously, ranging from converted carriage bodies to articulated wagons, and in some cases multi-deck transporters. In the case of diesel traction, Class 66s have generally been rostered on this type of working; however, as the accompanying photograph depicts, a Class 60 was allocated to it for a short time. At that time, Class 60s were quite rare at Bristol Temple Meads, though as mentioned later in this chapter, they were often seen passing through whilst working the china clay diagrams.

On a very dull morning 60040 *The Territorial Army Centenary* passes through Bristol Temple Meads whilst working 6V51, 03:05 Warrington Arpley–Portbury Dock car train on 22 March 2013.
EDWARD GLEED

Oil and its Derivatives

It is important to further detail the actual commodities and wagon types that Class 60s can be seen hauling. Some of the UK's heaviest trains emanate from the oil refineries of Robeston in south-west Wales, and from the Lindsey and Humber refineries on Humberside, and these are well suited to the Class 60, in many cases because the overall weight of the train is too heavy for the Class 66 (depending on the route). Since the latter part of 2014, Colas Rail UK has taken over a number of workings that were previously operated by DB Schenker Rail UK.

The Robeston (Murco) refinery generally caters for oil traffic to and from Westerleigh, Theale, and on occasions Bedworth near Coventry, whilst the Lindsey refinery (Total, Petrofina) and also Humber (Phillips 66)

handle traffic to Rectory Junction at Colwick, Westerleigh (Bristol), Colnbrook (Slough), Jarrow (South Tyneside), Kingsbury (Tamworth) and Bedworth (Coventry). One working that has been consistently hauled by the Class 60 for many years is the heavy Lindsey–Colnbrook (Elf) working. This runs as 6V70 Lindsey–Colnbrook, while the return working runs as 6E38 15:50, which is routed via the North London line and joins the Midland main line at Brent Curve Junction at Cricklewood. This service used to be operated by DBS, but has recently transferred to Colas Rail, who assigned it to their Class 60 fleet. Another working for which the Class 60 has been used over the years is between Stanlow (Leeds) and Jarrow (South Tyneside), where two-axle TTA tank wagons were used. Class 60s were also employed on workings between Lindsey and Eggborough.

Drax-liveried 60066 passes through the small hamlet of Gossington whilst working 6B13 05:05 Robeston–Westerleigh 'Murco' tanks on a very warm 17 March 2015. EDWARD GLEED

On a beautiful summer's evening Loadhaul-liveried 60059 *Swinden Dalesman* approaches Sedbury, near Chepstow, atop 6B47 18:25 Westerleigh–Robeston discharged tanks on 17 August 2009. EDWARD GLEED

The delightful location of Ram Hill, situated between Westerleigh Junction and Bristol Parkway, sees 60001 powering 6B33 13:30 Theale Margam 'Murco' tanks on a glorious 7 March 2014. EDWARD GLEED

60044, wearing the former Mainline Freight livery, works 6E41 11:35 Westerleigh–Lindsey through Rangeworthy during February 2009. The loaded working departed Lindsey the previous evening as 6V98 to Westerleigh. EDWARD GLEED

A popular working that has long been photographed by enthusiasts is the 6D43 Jarrow–Lindsey empties, the loaded working being 6N03 Lindsey–Jarrow, which like 6V70 has always been a solid Class 60 turn. It is understood that the 6N03 and 6D43 no longer run, as the fuel is supplied to Jarrow by pipeline. A further working is 6Y32 08:24

Photographed under the most appalling weather conditions, DBS 60092 wheels 6E38 13:54 Colnbrook–Lindsey along the Midland main line at Kangaroo Spinney, near Wellingborough, on 20 October 2014. EDWARD GLEED

On a beautiful summer's evening 60017 travels through the Vale of York at the helm of 6D43 17:25 Jarrow–Lindsey empties. The working has just past Colton junction, a few miles to the south of York, on 16 June 2014. EDWARD GLEED

Fawley–Holybourne crude oil tanks. This service is routed via Alton and is normally worked by a Class 66; however, on one occasion 60011 was reported to have worked this diagram. Class 60s in the Southampton area are not that common; however, the 6B49 12:00 Fawley–Eastleigh Yard working can on occasions produce a Class 60. Another diagram that the Class 60s have operated is the 6D49 13:55 Ferrybridge–Lindsey fuel oil empties, along with 6N71 17:05 Linkswood–Mossend empties – loaded, these had conveyed aviation fuel for RAF Leuchars.

On 25 April 2014, 60059 hauls fifteen TTAs through Southampton Maritime FLT with 6B49 12:00 Fawley–Eastleigh Yard. MARK V. PIKE

60056 brings a late-running Grangemouth–Linkswood aviation fuel train over the Forth Bridge and approaches North Queensferry on 20 February 2002.
IAN LOTHIAN

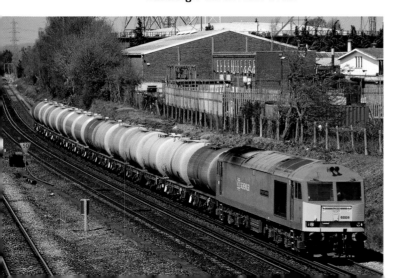

Having received a signal check as the train approached Camelon, 60048 *Eastern* powers a lengthy Dalston–Grangemouth working, composed of 100-tonne BP-liveried TEAs, on 4 January 2001. IAN LOTHIAN

The Grangemouth refinery in Scotland caters for oil traffic to destinations such as Motherwell, Linkswood, Prestwick and Dalston. These workings either utilize two-axle TTA tanks or the 100-tonne TEA tanks. One working, namely 6N36 Mossend–Grangemouth, has seen the service operate with twenty BP (British Petroleum) TTAs in tow. Similar to the 100-tonne TEAs, these tanks are liveried green, as the Grangemouth refinery is operated by BP. It is usual for the Dalston–Grangemouth tanks to be formed of entirely 100-tonne TEAs, and these would require the use of a Type 5 locomotive as the route involves the punishingly stiff gradient of Beattock; therefore the Class 60 is ideally suited to this diagram. In contrast, short workings such as the Grangemouth–Motherwell TMD tanks have been formed with as few as five TTAs, and a working of this kind for the Class 60 would be nugatory.

A further working for which Class 60 haulage was used was 6D96 13:00 Welton–Immingham oil tanks. For a long time the Waterston refinery in south-west Wales (near to the current Robeston refinery) despatched fuel to places

such as Langley, haulage that at one time was operated by pairs of Class 37s.

Other diagrams operated by the Class 60 over the years were 6V32 Albion–Waterston, 6B24 15:33 Didcot P.S.–Cardiff Tidal, and 6E27 10:19 Bedworth–Humber. Fuel oil is also brought to Peak Forest in two-axle TTA tanks.

A beautiful evening view of 60099, at Margam engaged in shunting duties. 16 September 2013.
LEIGHTON PRADO

It is half-past six at Peak Forest on a lovely summer's morning, and 60010 is resting between duties at the fuelling point on 2 June 2006. EDWARD GLEED

One notable working for the Class 60 is the conveyance of bitumen from the Lindsey oil refinery to Preston docks. The loaded working runs as 6M32 to Preston, while the empty working returns as 6E32 08:55 (MWFO) Preston Docks–Lindsey. This service is routed via the Copy Pit line and joins the Calder Valley main line via Hebden Bridge at Hall Royd Junction. This is one of many services that terminate at the Lindsey refinery, which provides many opportunities for viewing Class 60s in this area. Under DBS operation, this was very often in the hands of the Class 60.

Summer fauna at the lineside at Hatfield and Stainforth as 60085 passes by atop 6E32 Preston Docks–Lindsey bitumen tanks on 15 June 2015. EDWARD GLEED

However, during December 2014, Colas Rail undertook driver training duties with a view to taking over this working from DBS in January 2015. On 5 January, 60087 *CLIC Sargent* provided the motive power for this working.

LPG (liquefied petroleum gas) has also been carried by rail. A very popular working used to operate between Furzebrook and Hallen Marsh: it ran as 6V13 and was Class 60 hauled. The service commenced during 1990, but sadly no longer runs – the last working was reportedly on 22 July 2005, though it is understood a Class 66 operated on this particular occasion. A further diagram that has seen the Class 60 operate on this traffic is 6M23 15:54 Fawley–Longport LPG. This service has also been known to have additional bitumen tanks attached.

Coal

Coal traffic has long been hauled by the Class 60s, ever since their introduction. During their early years of operation they have had many workings throughout many parts of the country – for example, South Wales and the South West, the East Midlands, the North West, Yorkshire and Scotland. These workings consisted of lengthy rafts of HAA MGR ('merry-go-round') wagons going to destinations such as Fiddler's

A light dusting of snow lies on the ground as 60046 *William Wilberforce* takes the Cumbernauld Line at Greenhill Lower Junction with a loaded coal from Grangemouth to Fiddler's Ferry on 4 March 2005.
IAN LOTHIAN

Ferry, Didcot and Drax, to name just three. Following the demise of the long-established HAA wagon, HTA bogie hoppers have taken over, and since the Class 60s are not fitted with swing-head buckeye couplers (unlike the Class 59s and 66s), they have been virtually ruled out of this type of work, bar one or two exceptions.

In order for the Class 60s to haul HTA sets, several HTA wagons have been converted to traditional buffer and screw

A lengthy MRG working passes through Oxford, with 60073 *Liathach* providing the motive power as it heads north with a Didcot–Three Spires Junction working on 22 July 1993. JOHN STRETTON

60094 *Rugby Flyer* passes Saughton on the outskirts of Edinburgh with the 08:46 Westfield–Millerhill Drax-loaded MGR working on 27 September 2005. IAN LOTHIAN

EWS-liveried 60096 passes Winwick Quay atop a Fiddlers Ferry–Liverpool bulk terminal working on 15 September 2009. EDWARD GLEED

coupling operation – in effect translator wagons so that Class 60s can handle this traffic. Several workings have been made utilizing converted HTAs, one of which still operates between Liverpool Bulk Handling Terminal and Fiddler's Ferry. It is understood that plans are being considered to equip the Class 60 fleet with buckeye couplers in the near future.

A further operation that used the converted wagons ran between Onllwyn and Aberthaw power station. In recent years the South Wales area, like many parts of the UK, has seen a sharp decline in both the mining and steel industries, resulting in reduced workings. To date the Onllwyn–Aberthaw route is served by Class 66s in a much reduced schedule. However, a number of Class 60 workings have been noted working in the Cardiff valleys. On 27 June 2014, 60065 *Spirit of Jaguar* was reported to have worked 00:22

Hope (Earle's Sidings)–Cwmbargoed. It is understood that the last time Class 60s worked on this section of line on coal duties would have been in the late 1990s, though other freight has been reported in more recent times. For many years MGR traffic was hauled by Class 47s and 56s, and the Class 60s have also been employed on this type of traffic.

During 2001, the section of railway between Portbury Dock and Ashton Junction was brought back into use, carrying commodities ranging from steel slab, automotive products and coal. During the first year or so, coal was transported by MGR wagons, and one such working employed 60041. Since then the HTAs have not only ousted the MGR wagons, but also in most cases the Class 60s on this and many other locations in England such as Ratcliffe, Immingham dock and Oxcroft Colliery. In Scotland over the years, places such as Falkland Road Yard, Hunterston and

During the first years of operation from Portbury Dock, MGR wagons were still very much in operation, as depicted here at Bristol. One such working is seen with 60041 at the helm on 19 September 2006. EDWARD GLEED

Menacing clouds loom overhead as 60076 *Suilven* threads its way through the encroaching undergrowth at Knockshincock disposal point. JOHN WHITEHOUSE

With the cooling towers of Didcot power station dominating the background, 60078 is photographed on one of the many Avonmouth–Didcot coal diagrams. 5 March 1997. JOHN STRETTON

Longannett power station via New Cumnock were served by the Class 60s, but have subsequently been replaced by Class 66s.

During 1992, the new Bristol Bulk Handling Terminal (BBHT) at Avonmouth was brought into use. Coal is docked at Portbury and is either loaded to rail at that location, or transported by a series of conveyors to Avonmouth for onward shipment to various locations such as Fifoots and Aberthaw power stations, both in South Wales. Most importantly the BBHT served Didcot power station until March 2013, when the power station switched to gas-fired operation. During the early years of operation, the Class 60s reigned supreme on these services, which consisted of lengthy rafts of MGR wagons. But when General Motors' Class 66s commenced operations during the late 1990s, the Class 60s ceased service on these flows because their different coupling arrangements meant that they were unable to haul the new HTA coal hoppers.

On a very busy section of the WCML at Sytch Lane to the north of Stafford former Mainline Freight 60011 is working what is thought to be the Walsall–Tunstead cement on 28 July 2009. EDWARD GLEED

Cement

Cement has long been transported by rail, and wagon types have varied over the years, including the 'Prestflows' and twin-silo wagons. Some of the workings to which the Class 60s were assigned include 6M22 12:40 Hunslet–Tunstead, 6M68 Dewsbury–Earles sidings, and 6F93 11:03 St Pancras–Ketton cement empties. This service uses the two-axle PCA tanks with Castle Cement branding.

China Clay

Other workings that the Class 60s used to operate were the 6M72 16:58 St Blazey–Cliffe Vale, which conveyed JIA

6V70 Cliffe Vale–St Blazey, a popular china clay working that no longer runs, photographed here under beautiful sunshine at Cogload Junction with 60039 providing the traction on 2 April 2004. BRIAN GARRETT

bogie hoppers and IWB vans with bagged clay, and the return working 6V70 Cliffe Vale–St Blazey. In both workings pairs of 37s were displaced in favour of a single Class 60 locomotive. This is one of the many reasons why British Rail required a new Type 5 freight loco, to displace pairs of locomotives where a single unit could be used instead, which could reap huge savings in fuel costs. Neither 6M72 nor 6V70 services run any more. China clay has been despatched to locations such as Cliffe Vale and also to Irvine in West Scotland. The Cliffe Vale workings convey PBA china clay bogie wagons, together with ferry wagons carrying bagged clay.

For many years china clay slurry has also been transported by rail from Burngullow in Cornwall to the Caledonian paper mill at Irvine. One service in particular, 6S55 Burngullow–Irvine, was entrusted to pairs of Class 37s, china clay being used both by the paper and pharmaceutical industries. The locomotives ran throughout the entire journey and were

EWS-liveried 60020 at Par, hauling a china clay slurry working on 31 March 1998. JOHN STRETTON

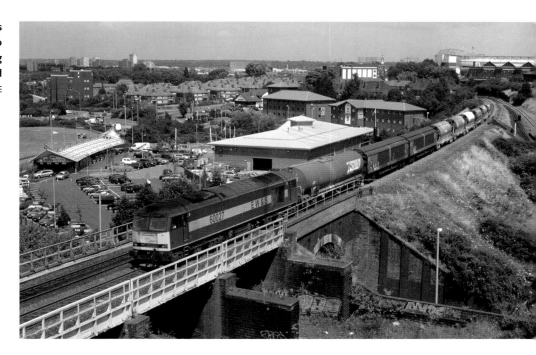

The sprawl of Birmingham forms the backdrop for 60027 at Camp Hill Bordesley junction, hauling a selection of PBA 'Polybulk' and ferry wagons. JOHN WHITEHOUSE

Another photograph depicting a Cliffe Vale working at St Andrews in Birmingham: 60091 hauling a mixture of PBAs, PCA two-axle tanks, ferry wagons and a solitary JIA wagon. JOHN WHITEHOUSE

at one time operating the longest-running freight train on British Rail. This service was notable during 1989 when it began to haul new French-built ICA slurry tanks, and when the Class 60s were in the first stages of construction. The Class 60 can still be seen hauling these wagons, though usually it is to transport them to and from repair works.

Due to their polished stainless-steel finish, enthusiasts nick-named the train the 'Silver Bullet'.

During the mid-1990s, the Class 37s were displaced from this working in favour of the then new Class 60s. As mentioned above, the assignment of the Class 60s to this service had the added advantage that a pair of 37s was more costly to

A short train of slurry tanks is hauled by 'Super 60' refurbished 60063, on 29 March 2012 atop 6Z15 Burton Wetmore sidings–Warrington Arpley. JOHN TUFFS

The re-timed 6A56, 22:54 Calvert to Northolt RTS West Waste 'binliner' approaches West Ruislip on 28 April 2008, hauled by EWS Class 60 No. 60063 *James Murray.* BRIAN MORRISON

operate than a single Class 60, both in terms of fuel and maintenance. The 6S55 working was almost as heavy as certain oil traffic, grossing 1,800 tonnes, and while pairs of 37s could haul this working over the northern summits of Shap and Beattock and the gradients in Devon and Cornwall, a single Class 60 would handle it with considerable ease. Sadly this service no longer runs from Burngullow as china clay now emanates from mainland Europe, and the resultant flows have been entrusted to the Class 92 25kV electric locomotives.

The Transportation of Refuse

A regular diagram for the Class 60 was the transportation of household refuse between Bredbury and Roxby, colloquially named by rail enthusiasts as the 'Binliner'. Over the years, three services have operated to and from Roxby (Gullet): 6E01 01:52 Northenden–Roxby, 6E06 09:40 Bredbury–Roxby, 6E07 20:49 Pendleton–Roxby. The return workings were believed to be 6M05 09:20 Roxby–Northenden, 6M07 10:45 Roxby–Pendleton and 6M06 17:19 Roxby–Bredbury.

At one time, refuse was transported from the cities of Bath and Bristol to Calvert in Oxfordshire. This ran as 6C13 (latterly 4V60), going out empty from Calvert and returning loaded as 4M60. This service was known by many as 'Dusty

bins' and was operated on behalf of what was then Avon County Council; it has recently ceased to operate. The aforementioned 6C13 and 4V60 were never a long-standing diagram for the Class 60, though it is believed that the class was regularly assigned to the service for a short period.

With Cowburn tunnel in the background, EWS Class 60 60078 approaches Chinley East Junction with the evening Roxby–Bredbury 'Binliner' on 5 June 2007. NIGEL CAPELLE

60039 at work under the wires on the ECML between Drem and Longniddry with the empty bins from Oxwellmains to Powderhall on 9 August 2007. IAN LOTHIAN

A further 'Binliner' working operated in Scotland between Powderhall and Oxwellmains. It employed Classes 37 and 67, though Class 60s were called upon to operate this diagram on occasions.

Intermodal Workings

Intermodal workings are not generally hauled by Class 60s, probably because of their overall permitted top speed. Most container traffic is timed to run as a Class 4 freight, and this classification is permitted to run at up to 75mph (120km/h), loaded or empty (whether the containers themselves are loaded or empty is of no significance). Since the Class 60s can only attain a top speed of 60mph (96km/h), this automatically precludes them from many of these workings. However, if the overall line speed of a given journey was no more than 60mph, then in theory a Class 60 could work the train, provided the 'route availability' criterion could be met. But on routes with a higher line speed, this would have a

One of the few intermodal workings hauled by the Class 60 at Denton Mains between Carlisle and Newcastle: an intermodal working bound for Teeside hauled by 60065 on 27 October 2012.
NIGEL CAPELLE

A mixed working containing intermodal containers, ferry and covered steel wagons with 60084 *Cross Fell* at the helm on 18 March 2003. Unusually, 60036 *GEFCO* is tucked inside. RICHARD TUPLIN

detrimental effect on the service as it would take longer for the working to arrive at its destination. No train operation company would tolerate such a situation, unless, for instance, a booked locomotive had failed and there was no other available, in which case the Class 60 could work the train but would probably be detached at the earliest opportunity.

However, there are always exceptions. The photograph shows an impressive working where a double-headed Class 60 is hauling intermodal container traffic; ferry vans and covered steel wagons had been attached to the rear, and this had reduced the working to a speed at which a Class 60 was permitted to haul the train. All rolling stock that is

permitted to run at a set given speed will always run at the speed of the slowest vehicle. Occasionally Class 60s have been employed at Eastleigh Yard to act as 'super shunters', and are sometimes called upon to haul 'trip' workings that run between Southampton Western Docks and Eastleigh Yard; these usually consist of intermodal boxes and other wagonload movements. During 2014/2015, Class 60s were used for the 6B43 09:38 Eastleigh Yard–Southampton Western Docks, together with the 6B44 12:07 Southampton Western Docks–Eastleigh Yard diagram.

Certain types of steel traffic use freightliner flats with containerized steel loaded on to the flats, while on

60065 passing Mount Pleasant just south of St Deny's with 6B43 09:39 Eastleigh Yard–Southampton Western Docks trip working on 2 August 2013. MARK V. PIKE

60014 *Alexander Fleming* passes Greenhill Lower Junction with the Grangemouth–Trafford Park intermodal on 30 July 2004.

IAN LOTHIAN

some enterprise workings containerized traffic has been marshalled in the train. Containerized traffic between Grangemouth and Trafford Park employed Class 60s on occasions. Workings on the Southern Region have also seen Class 60s operate, namely the Transfesa working, which conveys components for the Ford Motor Company.

MoD Traffic

Class 60s have also been called upon to work traffic for the Ministry of Defence. In the accompanying photograph, a short working is seen at Newport. It will be noticed that the

working conveys containers with both VGA and VDA vans on either side, acting as barrier vehicles.

Nuclear Waste Traffic

The Class 60s have no involvement with nuclear waste traffic. This is because Direct Rail Services operate all these services and they have no Class 60s, and the loads are sufficiently light for other classes of locomotive to haul. Furthermore, DB Schenker Rail UK and Colas Rail UK, who are the current owners and operators of the Class 60s, do not have any contract for traffic of this nature at present.

The Transfesa 'Blue Train' 7L23, 09:31 from Dollands Moor to Dagenham passes Bickley Junction on 4 July 2008, unusually hauled by an EWS Class 60, No. 60041.

BRIAN MORRISON

60100 *Pride of Acton* at Newport working the 6B24 Didcot–Wentloog MoD train on 13 October 2007.

BRIAN GARRETT

A solitary track machine is hauled through Bolton Percy by Corus-liveried 60033 *Tees Steel Express* on 17 August 2001. RICHARD TUPLIN

60040 *The Territorial Army Centenary* deputises for the Class 66 that normally works this service, passing through Lawrence Hill on 6B65 Westbury–ADJ engineers' train on 3 May 2011. EDWARD GLEED

Engineers' Traffic

Engineering traffic has for many years seen the Class 60 in use on a variety of workings, ranging from short-formed workings with only a handful of OCA wagons or even track maintenance vehicles, to very lengthy workings that have been known to comprise a mixture of forty-three loaded/ empty MFAs, MTAs and PNAs. Autoballasters (JJAs and HQAGs), MRA side-tipping wagons, 'Salmons', 'IOA' interna-

tionally registered bogie ballast wagons and YEA long welded rail carriers are another area of operation for the Class 60. The very long HOBC (high output ballast) train has very occasionally seen a Class 60 employed, though pairs of Class 66s are normally used in a 'top and tail' mode.

In recent years Class 60s have been diagrammed to work more engineers' trains, as more have been put through the

A lengthy engineers' train comprising both YEA and MFA wagons passes through Willington with 60024 at the helm. The cooling towers of the closed Willington power station are seen in the distance. JOHN TUFFS

60045 the *Permanent Way Institution* and 60071 *Ribblehead Viaduct* pass through Burton-on-Trent with a long welded rail train. JOHN TUFFS

A resident supershunter: 60071 *Ribblehead Viaduct* busy going about its duties in Eastleigh Yard on 3 May 2011. MARK V. PIKE

'Super 60' programme. Class 60s have also been gainfully employed to act as a super shunter at certain locations, Eastleigh being one of them. Now that Colas Rail UK operates a number of Class 60s, it is understood that they will be used on infrastructure duties. Even when the Class 60s in service dropped to single figures, they could also be allocated on engineering diagrams, 6K05 Carlisle Yard–Crewe Basford Hall diagram being one of them. The Colas Class 60s have also undertaken workings hauling the Rail-Vac unit across parts of the country.

The barren landscape of the S&C is the backdrop for 60091 as it crosses Arten Gill viaduct, the roof of England, with 6K05 Carlisle–Crewe Basford Hall engineer's train on 24 April 2012. NIGEL CAPELLE

Iron Ore and Steel

After the withdrawal of the Class 37s and Class 56s from the heavy iron-ore trains between Port Talbot and Llanwern steelworks, and the triple-headed Class 37s on the Hunterston and Ravenscraig workings, Class 60s took over and operated these workings until these services were closed down, the result of the rationalization of the steelworks at these places. Over the years, the 60s have worked steel traffic in varying forms, such as iron ore from Port Talbot to Llanwern. Another regular diagram for Class 60 iron-ore traffic operates between Immingham and Santon; it always consists of JTA and JUA bogie hoppers.

60001 at Brockelsby junction atop 6T27, Immingham–Santon iron ore, on 16 June 2014. The Lindsey oil refinery dominates the skyline. EDWARD GLEED

60001 passing through Barnetby on its return journey to Immingham whilst working 6K23 Santon–Immingham on 16 June 2014. EDWARD GLEED

60500 *Raid Magazine* approaches Lanark Junction on its way south with the Dalzell–Lackenby empty steel on 6 December 2005. This was the only Class 60 to be renumbered: formerly it was 60016. IAN LOTHIAN

60052 heads south along the Midland main line at Clay Cross with a Lackenby to South Wales steel service on 5 March 2003. RICHARD TUPLIN

It is quite normal to see a Class 60 that has been allocated to one of these diagrams working many trips between Immingham and Santon. Steel slab has also been conveyed from Dalzell to Lackenby, and from Lackenby to Llanwern, steel coil (Lackenby–Corby) and steel scrap from both Exeter Alphington Road and Beeston, and hot rolled coil between Dazell and Lackenby. The automotive industry uses steel coil brought in by rail, and needs it to be conveyed in covered wagons; these are generally of the telescopic cowl type.

Class 60s have also hauled other steel workings such as 6O26 14:22 Scunthorpe–Dollands Moor service, which is ultimately bound for Ebange in France and consists of FIAs loaded with steel slab. The Class 60 hands over to a Class 92 at Doncaster for the run to Dollands Moor.

In further workings on the ECML Class 60s have been engaged on flows between Scunthorpe and Redcar hauling SSA scrap steel wagons, namely 6N45 Scunthorpe–Redcar empties. Occasionally a Class 60 is assigned to steel workings between Llanwern and Swindon running as 6B49 and

On a very hot 22 July 2014, 60024 crosses Coalpit Heath viaduct atop 6B50 Swindon Stores–Llanwern steel. This is another service often hauled by a Class 66. EDWARD GLEED

On a beautiful warm and sunny morning, 60020 passes Portskewett with 6V05 Round Oak–Margam, with curtain-sided IHA wagons dominating the working,on 20 March 2014. EDWARD GLEED

Semaphore signals reign supreme at Barnetby, but for how much longer? 60024 *Clitheroe Castle* passes through atop 6V19 Immingham–Llanwern steel on 15 June 2015. EDWARD GLEED

return 6B50. There are also workings between Margam and Round Oak near Brierly Hill (Birmingham) when a Class 60 hauls telescopic BYAs and canvas-sided IHAs. Notable workings are 6V05 and 6V07.

Class 60s have also been employed for workings between Humberside and South Wales – for example, 6V19 17:22 Immingham–Margam empty steel, again with telescopic BYAs in tow – and for workings also bound for Rotherham.

One notable working worthy of mention is 6E08 Wolverhampton–Immingham, which is more or less guaran-

teed to be worked by a Class 60. This working is interesting as it sometimes conveys only a handful of wagons, though like other steel workings, it can convey many BYAs as well as BDAs. The North East also sees Class 60s, notably at Tees Yard. The accompanying photograph depicts 60039 engaged on shunting duties.

A further working of note is 6V62, which until July 2014 was usually in the hands of a Class 66. This service departs at 10:27, and can run as 6Z62 Tilbury–Llanwern Exchange sidings; this particular diagram commenced during

Due to a derailment in the Gloucester area, 60049 passes through Ram Hill atop the diverted 6V05 Round Oak–Margam steel on 18 October 2013. EDWARD GLEED

60040 *The Territorial Army Centenary* hammers through Hatfield and Stainforth with a Hedon Road sidings– Rotherham covered steel working on 15 June 2015.

EDWARD GLEED

Tees Yard is now a shadow of its former glory. Here, 60039 is shunting steel slab carriers on 17 June 2014.
EDWARD GLEED

A lengthy 6E08 Wolverhampton Steel Terminal–Immingham is wheeled through Dudley Port with 60059 *Swinden Dalesman* at the helm on 15 July 2014.
EDWARD GLEED

November 2013. This service is operated by Colas Rail, and has utilized their Class 56s, 66s and 70s, but Colas Rail UK purchased a consignment of ten Class 60s from DBS, and on 23 July 2014 the first Colas Class 60, 60087, was assigned to this diagram. However, during its maiden journey on this service the Class 60 failed at Hullavington Loop and remained there for four hours. Colas Class 70, 70804, gave assistance, with 60087 dead in tow. The Class 60, No. 60087 was deemed a failure, which was attributed to GSM-R

Emerging from the 4,064m (4,444yd) Chipping Sodbury tunnel, 60085 has charge of 6V62 Tilbury–Llanwern on 20 March 2015. The delightful village of Old Sodbury is also seen. EDWARD GLEED

On a scorching afternoon at Llanfihangel Crucorney, 60063 passes through in the blistering heat while working 6V75 Dee Marsh–Margam on 5 July 2013.
EDWARD GLEED

Shrewsbury Abbey is seen in the distance as 60004 hauls a southbound steel working. Semaphore signalling is very much in abundance in this part of the country. JOHN WHITEHOUSE

problems, and it was ultimately tripped to Toton for repair. But the Class 60s have redeemed themselves, and to date 60021, 60087, 60076, 60085 and 60096 have been assigned to this diagram.

Quite often a Class 60 is allocated to workings to and from Dee Marsh and Margam, notably 6M11 Margam–Dee Marsh, which is sometimes required to run via Llanwern to attach/detach wagons, the return working running as 6V75.

During December 2013, Class 60, No. 60066, which had recently been outshopped in silver with Biomass branding, was called upon to work this service. Similar to 6V05, this 6V75 working will quite often be very lengthy and include canvas-sided IHAs and telescopic BYAs. Workings using steel cradles have also been seen over the years. Other workings that the Class 60s have hauled include aluminium from North Wales.

Recently outshopped in the Biomass livery, an immaculate 60066 thunders through Cwmbran atop 6V75 Dee Marsh–Margam on 16 December 2013.
EDWARD GLEED

EWS-branded Mainline-liveried 60044 wheels the Holyhead–Warrington aluminium train as it passes through Valley on a dull 26 April 2008.
JOHN WHITEHOUSE

Kirkby Stephen on the S&C plays host to 60028 *John Flamsteed*, which is working the Newbiggin–Drax gypsum on 28 July 2007.
JOHN WHITEHOUSE

Gypsum/Fly-Ash Traffic

The Class 60s operate gypsum traffic from various locations utilizing 20ft (6m) containers loaded on PFA and FGA wagons or container flats. As a by-product of the power station functions, gypsum is a very green recycling exercise and is used in the manufacture of plasterboard. The traffic is carried in containerized form, and operates from locations such as Drax–Newbiggin (6M08, 6M52 and 6M20) via the Settle & Carlisle, Newbiggin–Milford (6E12 and 6E13), Newbiggin–Warrington Arpley and Newbiggin–Knottingley. Workings conveying fly ash have reached into Scotland, as depicted in the accompanying photograph.

The desolate fells and almost barren moorlands typify the scenery of the S&C, as seen in this view of 60035 and 60039 passing through Waitby on a Drax–Newbiggin gypsum working on 23 March 2002.
IAN LOTHIAN

60021 *Pen-y-Ghent* has just departed from Longannet power station on 23 February 1999, with loaded fly-ash tanks for Westbury for use in the construction of breeze blocks. IAN LOTHIAN

Timber

Like many other commodities conveyed by rail, timber traffic has seen an increase during recent years. Long before the Class 60s were constructed, Class 26s had operated timber log traffic from the Highlands of Scotland to the paper mill at Corpach. In recent years, timber traffic from Ribblehead, Baglan Bay and Teigngrace in Devon has been operated by Colas Rail's fleet of Class 56s, 66s and 70s. Class 60s have now started to operate these diagrams, the first of which ran as 6V54 to Baglan Bay, followed by the working to Teigngrace, also running as 6V54 and returning as 6M51.

60090 *Quinag* was the unusual choice of motive power for the afternoon Mossend–Aberdeen freight, here passing Plean on 28 March 1997. IAN LOTHIAN

A pleasant aroma of timber is enjoyed as Colas 60076 wheels the loaded 6M51 Teigngrace–Chirk through Pilning on a glorious evening on 29 May 2015.
EDWARD GLEED

Low cloud and mist swirl around as 60059 *Swinden Dalesman* shunts MBA Monster-Box wagons at Peak Forest at 7:00am on a dreary 1 June 2006. An unidentified Class 60 is also seen in the background.
EDWARD GLEED

Aggregate

For many years Class 60s have been engaged on stone traffic, and like some of the oil workings, certain stone diagrams are regularly hauled by a Class 60. There are a number of major quarrying locations in the UK, including Peak Forest situated in the High Peak, the quarries of Merehead and Whatley in Somerset, and Meldon quarry in Devon. Although Merehead, Whatley and Meldon quarries very rarely see Class 60s, Peak

Forest, on the other hand, has Class 60s virtually on a daily basis, with as many as three at the same time. A very popular working that is often hauled by a Class 60 from this area is 6F05 Tunstead–Oakleigh (Manchester), utilizing 100-tonne 'Brunner-Mond' limestone hoppers. The Class 60s have also hauled the short trip between Tunstead and Hindlow, using BLI (Buxton Lime Industries) hoppers in their familiar livery.

In the High Peak, 60012 approaches Edale amidst the drystone walls that typify the landscape in this area.
9 September 2004. NIGEL CAPELLE

Maximum power is required to haul the heavy 6F05, 15:05 Tunstead–Oakleigh working up the stiff gradient to Peak Forest and beyond, with 60091 providing the motive power on a searingly hot 23 July 2013.
EDWARD GLEED

DBS 60074 *Teenage Spirit* with its front end coated in stone dust, passes through Wellingborough on 17 October 2009, atop 6M34 Crawley to Peak Forest.
BRIAN MORRISON

Vast tonnages of stone are quarried from Peak Forest, Hindlow, Rylstone (6D48 Rylstone–Heck) and also from the Mendips to destinations such as Ely (Papworth), Stourton (Leeds), Bletchley, Purley, Acton, Woking and Hull (Dairycoats) hauling stone-covered hoppers in Tarmac livery. Services between Ashburys and Dowlow have used Class 60s to operate this diagram, whilst another popular working was the heavy 6M85 11:55 Tunstead–Ratcliffe aggregate. Much of the aggregate which emanates from the quarries of Whatley and Merehead is generally in the hands of the General Motors Class 59s, though a Class 60 has occasionally been allocated to one particular working, 6M20 11:00 Whatley–St Pancras. However, Class 66s appear to be the normal motive power for this service.

Another view of 60074 *Teenage Spirit*: on this occasion it is hauling yet another stone train as it crosses the swing bridge at Selby, bound for Peak Forest, on 4 August 2009. RICHARD TUPLIN

EWS-branded DBS Class 60 No. 60077 hauls 7O80 Luton Limbury Road to Angerstein Wharf, passing between Bexley and Crayford on 22 September 2009. BRIAN MORRISON

Interestingly, during the first two weeks of November 2014, Class 60s returned to the Westbury area, namely 60001 and 60049. DBS-liveried 60001 was reported to have worked 7V16 from Fareham to Whatley, whilst EWS-liveried 60049 worked the engineers' working 6041 from Westbury to Eastleigh. Further to this, 60001 worked 7V82 Crawley to Merehead, while 60049 was assigned to work

7C54 Oxford Banbury Road to Westbury aggregate, 60049 having worked from Merehead earlier that day. Aggregate to and from Mountsorrell quarry has seen Class 60 haulage over the years, the 6C31 08:37 Mountsorrell–Radlett 'Redland' self-discharge stone train being one of them.

The Class 60s have also operated along the North Wales coast on workings from Penmaenmawr quarry to various

60064 traversing the Midland mainline at Cossington on the Mountsorrell–Redland stone working on 14 June 1991.

JOHN STRETTON

Deep in the heart of London, 60099 *Ben More Assynt* passes Kensington Olympia on 25 March 1995. In 2015 this locomotive is still in active service, wearing the silver TATA steel livery. JOHN STRETTON

High in the Cumbrian Fells, EWS-liveried 60089 *The Railway Horse* climbs past Little Strickland on 14 June 2003 with the Redcar–Hardendale lime covhops.

IAN LOTHIAN

locations, including Crewe. Stone traffic in and around London is seen on a regular basis, notably around Acton. Many stone workings that have come from the Somerset quarries arrive at Acton, where several portions depart to locations such as Bat and Ball, among others.

With the Marks Tey signalbox in view, 60043 *Yes Tor* leaves Marks Tey under the wires with a loaded sand working bound for Hayes on 14 June 1996.

JOHN WHITEHOUSE

In Kent, Class 60s have been employed on the Stud Farm–Hothfield grit working, and in North Yorkshire they hauled stone traffic on the Redmire branch. At one time this section of railway linked the East Coast main line with the Settle and Carlisle railway. Though passenger services ceased operation in 1954, the line remained open for stone traffic to the quarry at Redmire. MoD traffic also used the branch serving Catterick camp. Sand is another commodity that has been conveyed by rail, with departures from Marks Tey being one of them.

Limestone has also been transported by rail to steelworks where it is used for steelmaking, though some workings no longer run. One of these diagrams was 6M46, which ran between Redcar and Hardendale, the return working being 6E46 Hardendale to Redcar, both of which have seen Class 60 haulage over the years. Following the announcement by the steelmaker Corus in December 2009 that steel production was to be reduced at its Teesside Cast Products factory, these runs ceased. The route for this working was via the picturesque Tyne valley and on to Carlisle; departing Carlisle, it then ran along the WCML to its destination, passing through delightful locations such as Little Strickland. The service used HGA lime hopper wagons.

Similar workings operated between Redcar and Scunthorpe carrying surplus stocks of iron ore; other workings included 6A03 Redcar–Santon. A by-product of the smelting process known as 'furnace burden' was also carried in JUA/JTA bogie tipplers; these workings included 6N02 Santon–Redcar and 6D02 Redcar–Santon, to name just two.

Railhead Treatment Trains

Railhead treatment trains carry equipment that removes leaf-fall detritus from the railhead during the autumn and early winter, to restore adhesion between rail and wheel. They are worked by Class 60s, usually those with high engine hours, which effectively form a reserve or part-time fleet.

Railtours

Having gained a following of committed railway enthusiasts, railtour operators requested the use of the Class 60 for railtour operations, much to the delight of its admirers. During their career, the Class 60s have operated many railtours, one of which was 'The Coal Scuttler' operated by Pathfinder Railtours. This railtour ran in connection with the Coalville depot open day held between 25 and 26 May 2001. Two Class 60s were used, 60057 *Adam Smith* and 60032 *William Booth*, both belonging to the coal subsector. Some of the railtours headed by a Class 60 have taken enthusiasts to locations that would normally be served by freight traffic, giving them an insight into Class 60 use within the freight industry.

'The Coal Scuttler', operated by Pathfinder Railtours, used 60057 *Adam Smith* with 60032 *William Booth*, seen here at Coalville during the open day held on 25 and 26 May 1991. ROY HUTCHINSON

One railtour that focused the enthusiasm of supporters took place during August 2013 and used two Class 60s, namely 60017 and 60063. It was aptly called 'The Taffy Tug' and operated over selected routes in the Cardiff valleys, commencing at Bristol Temple Meads. The locomotives had been despatched from Margam the previous evening as 0Z85 (19:44, Margam–Bristol Barton Hill). It is highly probable that one of the locomotives would have worked the regular 6B33 13:30 Theale–Margam 'Murco' tanks earlier that afternoon, and the other Class 60 might previously have worked a steel diagram in the South Wales area. This would

With semaphores firmly in the 'OFF' position, 60074 *Teenage Spirit* coasts through Barnetby on the 1Z28 Cleethorpes–Bristol Temple Meads charter on 2 April 2011. BRIAN GARRETT

Coal subsector 60060 *James Watt* at Buxton during one of the many railtours that have been hauled by a Class 60. 1 May 2004. BRIAN GARRETT

In the delightful setting of Ystrad Mynach up in the Cardiff valleys, 60017 and 60063 are at the helm of 'The Taffy Tug' on a gloriously sunny 25 August 2013.
EDWARD GLEED

have been very convenient in that both locomotives could then be despatched to Bristol that evening.

Following the railtour, both Class 60s were despatched to South Wales as 0Z61 23:01 Bristol Barton Hill–Margam, arriving at 01:04 – again, both Class 60s being conveniently placed to take up duties, with almost certainly one 60 being assigned to 6B13 05:05 Robeston–Westerleigh tanks, the other possibly to one of the many steel workings in the area. This again proves that these are very versatile locomo-

tives, and looking at the details of the railtour in its entirety provides evidence that DBS's assets were undoubtedly being maximized.

During August 2014, Pathfinder tours operated 'The Taffy Tug ii', which was similar to the original 'Taffy Tug' of 2013. On this occasion there were three legs of 'The Taffy Tug ii' (*see* Appendix). On this occasion, DBS supplied Class 60s, 60039 and 60040 *The Territorial Army Centenary*, both locomotives returning to Margam later that evening.

Deep in South Wales, 60039 and 60040 *The Territorial Army Centenary* work 1Z61 'Taffy Tug ii', here passing Tondu signalbox on 24 August 2014. EDWARD GLEED

60061 *Alexander Graham Bell* and 60044 *Ailsa Craig* near Mostyn on 11 August 1991, working the 14:30 Crewe–Llandudno special sponsored by Trainload Coal. JOHN TUFFS

60010 at Brush, undergoing repair following collision damage. This particular locomotive is gainfully employed with DB Schenker Rail UK. 12 September 1997. JOHN STRETTON

The early railtours included 'The Greenford Grinder', operated on 18 August 1991 as part of the Old Oak Common open day, when Class 60 60047 *Robert Owen* worked in partnership with Class 59 59005 *Kenneth J Painter*.

Although not railtour associated, on 14 September 1991 Network South East operated certain passenger services along the Middleton Towers route to Kings Lynn. On this occasion 60048 *Saddleback* hauled two NSE-liveried Class 312 EMU sets. The Chester to Holyhead main line has also seen Class 60s on railtours; one in particular was the 14:50 Crewe–Llandudno special sponsored by Trainload Coal.

The Class 60 in Works and Depot

Having discussed the many workings that the Class 60 has worked during its career, it is also important to briefly describe its role whilst in attendance at main workshops, depots, stabling and fuelling points throughout many parts of the UK. It would be impossible to detail every depot to which the Class 60s have been allocated, therefore just a small selection of photographs has been included to afford readers an insight into the variety of depots that the Class 60 has attended. Major traction maintenance depots such as Toton have undertaken significant work on locomotives, for instance the on-going 'Super 60' refurbishment programme, detailed in Chapter 6. Indeed, Class 60s have been returned to Brush Traction over the years for collision damage repair, work that could not have been done at maintenance depots,

An interesting view inside Brush, with 60025 being prepared for repainting into Loadhaul livery on 30 January 1996. JOHN STRETTON

Thornaby depot, where metals-allocated Class 60s 60049 *Scafell* and 60023 *The Cheviot* are awaiting their next turn of duty. JOHN STRETTON

in addition to refurbishment programmes that had been undertaken earlier.

Following the construction of the Class 60, Brush had service engineers for the first five years at a number of depots, namely Toton, Immingham, Thornaby, Stewarts

Two Class 60s on Leicester depot wearing the two-tone grey livery with the Mainline branding: 60048 *Saddleback* and 60071 *Dorothy Garrod*. 24 December 1995. JOHN STRETTON

One of the smaller depots for locomotive maintenance was Westbury: here, 60008 *Moel Fammau* is seen at the depot on 24 February 1991. JOHN STRETTON

Lane, Motherwell and Cardiff Canton. Other maintenance depots have undertaken general servicing and routine maintenance work, for example Thornaby, Leicester and Westbury, while smaller facilities such as Didcot and Peak Forest are simply stabling or fuelling points.

As detailed earlier in this chapter, Peak Forest in the High Peak has always been a place of interest for rail enthusiasts, and has often been the host of railtours. It has also been a place of interest for photographers, myself included. What could be more pleasing than to sit on the surrounding grass banks on a warm and sunny afternoon with a Bakewell pudding in one hand and a mug of tea in the other, watching the shunting operations. A year or so ago, I visited the location with my family whilst on holiday in the surrounding area, and although I was only there for not much above half an hour, the activity was intense. Trains are constantly

The light is fading fast as 60099 pauses opposite the fuelling point at Peak Forest on a gloomy 11 November 2013. EDWARD GLEED

in operation for hours on end, and on that occasion there were two Class 60s (another reason for the popularity of the Peak Forest!).

Although the Class 60s were designed for heavy freight haulage, as has been mentioned earlier in this book, latterly certain members of the class have been relegated to more mundane duties, having been employed as the yard pilot. Such locos have included 60010, 60049, 60065, 60071 and 60073, and these have been used at locations such as Westbury yard, Eastleigh and Hinksey yard (Oxford). Usually these duties have been allocated to a locomotive with high engine hours, or sometimes following an overhaul to prove that nothing troublesome, or potentially troublesome, is present before committing it to the main line.

In freak lighting conditions, 60065 Spirit of Jaguar draws stone hoppers through the loading terminal at Peak Forest on 16 August 2011. EDWARD GLEED

CHAPTER FIVE

LIVERIES, NUMBERS AND NAMES

Liveries

During the late 1980s, the railway industry was going through a major change. Transported commodities were being divided up into different categories, known as sectorization; for example, commodities such as oil were to be clas-sified as being part of the Petroleum sector, while steel and associated products came under the Metals sector. In total there were six Trainload sectors: Coal, Construction, Metals, Petroleum, Distribution and General.

Of the six sectors, only four were allocated to the Class 60 fleet; Distribution and General subsectors were not

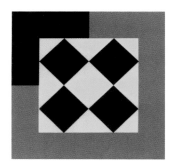

The Trainload Freight Coal subsector logo (designed by Roundel Design Group for British Rail/Trainload Freight).

The Trainload Freight Metals/Automotive subsector logo (designed by Roundel Design Group for British Rail/Trainload Freight).

The Trainload Freight Construction subsector logo (designed by Roundel Design Group for British Rail/ Trainload Freight).

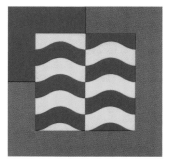

The Trainload Freight Petroleum subsector logo (designed by Roundel Design Group for British Rail/ Trainload Freight).

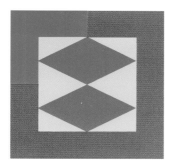

The Trainload Freight Distribution subsector logo (designed by Roundel Design Group for British Rail/ Trainload Freight).

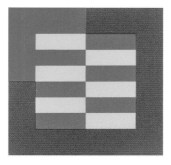

The Trainload Freight General User subsector logo (designed by Roundel Design Group for British Rail/ Trainload Freight).

allocated. The original concept of the Trainload sectors was for locomotives to work within their allocated sectors; for example, a Class 60 allocated to the Coal sector would specifically work coal traffic. However, in reality this did not always go to plan – for instance, in cases of failure, a Class 60 allocated to the Coal sector could be called upon to work a train under the Metals sector, and so on. The Class 60s were all outshopped in their own distinct Trainload liveries according to their classification in the sector, rather than the Railfreight liveries as worn by other classes. Other classes, for example 31s, 37s and 47s, would also be outshopped in the Trainload liveries, according to their allocated sectors.

From the outset the Class 60 was painted using the industry-known procedure of 'two-pack' painting. The Class 60 bodyshells were fabricated by Procor at their workshops in Wakefield and were delivered to Brush Traction in Loughborough by road, each bodyshell having been fully painted at the point of manufacture (see Chapter 3). The

two-pack method not only gives a far superior finish over the traditional hand-painting methods employed on rolling stock hitherto, but is also very durable and resilient to such wear and tear as might occur in the course of its duty – for example, stone chipping. However, two-pack painting is a completely different process, and carries with it a much higher implication first in terms of cost, and also because much higher standards of health and safety are needed in the work procedures.

With the traditional painting methods as used in the past, it was a relatively straightforward process to rub down, prime and repaint in the event of damage caused to the bodywork that required either a partial or a complete repaint. Necessary protective equipment had to be worn, and in the case of spraying, the use of breathing apparatus was (and still is) required. With a repaint using two-pack, specialist equipment is required because when two-pack is rubbed down, cyanide particles are released, which must be safely contained.

The application of advertising branding has developed vastly in recent years. Most train-operating companies (TOCs) who inherit rolling stock from other TOCs may wish to rebrand their newly acquired stock into the respective 'house colours', and in an attempt to keep costs down, the use of vinyl is widely employed. It has to be stressed that the application of vinyl is not an easy task. First, the body to which the vinyl is to be affixed must be thoroughly cleaned. Vinyl is usually applied in sections, and these must be carefully lined up in relation to the adjoining pieces of bodyline of the rolling stock. During recent years, certain members of the Class 60 fleet have had special liveries applied, and in some cases with additional content. Two notable liveries have been applied, 60040 wearing an all-over maroon base colour with the Territorial Army logo applied, and 60074, which was outshopped in light blue with the 'Teenage Cancer Trust' logo. These logos would no doubt be hugely expensive were they to be painted by hand, therefore the use of vinyl is almost certainly more cost effective.

In order to discuss the many liveries worn by the Class 60s over the years, it is important to detail those applied to other locomotives hitherto, as this may well have had a bearing on British Rail's decision to introduce the new Trainload liveries. From the late 1960s, the ubiquitous BR blue and blue/grey livery scheme was much in abundance. It could be argued that the introduction of the HSTs initiated the livery change. To some, the HSTs were affectionately known as the 'Flying Banana', partly because of the warning yellow applied to the front of the cab, which also extended some way along the body side of the power car.

During 1978, a variant to the BR blue livery was applied to Class 56, 56036 being the first to receive what became known as the 'large logo' livery. This livery was steadily applied to certain classes of main-line locomotives, namely Classes 37, 47, 50 and 56. It was certainly eye-catching with its light grey roof, blue body sides and wraparound yellow cabs with black window surrounds.

A year or so later another change was taking place: breaking tradition with the BR corporate livery of blue/grey, the new livery became known by many as the 'executive' livery, and was applied to both the advanced passenger trains (APTs) and the HSTs. A few years later, another version of the large logo was being applied to freight locomotives. Instead of the blue and light grey sections, dark grey was used, and called Railfreight grey. In a further derivative a red stripe was applied at waist level, including, in most cases, the buffer beam. It was colloquially known as 'Railfreight red stripe'.

However, during the mid- to late 1980s another livery change was under way, that of outshopping locomotives according to their specific sectors. In more recent times, the choice of liveries has been widened. Certainly this is true from the BR perspective, because during the BR blue/grey era, any departure from this livery was frowned upon and would necessitate special permission from senior management.

A New Corporate Identity

For the Class 60 'Trainload' liveries and accompanying elements, BR sought the expertise of the industrial design consultancy Jones Garrard Limited – at present trading as Jones Garrard Move – who in turn commissioned Roundel Design Group to design the new logo and livery. Jones Garrard Limited had a great deal of experience in the railway industry over the years, and had much expertise in terms of livery application, seating design and technical studies of railway engineering, and had provided broad designs to the transportation industry. The company had also undertaken projects for the Class 319 and 442 electric multiple units. Like Jones Garrard Limited, Roundel Design Group (now rebranded as Chaos) was no stranger to the railway industry either, being involved with the livery design for both UK and international companies. These have ranged from

the UK-based companies of London Transport, London Overground, Southern Railway and Heathrow Express, for the international markets Canton and Kowloon Railway, for Union Railways, and for many other companies, some of whom are not associated with the railway industry, for example The National Trust.[5]

In order for the design of the Class 60 to denote the purpose for which it was constructed, BR's Chairman Sir Robert Reid wrote to Mr B. R. Oliver:

> As you may be aware, the Class 60 has been designed specifically for freight operations, to provide greatly increased hauling power and improved efficiency over locomotives currently in use. . . It is therefore appropriate that the design should communicate power, strength and robustness as the main attributes of this locomotive, whilst the livery maintains the corporate Railfreight identity.[4]

Jones Garrard was of the opinion that a powerful new corporate identity for locomotives was needed, which would then be partially extended across the company to staff mess rooms and corporate literature.[5]

Although the Class 60s were constructed as heavy freight locomotives, their livery application was subjected to as much scrutiny as that of a passenger locomotive. Even though freight locomotives are out of the public 'eye' for much of the time, the attention to detail had to be upheld.

The Class 60 brochure (designed and produced by Roundel Design Group for British Rail/Trainload Freight).

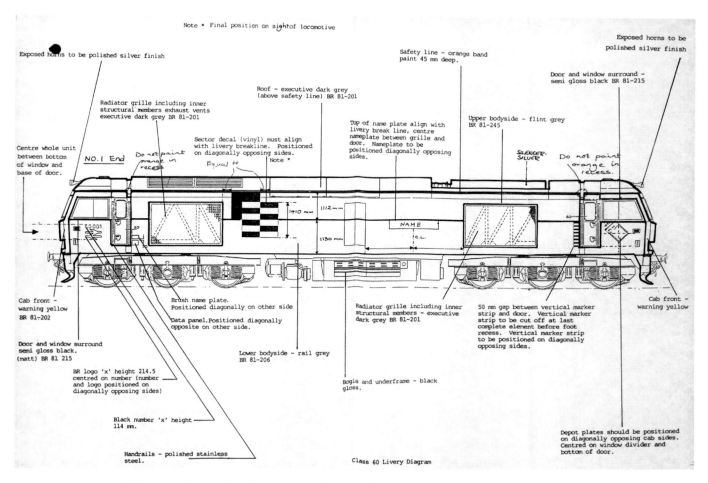

The Class 60 livery plan, indicating the positioning of the various Trainload Freight livery elements.
THE NATIONAL ARCHIVES

British Rail laid down strict guidelines, which were detailed in the Class 60 specification on how the livery would appear on the locomotive, and requiring it to be painted in accordance with the BR painting schedule; however, it was recognized that a contractor might wish to submit their own painting system.

The specification further stipulated that painting was not permitted to adhere to any surface in a way that might adversely affect the operation or performance of any equipment. Warning notices, standard signings and symbols were to be included at the direction of the engineer. Subcontractor's equipment (in this case the Class 60 body) had to be painted by the manufacturer (Procor), and was to be adequately protected from the elements before it left their works.

Detailed livery drawings were produced to indicate the positioning of the subsector symbols, and also the actual demarcation point from one colour to another. The internal components were just as important as the external livery, and had to conform to the established distinguishing colours so they could be easily identified by maintenance staff. In the case of the engine itself, this was off-white or grey, and attention was given to the cabs (*see* Chapter 3). It must be noted that an interior repaint is hugely expensive because a deep clean is required, and all the pipework and conduit must be masked, and although the Class 60s have been put through more refurbishment programmes in subsequent years, under the 'Super 60' programme the internal colours remained the same. Externally this new livery was a major change from the livery application used in driving cabs since

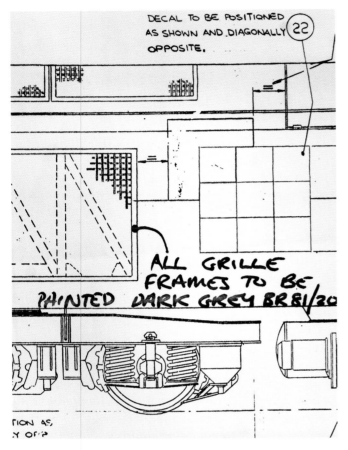

Class 60 Construction subsector livery application diagram. This application was always a high priority for British Rail. THE NATIONAL ARCHIVES

the 1955 modernization programme, which employed the services of the British Transport design consultants Wilkes & Ashmore.

Livery Launch

As with any locomotive, performance is of paramount importance; however, it is not just about the locomotive's haulage credentials, it must also look its best, and the end product must be very pleasing to the eye. The ubiquitous BR blue had been scorned by some enthusiasts for its bland and unimaginative design, sometimes appearing drab after only being in service for a matter of weeks. Overseas, railway advertising has played a major part in the way locomotives are presented to the wider industry and public. For many

years BR had its own highly skilled painters and sign writers to apply legends and insignia.

In latter years the railway industry has gone to significant expense to adopt new liveries for their locomotives and rolling stock, and has appointed outside companies to devise specific styles of livery, many of which are hugely complex, depicting a range of products from cheeses to white goods and confectionary to model railway manufacturers. Indeed, one model manufacturer had one of its models displayed on the sides of its full-size counterpart. Similarly for many years the railway authorities have been keen to exhibit their credentials, in many cases incurring significant expense. One example is 60099, which was repainted in the house colours of the Indian-owned TATA Steel Company. The locomotive was then strategically positioned in front of a steel ladle that had been placed on an embankment with its contents spewing down to the locomotive.

The livery applications to the Class 60 are numerous. A list of these is given below, including 'one-offs' and specials. An exhaustive list of livery applications, their meanings and ownership is detailed further in this chapter. A full appraisal also details which class member wore each livery.

Trainload Freight Liveries

The Trainload Freight livery was based on the Railfreight livery that had been applied to many of the freight-allocated locomotives during the mid- to late 1980s. The Railfreight 'red stripe' livery was a further derivative of the Railfreight livery, and involved a red stripe being applied to the solebar and in many cases continuing over the buffer beam. It was mandatory for all UK locomotives to employ yellow lower cab fronts as a visual warning approach, the upper half being two large windows with black window surrounds, along with a compulsory orange cant-rail stripe. This stripe warns fitters/cleaners of the safe working height, thus preventing possible electric shock from OHLE (overhead line equipment) present on electrified railways.

When sectorization commenced towards the end of the 1980s, the new Trainload liveries were introduced. These were totally different from the liveries that had been applied hitherto. The base livery was to be known as two-tone grey: a deep band of light grey was applied from the solebar to mid-height of the locomotive, and from here to the cant-rail stripe, a darker shade of grey was employed. The roof was also a slightly darker shade of grey. All six of the subsector

Traced overlay indicating the wrong placement of the Trainload Construction element, in this instance on 60001 *Steadfast***.**
THE NATIONAL ARCHIVES

classes used this base livery. The way in which the individual subsector liveries were defined is described below. Detailed livery plans had been submitted for approval by BR; even small items such as the mesh frames were specified and were to be painted dark grey. In the case of the Trainload livery elements – Coal, Metals, Petroleum and Construction – there were to be absolutely no divisions between colours within the sub-sector symbols.

Once the Trainload liveries had been approved by the BRB and subsequently applied, the position was regarded by some as incorrect and drew negative comments as it was deemed to be causing interference with the roof panel joints and lifting handle. The first proposed remedy had been rejected because it would have impacted on the name-plate fixings, which were in a pre-determined position. In a letter from Martyn Cornwell (Business Design Manager) to J.G. Tidmarsh (Project Manager for the Class 60s), the Roundel Design Group was asked to provide a solution that would not require the re-positioning of the nameplates. A new proposition was put forward which Cornwell believed would resolve the issue, thus responding to the initial placement criticisms, whilst at the same time only creating minimal disruption for Brush.

Supplied with the letter (dated 28 November 1989) was a photograph of 60001 *Steadfast*, having been allocated to the Construction subsector, with a traced overlay outlining the proposed new position of the element in relation to the current location of the logo. However, it would appear that the new proposal was not implemented by British Rail as the Trainload elements continued to be applied to the original location on the bodyside, these being placed on the body sides where there were no roof panel joints, which would in turn allow the element to be placed on the bodyside, directly below and between the roof opening hatches and silencer. With any livery change, such an alteration can have implications as to where the nameplate is to be affixed. The positioning of the plates will be governed to some extent by the nature of the locomotive superstructure, as they may hinder the application of nameplate fixings. Interestingly 60001 underwent a full repaint a year or so after delivery owing to the paint finish having an 'orange peel' effect, allowing general rail grime to settle in the small imperfections.[4, 11]

Much thought went into the actual meaning of the individual Trainload elements, as described below.

Coal Subsector Livery

Black diamonds were thought to be appropriate for this symbol, as coal had long been known as 'black diamond'. The design consists of two offset squares, the upper one slightly to the left is black, while the lower square is yellow. On top of the yellow square, four small black diamonds, two above

two, are applied. Directly to the side of the driver's door is a small, vertical yellow band with black diamonds arranged vertically.

Further to the standard livery application of two-tone grey, a select number of locomotives had their key components given additional details in paint: thus their wheel rims were picked out in white, their bogie dampers in grey, and buffer crowns in white/grey. Such a high degree of workmanship might have been thought a little extravagant in terms of cost for a railtour, but it must not be forgotten that the locomotives were very much in the 'public eye'; equally, it might have been considered an extravagance that would be more appreciated by a rail enthusiast than by a customer of Trainload Freight. Nevertheless, both rail enthusiast and customer alike might wish to have a photograph of a given locomotive on their home or office wall, so these logos would be prominent in the resultant images, against a black background.

Construction Subsector Livery

The construction element in this livery is made up of blocks, reflecting building blocks. It is composed of two offset squares, the upper one slightly to the left being blue, while the lower square is yellow. On top of the yellow square are five smaller blue squares, the fifth square being integrated into the upper blue square. The arrangement is thus two, staggered by two, staggered by two, which is repeated in a similar fashion directly behind the driver's door.

Petroleum Subsector Livery

The 'wave' in the Trainload element depicts the liquid nature of the products conveyed, and is almost a repeat of the Construction livery, but instead of the blue squares, thin wavebands of alternating blue and yellow are used. It is

60001 *Steadfast* wearing the Construction subsector livery at Stewart's Lane depot in London on 27 July 1992. Note the inward-opening engine-room doors (*see* **Chapter 2**). JOHN STRETTON

Allocated to the Petroleum subsector, 60054 *Charles Babbage* heads an engineers' working on the 'up through' line at Bristol Temple Meads on 12 February 2006. EDWARD GLEED

worth noting that when 60054 *Charles Babbage* was taken into service it was painted in the Petroleum sector livery, and remained so until recently when it was repainted into the current company's – DBS – house colours of red and grey. Prior to the application of the DBS livery, this was the only locomotive that had worn a single livery throughout its entire career, having escaped the interim liveries of Transrail Freight, Mainline Freight, Loadhaul and the later EWS livery (described in later sections).

Metals Subsector Livery

The Metals logo is again almost a repeat of the Construction elements, but instead of the blue squares, vertical blue and yellow chevrons were affixed to the larger yellow square. The angular quality of this mark was considered appropriate for this subsector.

Three New Liveries

During the mid-1990s, the erstwhile Trainload Freight livery was superseded by three new liveries, which were to be known as Mainline Freight, Transrail Freight and Loadhaul. The Loadhaul livery was applied to five members of the fleet, which are listed below and were originally designated to the North East region. Only three Class 60s had the full Mainline Freight livery applied, and these were allocated to the former BR Southern Region, being based at Hither Green. The remaining Class 60s that were operated by Mainline Freight and which were not given a full repaint had the Mainline logos applied on top of the two-tone grey livery.

The remainder of the fleet came under the Transrail branding. This was by far the easiest and cheapest livery to alter, but it was the biggest fleet allocation requiring change. These members had their original Trainload elements

In beautiful light, 60031 *Ben Lui* wears the Metals subsector branding while on depot at Leicester on 14 April 1991. JOHN STRETTON

Following removal of its original Coal subsector logo, unbranded 60067 *James Clerk-Maxwell* **passes Sytch Lane on the WCML, hauling a lengthy raft of MBA 'Monster' box wagons on 22 June 2001.**
EDWARD GLEED

removed, to be replaced by what was colloquially known as the 'Big T' that represented Transrail. Other classes of locomotive also had this 'Big T' affixed over older liveries – as with, for example, the acclaimed Dutch livery, which then became known as Transrail-Dutch. However, none of the Class 60 fleet wore this livery.

Certain members of the Loadhaul and Mainline Freight fleet just had their respective logos applied on top of the two-tone grey livery. This was almost certainly done on the grounds of cost, though in my opinion it did not look

as aesthetically pleasing. A number of Class 60s had no branding at all, and thus wore the original two-tone grey livery scheme.

The Loadhaul Livery

The Loadhaul livery was predominantly black, with orange lower cab sides finishing at an angle; this angle was also repeated at the front of the loco cab. On certain Loadhaul locomotives the tapered angle was symmetrical on each side

The Loadhaul livery applied to 60059 *Swinden Dalesman,* **on shunting duties, adds a little colour to the scene at Peak Forest on a dreadfully wet 1 June 2006.**
EDWARD GLEED

A variation on the Loadhaul livery: 60070 *John Loudon McAdam* **in two-tone grey with Loadhaul branding, at Peak Forest on 26 April 2004.** BRIAN MORRISON

of the lower cab front, while others had the angle tapering downwards (personally I thought this arrangement looked neater). The Loadhaul branding was a white upper and grey lower background, with the word 'Loadhaul' slanted forwards in black. Nameplates, where fitted, were of a standard design, but instead of a red background as on many other namings of the era, the Loadhaul nameplate background was black, with the exception of the *Gypsum Queen ii* nameplate, where the background colour to the nameplate was red, although this was later changed to black.

The Mainline Freight Livery

The three Mainline Freight Class 60s that received a completely new livery were painted in a rather pleasing aircraft blue – with the exception of the roof, which was painted dark grey – with the lower cab fronts in yellow. This was finished off with a mid-height thin silver band that ran the entire length of the locomotive, though it was interrupted where any nameplates were affixed. The livery also included three silver wheels, which were segmented along the sides. The locomotive running number was the same silver shade as the band, though the number was blue on the cab front. The nameplate was overall silver with a raised perimeter and wording highlighted to match the livery of the bodyside.

On the remaining Mainline fleet the nameplates were of standard design, and the locomotives just had Mainline Freight branding. The Mainline logos that were affixed to the two-tone grey livery were subtly different from the silver logo applied to the fully repainted locomotives. Although the

Under threatening skies, 60071 *Dorothy Garrod* stands in Falkland Yard at Ayr at the helm of an MGR working. The locomotive wears two-tone grey with Mainline branding. JOHN WHITEHOUSE

design was the same, these smaller wheel logos were blue with the addition of yellow and blue segments at the wheel edge, with a full yellow circular pin-stripe, which contrasted well with the grey. The grey cab-side air grille remained silver, unlike those in the Loadhaul livery, which remained black.

Allocated to the Construction subsector, 60044 *Ailsa Craig*, in attendance at Leicester depot on 6 April 1996, shows off the Mainline Freight livery of aircraft blue. JOHN STRETTON

60078 just north of Clay Mills, wearing the original Mainline Freight livery but with the additional EWS 'Big Beastie' logo, on 29 April 2006. JOHN TUFFS

A heavy load of steel coil strip descends from Bishton flyover near Magor with 60011 providing traction. It is now virtually devoid of its Mainline Freight branding. 12 November 2009. EDWARD GLEED

Transrail Freight

As already mentioned, the Transrail livery was by far the cheapest to alter. This was because the basis for the livery was two-tone grey, just as the Trainload liveries, though instead of the base yellow squares with the varying legend, the so-called 'Big T' was applied. This consisted of a white roundel with a

red-coloured band and a full blue circle patch, on top of which was a large white 'T' – hence 'Big T'. Two red oblong bands are situated below the 'T'. Of interest, many other classes had this logo applied, namely Classes 31, 37 and 56.

EW&S (English, Welsh & Scottish Railway) Livery

The erstwhile EW&S livery – the ampersand was later removed, to become EWS – was adopted from its parent company Wisconsin Central Railroad Company in the USA. At the time, the Wisconsin Company wore the livery of all-over maroon with a thick mid-waistband of pale yellowish cream. After EW&S had acquired the complete assets (including freight rolling stock) from Loadhaul, Mainline Freight and Transrail Freight, the company wanted to mark the locomotives with their own branding, though there was uncertainty at that time as to which shade of maroon to use. It was therefore decided to outshop a number of locomotives – not just the Class 60s – in plain undercoat until a decision could be reached.

Inevitably general rail grime quickly built up, necessitating an intensive clean before the repaint into the respective 'house colour' of the owner could take place. Tremendous skill was expended in applying a superior lasting finish, but sadly even this was soon covered in grime. It was not until the late 1990s that an agreement was reached as to which

Transrail was one of the three post-Trainload Freight liveries. Here, 60015 *Bow Fell* displays the livery as it heads the Bletchley–Tunstead through Lichfield Trent Valley in 2005. JOHN WHITEHOUSE

60041, formerly named *High Willhays*, at Bristol Temple Meads showing off the EW&S livery. Note the ampersand legend in the EW&S lettering. 19 February 2006. EDWARD GLEED

insignia and logo was to be used across the EW&S fleet, though the livery had been quickly decided.

The actual EW&S legend was the result of a competition run in a popular railway periodical of the time, *Rail*. The motif depicted three heads representing the heads of the lion of England, the dragon of Wales and the stag of Scotland. This emblem was applied and came to be known colloquially as the 'Beasties'. The livery for the three 'Beastie' heads was yellow and affixed to the lower cab sides (*see* next section).

The EWS 'Big Beastie' Logo

The 'Big Beastie' name and subsequent 'Big Beastie' legend materialized after an EWS shunting locomotive had been scrapped and the scrap dealer was under the impression that it was not an EWS locomotive. Therefore, the 'Beastie' logos were then affixed to Class 60 (and a number of Class 92) locomotives with matching EWS legend of maroon with a matching underline, which is overlaid on a yellow background. There are two different sizes of logo, which are shown below; (4 025) (4 026) (4 027) and the 'Big Beastie' name was derived from the three heads of England, Wales and Scotland, which are depicted in its logo.

On 5 March 2010, EWS Class 60, No. 60071 'Ribblehead Viaduct' is seen between Gossington and Dursley at the helm of 6E41 Westerleigh-Lindsey tanks. EDWARD GLEED

In further repaints on **EW&S** locomotives, the ampersand was removed to read **EWS**. Here at Westerleigh, 60085 *MINI-Pride of Oxford* belches thick exhaust smoke as it gets underway with 6E41 to Lindsey oil refinery on 2 June 2009. EDWARD GLEED

EWS locomotives not receiving a full repaint had **EWS** 'Big Beastie' logos applied. One of the locomotives so treated is 60013 *Robert Boyle* at Undy working the 6B13 Robeston–Westerleigh on 17 July 2007. EDWARD GLEED

Ever-encroaching weeds grow in Toton Yard as 60060 (formerly *James Watt*) awaits its fate. It depicts the large **EWS** 'Big Beastie' logo as applied to some non-repainted **EWS** locomotives. 20 October 2014. EDWARD GLEED

The small version of the **EWS** 'Big Beastie' logos on 60067 (formerly *James Clerk-Maxwell*) as it, too, awaits a decision on its future at Toton Yard on 20 October 2014. EDWARD GLEED

60006 *Scunthorpe Ironmaster* wearing the British Steel blue livery, running along the sea wall at Culross with a loaded MGR from Inverkeithing Yard to Longannet on 30 October 1998.
IAN LOTHIAN

British Steel

During 1997 two Class 60s, still under the auspices of EWS, were selected to be repainted in British Steel blue livery. This livery was applied to locomotives 60006 and 60033 in a joint ceremony to signify the twinning of EWS and British Steel. The livery was all over, applied with the necessary yellow lower cab fronts, as other Trainload liveries. A yellow, high visibility reflective self-adhesive band was also applied at solebar level, this being the standard practice for all EWS-liveried locomotives. The locomotives were named *Scunthorpe Ironmaster* (60006) and *Tees Steel Express* (60033). The familiar British Steel logo was applied to both body sides, using white vinyl.

Corus Steel

Following the repainting of the aforementioned locomotives in British Steel blue livery during 1997, 60006 and 60033 were repainted again into the house colours of the steel manufacturer 'Corus'. The livery was most striking indeed, all-over silver, and as the previous livery, with the obligatory half yellow warning panel and reflective solebar band. The red Corus logo was applied to both body sides. At the time of preparing this book, both Corus-liveried locomotives, 60006 and 60033, have been placed into store and remain at Toton.

60006 *Scunthorpe Ironmaster*, this time at Bristol Temple Meads and now wearing the Corus Steel livery during 2001. EDWARD GLEED

TATA Steel

The third steel manufacturer to adopt rail to transport its products in the United Kingdom was the Indian steel company 'TATA'. However, to date, the only Class 60 to have been repainted into the house colour of TATA silver grey is

A steel ladle spews slag down
the bank in a staged photo shoot
to unveil the **TATA** Steel livery
applied to 60099 at Scunthorpe
steelworks. 2 September 2009.
RICHARD TUPLIN

The TATA Steel logo applied to 60099. 4 January 2014.
EDWARD GLEED

The TATA Steel branding on 60099, 4 January 2014.
EDWARD GLEED

60099, formerly named *Ben Moore Assynt*. Also, red has been
used in place of the reflective yellow band on the solebar.
The light blue 'TATA Steel' logo has been applied to either
side of the body, with DB SCHENKER branding applied in
black below each secondman's cab side window.

The Great Western

The Great Western name is not to be confused with 'First
Group' or 'First Great Western'. Only one Class 60, 60081,
was outshopped in Great Western green, which was unveiled
at the Old Oak Common open day on 2 August 2000. After
the repaint it was named after the GWR's chief engineer
and one of the most celebrated railway engineers, Isambard
Kingdom Brunel. The Brunswick Chrome green livery was
applied overall, with the exception of the obligatory half
yellow, lower cab front warning panel. On each of the body
sides a triple 'pin-stripe' lining was applied as a panel. This
followed standard Great Western Railway signature livery of
a thin orange band pin-stripe, then a wide black band, then
a repeat of the thin orange band. The triple pin-stripe was
neatly rounded off on each corner.

The name and number plates were cast in brass with a
black background. This also contained a thin red band an
inch or so inside from the perimeter of the edge; the plate
was also rounded to match the pin-stripe.

The 'EWS Big Beastie' three heads were cast in brass and affixed below the secondman's cab side window. To further enhance this livery, the warning horns were a matching colour to the 'EWS Beastie' casting. Another appropriate feature was the application of raised brass numerals of the locomotive number, mounted below the driver's cab side window, with black underlay and a red pin-stripe. The locomotive number was N° 081 in red, and it was affixed to the front yellow warning panel.

Sadly this locomotive suffered a catastrophic engine failure when the connecting rod punctured the engine casing (discussed earlier). However, it is understood that all the Class 60 locomotives currently stored at Toton could be brought back into service, although some would require more expenditure than others – and given the extent of the damage, 60081 *Isambard Kingdom Brunel* would require significant financial input for it to be brought back into traffic.[11]

Having arrived at Grangemouth on the empty tanks from Dalston, 60081 is wearing the acclaimed Great Western livery, which it received during the Old Oak Common open day. 29 March 2002. IAN LOTHIAN

DB Schenker Rail UK

On 28 June 2007, it was announced that an agreement had been reached for Deutsche Bahn to purchase EWS. Following European approval the sale was completed on 13 November 2007.

Initially it was stated that EWS rolling stock would not be rebranded; however, during 2009, DB Schenker Rail UK changed its mind, and several locomotives received DB Schenker branding. Rebranding commenced from 1 January

The corporate DB Schenker Rail UK livery is certainly vibrant. Here, 60040 arrives at Peak Forest on 22 July 2014. EDWARD GLEED

The lapping waters of the River Severn at Gatcombe, with 60007 the *Spirit of Tom Kendell* in charge of 6B13 05:05 Robeston–Westerleigh tanks on 29 September 2011. EDWARD GLEED

2009 with 59206, and in January 2009 the official rebranding from 'EWS' to 'DB Schenker Rail UK' took place. The first Class 60 to carry this livery was 60011 during February 2011, and as of 2015, twenty-one of the former EWS loco-

Logo depicting the DBS safety campaign affixed to 60007 *Spirit of Tom Kendell*, at Westerleigh on 29 September 2011. EDWARD GLEED

motives have received the striking DBS livery of red and grey. With the exception of the cab roof, the remainder of the roof has been painted a tasteful shade of mid-grey, along with a broad solebar band of the same colour. This band extends up to the lower part of the main air-intake body-side mesh, which is painted black. The remainder of the body is all-over DB red. The lower part of the yellow cab front remains.

To date there is one deviation to the livery: No. 60007 *The Spirit of Tom Kendell*. Although the locomotive is painted in the company's house colours, it has additional logos affixed to the body side, depicting a safety helmet with the words 'Switch on to Safety'. It is DB Schenker Rail UK's rail safety campaign for employees. The locomotive was named after the untimely death of Tom Kendell following an accident.

An autumn breeze causes trees to sway near Yate as 'Teenage Cancer Trust'-liveried 60074 *Teenage Spirit* **works the diverted 6V05 Round Oak–Margam steel on 17 October 2013.** EDWARD GLEED

Teenage Spirit

DB Schenker Rail UK and The Childhood Cancer Trust are one of many organizations to have teamed up to raise money for research to find a cure for cancer. To cement ties, DBS arranged for 60074 to be sent for repainting at Toton into a very striking all-over light blue livery, with the Teenage Cancer Trust logo affixed to each body side. Like other locomotives in the past that have been outshopped with high profile liveries, particular attention is also paid to the underframe. The cab steps and brake pipes were painted white, while the pipes connected with the parking brake were painted brown. It is sometimes the custom that the buffer crowns are painted white or silver, and in the case of 60074 the buffers were picked out in silver. In addition to the repainting, the locomotive was named *Teenage Spirit*, and on 1 March 2009 at the York National Railway Museum, the locomotive was unveiled by ITV Emmerdale actor Chris Chittell. The DB Schenker logo was affixed below the secondman's cab side window.

To further this fundraising, *Rail Express* magazine teamed up with the world-famous model railway manufacturer Hornby, who produced a limited edition (1,000 pieces) of the highly acclaimed Class 60, suitably attired in the Teenage Cancer Trust livery, together with etched nameplates and a numbered certificate.

60074 *Teenage Spirit* **depicts the logo of the 'Teenage Cancer Trust' at Westerleigh, 30 January 2014.**
EDWARD GLEED

Initially the locomotive was repainted without refurbishment; however, it was selected for refurbishment under the on-going 'Super 60' programme, and rather than a standard repaint into DBS colours, the company authorized a repaint into the Teenage Cancer Trust livery. During the five years that 60074 wore this unique livery, it was given a full refurbishment.

Following this, the locomotive was released from Toton having been repainted in this livery, although the front cab window frames were painted blue and the application of the DB logo was directly below the front cab windows. During September 2014, 60074 lost its unique blue livery and received the corporate DB Schenker red/grey livery at Toton.

Having attended the Cranmore 150 Quarry Gala at Merehead, a gleaming 60040 *The Territorial Army Centenary* passes **Dr Day's Junction, Bristol, on 18 July 2008.** EDWARD GLEED

60066 at Old Sodbury atop 6B33 Theale–Robeston; it is the third Class 60 to wear silver livery. It has the Drax 'powering tomorrow' logo affixed to the bodyside. 20 March 2015. EDWARD GLEED

Territorial Army

In a similar vein to the repainting of 60074 in its unique livery, on 14 June 2008 60040 was unveiled in the 'Army Be The Best' livery at the National Railway Museum at York. The locomotive was named *The Territorial Army Centenary* by HRH the Duke of York in a ceremony to mark the centenary of the Territorial Army. The actual livery is most striking, as the locomotive wears an all-over deep red colour except for the mandatory yellow warning panel and orange cant-rail stripe. Like other locomotives in promotional/advertising livery, it is generally the logos that make the locomotive noticeable. However, in the case of 60040, the insignia of the Union flag is most prominent, and also the bold white lettering, which reads: 'ARMY BE THE BEST REGULAR AND TERRITORIAL'. The Union flag has been very well rendered indeed, with differing shades of colour that give the impression that the flag is actually fluttering.[11]

Drax

In December 2013, 60066 was released from works having received the 'Super 60' refurbishment programme. In a departure from the DBS's house colour of red and grey, the locomotive was painted silver, replacing the area that would normally be DBS red. However, with the exception of the

cab roof, the main roof above the engine is the same colour as the lower body sides' band, which is grey. The yellow warning panel remains the same as that of other members of the Class 60 fleet under the DBS colour scheme.

Although the 'DB' logo is fixed to the front cab below the windscreen, there are no DB Schenker legends on the body sides. This has been replaced by the 'Drax Biomass' branding, incorporating a tasteful mix of graduating colours of black, blue and green; the blue is used predominantly for the

The colourful Drax logo affixed to 60066. 16 March 2015. EDWARD GLEED

The Drax branding applied to 60066. Note the absence of capitalization. 16 March 2015. EDWARD GLEED

main lettering, which reads 'powering tomorrow', written in lower case. This livery was applied in recognition of a trial run of Biomass traffic between Hull and Drax.

Colas Rail

Colas Rail is one of the leading suppliers of railway infrastructure services in Europe and the United Kingdom. In terms of traction, Colas Rail UK has a relatively small fleet of locomotives, though this is steadily growing. As of June 2015, the company has eight Class 60s in traffic, in addition to a fleet of ten brand new Class 70 locomotives that it acquired from GE Pennsylvania. Colas has purchased a small fleet of ten Class 60 locomotives from DBS. This vibrant livery, which had hitherto been applied to Classes 47, 56, 66 and 70 locomotives, has now been applied to its Class 60 fleet, with 60087 making its debut on the main line on 2 June 2014.

The livery is reminiscent of the Loadhaul livery of the mid-1990s, in that it has the black and orange as Loadhaul, but also a third colour, yellow, though as standard practice this differs slightly in shade from the warning panel, and is more a 'lemon' yellow. The roof, upper cab and body sides are high gloss black with the yellow and orange colours being applied to the lower body sides in a tapered slant towards the cab ends, both rising to a point between the body-side doors and mandatory orange cant-rail stripe. The demarcation between the orange and yellow is afforded by way of a slant, making the bodyside appear more contemporary. On the Class 60s, this slant rises to a peak just below cant-rail level, almost half way along the length of the body, and then

Colas-liveried 60087 *CLIC Sargent* on 0Z50 coasts through Lawrence Hill whilst en route to Cardiff Canton for crew familiarization duties on 21 July 2014. EDWARD GLEED

descends at an angle to the rear of the engine at cab side window level.

Looking at the side elevation of the locomotive, the yellow is positioned on the left-hand side while the orange is applied to the right-hand; this pattern is replicated on the other side. The lettering is black, as is the bodyside mesh.

The locomotive running number is black, and follows the now widely used practice of no gap between the class number and the individual locomotive number. The locomotive running numbers are applied below the four cab side windows, and also on the cab fronts below the driver's side cab window. The company logo, which depicts a safety helmet illustrating the Colas Rail branding, is also applied below each cab side window but above the running number, while the legend 'COLAS RAILFREIGHT' is coloured black and affixed to the body sides. The sixth, seventh and eighth Colas Class 60s to be released to traffic have introduced a variation on the company logo in that the Colas Rail helmet

is slanted backwards, whereas other members of the Colas fleet have the Colas Rail helmet in the horizontal position. The helmet is more in keeping with the French style of helmet, favoured by fire services.[11]

Running Numbers

There has also been much thought as to the placement of running numbers on the locomotive. In most cases it has been customary to place the locomotive running number directly below the driver's cab side window. In the pre-TOPS ('Total Operations Processing System': see below) era the locomotive number was repeated below the secondman's window, but where there were 'large logo' elements the numbers would have been too large to fit beneath the cab windows, so they were placed along the main body side. This is certainly the case as far as the EWS-branded Class 60s were concerned.

The fonts came under scrutiny as well, with two examples being given. For the EWS font, 'Gill Sans' was chosen, while under the British Rail era, the 'Rail Alphabet' was used, the latter being designed by Jock Kinnier and Margaret Calvert. Further to this, two Class 60s that had been outshopped in British Steel blue, 60006 and 60033, both had their locomotive running numbers applied to the body side, in white. During the blue/grey livery era, it was not usual for the locomotive running number to be placed on the cab front; however, the Class 60s wore their locomotive number placed below the driver's front cab window.

It will be noted that in the Trainload livery, the Class '60' number was omitted. Following on from the original Trainload liveries and the later Loadhaul and Transrail livery, the full locomotive running number was applied below the driver's cab side window and was repeated on the cab front. Interestingly, the Class 60s that had the Mainline Freight logo superimposed on the original two-tone grey livery retained only the locomotive running number as in the original Trainload liveries.

Identification Tables

The tables on pages 136–138 have been compiled so readers can identify which livery each Class 60 has worn. It will be noted that many Class 60s wore numerous liveries over successive years, so certain locomotives will appear under

Colas 60076 stands in the loco spur at Bristol Temple Meads. It depicts the company helmet as on 18 June 2015. Later repaints depict the fire helmet with a backward slant. EDWARD GLEED

several livery headings. The same method also applies to namings. As with most other construction classes of locomotive, the numbering sequence has remained much the same. In 1974, British Rail devised a new numbering system within TOPS, comprising a five-digit numbering sequence for mainline diesel and electric locomotives (steam locomotives are also reportable under the TOPS system, though their TOPS numbers do not reflect the running number on the locomotive). This is explained using two examples, as follows: Class 60, 60 001 and 60 100. Although the TOPS system was devised several years previously, the renumbering of locomotives did not commence until 1974.

Class	Sub Class	Locomotive Number
60	0	001–100

Initially, locomotive numbering was applied in the following manner, for example 60 001. The class of locomotive, in this

60020 at Westerleigh working the Robeston–Westerleigh tanks on 14 April 2014. Note that there is no space between the class and the locomotive number: thus 60020. EDWARD GLEED

case the number '60', is separated from the running numbers. However, in recent years, the application of locomotive numbers has altered. For example, in the case of the twentieth member of the class, 60020, there is no space between the numbers and it is applied thus: 60020.

Detail Differences

Since their introduction, the Class 60s have remained more or less the same in terms of their external bodywork. In contrast, many older classes, such as the 37s and 47s, of which hundreds were built, were subject to numerous alterations – for example altered cooler groups, cut-away buffer beams, repositioning of body-side grilles, to name but a few. In most cases with the Class 60s, any differences that are obviously recognizable are merely variations in terms of the

60001 at the Brush 125th anniversary open day in Loughborough on 3 August 2014; its number is depicted with the spacing between the class and the running number: thus 60 001. EDWARD GLEED

livery – although additional roof vents were incorporated, which did not lead to a change in the livery.

However, there have been some livery and numeral variations that are not so obvious. In the accompanying photographs, 60074 wears the 'Teenage Cancer Trust' blue livery. The aforementioned photographs were taken as the locomotive was hauling 6B13 05:05 Robeston–Westerleigh 'Murco' tanks, which was photographed near its destination of Westerleigh. Quite by chance the locomotive was oriented with cab No 2 on the 'A' side facing the photographer. In the photograph (right) (4 047) we see the locomotive as it had been released from the paint facility at Toton, complete with black window frames, and complete five digit numbering (class and running number) though without the 'DB' logo. In the photograph bottom-left (4 048) the locomotive is seen following its release from Toton following an authorized repaint. This is where the differences are to be noticed; the locomotive now wears blue front cab window frames, with just the locomotive running number and 'DB' logo. In the photograph bottom-right (4 049) the locomotive

60074 *Teenage Spirit* **with black window frames and full numbering. 8 May 2015.** EDWARD GLEED

60074 *Teenage Spirit* **with blue window frames and DB logo, with the running number 074. 6 March 2012.**
EDWARD GLEED

60074 *Teenage Spirit* **with blue window surrounds and DB logo, with full running number 60074. 24 May 2012.**
EDWARD GLEED

60054 *Charles Babbage* **at Bristol Temple Meads with the original secondman's cab side two-piece window on 12 February 2006.** EDWARD GLEED

60099 *TATA Steel* **at Westerleigh carrying a black snowplough on 14 December 2010.** EDWARD GLEED

60054 *Charles Babbage* **at Bristol Temple Meads with the three-piece window unit on 12 February 2006.**
EDWARD GLEED

still wears blue window frames and 'DB' logo and further to this, the locomotive running number now includes the Class to read 60074.

In the next two photographs, 60054 *Charles Babbage* is seen at Bristol Temple Meads, at the head of an engineering train. Being photographed from the same side, it is interesting to note that the driver's cab side window is divided into three sections, while the secondman's window has only two sections.

The one-piece snowplough has been painted in several colours over the years. 60001 was originally outshopped with a grey one (a photograph is shown of 60001 in the introduction), though the majority were painted black. A few snowploughs were painted yellow.

60039 with a yellow snowplough at Westerleigh whilst working 0E41, East Usk Yard–Westerleigh on 22 April 2010. EDWARD GLEED

Original Trainload Livery Allocations [1] [11]

Trainload Coal:

60004 60032 60045 60046
60047 60055 60056 60057
60058 60059 60060 60061
60066 60067 60068 60069
60070 60071 60072 60073
60074 60075 60076 60077
60078 60079 60086 60087
60088 60090 60091 60092
60093

Trainload Construction:

60001* 60005 60006 60010
60009 60011 60012 60015
60016 60017 60018 60019
60039 60040 60041 60042
60043 60048 60080 60081
60082 60083 60084 60085
60094 60095 60096 60097
60098 60099 60100

Model manufacturer Bassett-Lowke built a model of 60001 for Brush without name. It was painted in two-tone grey with Construction subsector decals.[4]

Trainload Distribution: Not used (though a further model of the proposed Class 60 was manufactured by Bassett-Lowke, which carried this livery and was numbered 60001).

Trainload General: Not used.

Trainload Metals:

60008 60020 60021 60022
60023 60024 60029 60030
60031 60034 60035 60036
60037 60038 60044 60049
60050 60052 60081 60093

Trainload Petroleum:

60002 60003 60007 60010
60013 60014 60024 60025
60026 60027 60028 60033
60051 60053 60054 60062
60063 60064 60065 60078
60079 60082 60089[1] [11]

Interim Companies Prior to EWS ownership

Unbranded: 60006 60010 60013 60015
60021 60028 60042 60046
60050 60067 60068 60069
60079 60087 60095

Loadhaul: 60007 60008 60025 60038
60059

Loadhaul logo on 2TG: 60050 60064 60070

Mainline Freight: 60011 60044 60078

Mainline logo on 2TG: 60072 60073 60074 60075
60076 60077 60079 60083
60086 60087 60088 60094
60099

Mainline Unbranded: 60011 (silver banding part-worn on both sides and Mainline logos missing).

Transrail: 60005 60015 60029 60032
60033 60034 60035 60036
60037 60045 60046 60047
60055 60056 60058 60061
60062 60063 60065 60066**
60080 60081 60082 60084
60085 60089 60092 60093
60096 60097

During the early days of EWS operation a livery had not been decided, and several locomotives under EWS owner-ship that had undergone overhaul were released into traffic in bare undercoat. The only Class 60 to be released in traffic in primer was 60022.

Interim Primer: 60022

EW&S: 60004 60010 60012 60017 60019 60020 60024
60026 60027 60040 60041 60047 60049 60050
60098

(**Transrail on one side only, coal on the other)

EWS: 60001 60002 60003 60005 60008 60009 60012
60016 60018 60021 60022 60023 60025 60029 60030
60031 60035 60036 60037 60038 60039 60042 60043
60045 60048 60051 60052 60053 60058 60062 60063
60065** 60069 60071 60075 60080 60083 60085 60087
60089 60093 60094 60096 60097 60100 60500*

Two-Tone Grey with EWS logo: 60007 60013 60014 60015
60028 60034 60044 60055
60056 60057 60059 60060
60063 60066 60068 60070
60073 60074 60076 60077
60078 60079 60082 60084
60090 60091 60092 60095
60099

Loadhaul with EWS logo: 60007 60059

Mainline with EWS logo: 60044 60078

DB Schenker Rail UK: 60001 60007 60010 60011
60015 60017 60019 60020
60039 60044 60054 60059
60062 60063 60074 60079
60091 60092 60100

Colas Rail: 6002 (5) 60021 (2) 6002 (6)
60047 (8) 60056 60076 (3)
60085 (4) 60087 (1) 60095 (7)
60096 (6)

Bracketed numbers after the locomotives' running numbers denote the order of Colas Class 60s being returned to traffic between May 2014 and June 2015. It is understood that the remaining Colas Class 60s will be refurbished should there be sufficient demand.

formerly 60016 and renumbered during 2004

** *During September 2014, DBS decided to commence removing the EWS branding from its locomotives. The first Class 60 to undergo this alteration was 60065. Instead of the EWS branding, the current DB logo has been affixed to below the secondman's cab side window, while on the front the logo has been placed directly below the front cab windows.*
In 2006 a decision was made by EWS to affix yellow stickers with both the maroon EWS legend and logo to their fleet of locomotives that were not to receive the full corporate EWS livery. Two sizes of logo were applied.

Specials

DB Schenker Rail UK

'Switch on to Safety':	60007
British Steel blue:	60006 60033
Corus Steel silver:	60006 60033
Territorial Army	60040
'Be The Best':	
Drax Biomass silver:	60066
Teenage Cancer Trust	
blue:	60074
GWR Chrome green:	60081
TATA Steel silver:	60099

Depot Plaques and Insignia Carried by the Class 60s

Canton	Goat
Immingham	Star
Stewarts Lane	Power station
Hither Green	Oast house
Thornaby	Kingfisher
Toton	Cooling tower
British Rail	Cast double arrow
GWR-style numberplates	60081

Detail Differences

Snowploughs

The entire Class 60 fleet was fitted with snowploughs from new, and the majority were painted black. However, three locomotives had different colours: 60001, which had a grey one (subsequently painted black); and 60016 and 60039, which had yellow ones.

Long-Range Fuel Tanks

Long-range fuel tanks of 1,150gal (5,228ltr) capacity were fitted to the following Class members:[11]

60002 60003 60004 60005 60007 60009 60010 60012
60015 60017 60020 60021 60022 60023 60024 60026
60027 60028 60030 60037 60038 60041 60042 60046
60047 60049 60050 60051 60052 60053 60054 60055
60056 60058 60059 60064 60067 60070 60071 60077
60080 60081 60089 60090 60091 60096 60098

Class 60 Names

The naming of locomotives has been a long-standing tradition within railway companies, dating back to the first days of steam traction. However, in more modern times the naming of locomotives waned to an extent. During 1977 it is understood that the late BRB Chairman, Sir Peter Parker, revised the naming policy of locomotives, allowing them to receive names, a practice that in most cases remains today, much to the delight of the rail enthusiast.

All 100 Class 60 locomotives received names, ranging from notable people in industry, innovators, inventors, mountains, substantial hills and peaks. The vast majority of the class received their names before being handed over to the BRB, with one or two exceptions, but even these received their names within a number of weeks following construction. In many cases, locomotive namings have helped to boost morale because locomotives were named after depots; others have been named after work colleagues who have made a significant contribution in their particular field to the railway industry; whilst yet others have received names in memorium for past colleagues. A small number of Class 60 names raised public awareness of charitable organizations such as The Teenage Cancer Trust.

This chapter will detail the entire allocation of names and numbers applied to the Class 60, and the many liveries that have been applied. Certain names allocated to the Class 60 follow in traditional style, whilst others are quite colourful and even exquisite with the addition of embellishments or crests. The numbering sequence for the Class 60 is relatively straightforward in that only 100 were constructed (unlike the ubiquitous Class 47, of which 512 were constructed over the many years, together with alterations to the subclasses, which has been problematic for the rail enthusiast). Of the 100, only one Class 60 has been renumbered, this being 60016 *Langdale Pikes*, which was renumbered 60500 and renamed *Rail Magazine*. This event took place during April 2000 to celebrate the 500th issue of the hugely popular magazine.

From new, all the Class 60s received names that had been planned well in advance by British Rail for fitment at the point of manufacture, and they were all named after notable people in industry, innovators, inventors, mountains, substantial hills and peaks. Some of the Class 60 locomotive names are familiar – for example *Florence Nightingale* and *Charles Babbage* – but others, such as *The Hundred of Hoo*, may not have been understood.

As well as their official individual names, like other classes of traction the Class 60 received a nickname: thus colloquially they are known as 'Tugs'. This name derived from the sound emitted from an engine installed in a barge or narrowboat, which in many cases has a low-sounding beat. In a similar vein to official names, nicknames were also bestowed upon certain locomotive by enthusiasts, and also unofficially by staff in the railway industry, some with affection, such as 'The Whistlers' for Class 40s, others less so, such as 'Bones' for Class 58s – which stems from their shape as seen from an aerial view – and 'Sheds' for Class 66s, whilst Class 31/0s were known as 'Toffee Apples' because of their removable power handle.

The first table depicts the Class 60s in their original guise and depot allocation.[5, 6]

Running number	Original name	Original livery	Allocated depot
60001	*Steadfast*	Construction	Hither Green
60002	*Capability Brown*	Petroleum	Immingham
60003	*Christopher Wren*	Petroleum	Immingham
60004	*Lochnagar*	Coal	Toton
60005	*Skiddaw*	Metals	Leicester
60006	*Great Gable*	Construction	Leicester
60007	*Robert Adam*	Petroleum	Immingham
60008	*Moel Fammau*	Metals	Thornaby
60009	*Carnedd Dafydd*	Construction	Leicester
60010	Pumlumon/Plynlimon	Petroleum	Leicester
60011	*Cader Idris*	Construction	Leicester
60012	*Glydr Fawr*	Construction	Leicester
60013	*Robert Boyle*	Petroleum	Immingham
60014	*Alexander Fleming*	Petroleum	Immingham
60015	*Bow Fell*	Construction	Hither Green
60016	*Langdale Pikes*	Construction	Stewarts Lane
60017	*Arenig Fawr*	Metals	Hither Green
60018	*Moel Siabod*	Construction	Hither Green
60019	*Wild Boar Fell*	Construction	Hither Green
60020	*Great Whernside*	Metals	Thornaby
60021	*Pen-y-Ghent*	Metals	Thornaby
60022	*Ingleborough*	Metals	Thornaby
60023	*The Cheviot*	Metals	Thornaby
60024	*Elizabeth Fry*	Metals	Cardiff Canton

Running number	Original name	Original livery	Allocated depot
60025	Joseph Lister	Petroleum	Cardiff Canton
60026	William Caxton	Petroleum	Immingham
60027	Joseph Banks	Petroleum	Immingham
60028	John Flamsteed	Petroleum	Thornaby
60029	Ben Nevis	Metals	Thornaby
60030	Cir Mhor	Metals	Thornaby
60031	Ben Lui	Metals	Thornaby
60032	William Booth	Coal	Immingham
60033	Anthony Ashley Cooper	Petroleum	Cardiff Canton
60034	Carnedd Llewellyn	Metals	Thornaby
60035	Florence Nightingale	Metals	Toton
60036	Sgurr Na Ciche	Metals	Thornaby
60037	Helvellyn	Metals	Thornaby
60038	Bidean Nam Bian	Metals	Thornaby
60039	Glastonbury Tor	Construction	Cardiff Canton
60040	Brecon Beacons	Construction	Cardiff Canton
60041	High Willhays	Construction	Toton
60042	Dunkery Beacon	Construction	Toton
60043	Yes Tor	Construction	Toton
60044	Ailsa Craig	Metals	Thornaby
60045	Josephine Butler	Coal	Stewarts Lane
60046	William Wilberforce	Coal	Stewarts Lane
60047	Robert Owen	Coal	Stewarts Lane
60048	Saddleback	Construction	Toton
60049	Scafell	Metals	Immingham
60050	Roseberry Topping	Metals	Thornaby
60051	Mary Somerville	Petroleum	Cardiff Canton
60052	Goat Fell	Metals	Thornaby
60053	John Reith	Petroleum	Immingham
60054	Charles Babbage	Petroleum	Immingham
60055	Thomas Barnardo	Coal	Toton
60056	William Beveridge	Coal	Immingham

Running number	Original name	Original livery	Allocated depot
60057	Adam Smith	Coal	Toton
60058	John Howard	Coal	Toton
60059	Samuel Plimsoll	Metals	Toton
60060	James Watt	Coal	Toton
60061	Alexander Graham Bell	Coal	Toton
60062	Samuel Johnson	Petroleum	Cardiff Canton
60063	James Murray	Petroleum	Cardiff Canton
60064	Back Tor	Petroleum	Immingham
60065	Kinder Low	Petroleum	Cardiff Canton
60066	John Logie Baird	Coal	Toton
60067	James Clerk Maxwell	Coal	Toton
60068	Charles Darwin	Coal	Toton
60069	Humphry Davy	Coal	Toton
60070	John Loudon McAdam	Coal	Toton
60071	Dorothy Garrod	Coal	Toton
60072	Cairn Toul	Coal	Toton
60073	Cairn Gorm	Coal	Toton
60074	Braeriach	Coal	Toton
60075	Liathach	Coal	Toton
60076	Suilven	Coal	Toton
60077	Canisp	Coal	Toton
60078	Stac Polliadh	Coal	Immingham
60079	Foinaven	Coal	Cardiff Canton
60080	Kinder Scout	Construction	Immingham
60081	Bleaklow Hill	Metals	Immingham
60082	Mam Tor	Construction	Immingham
60083	Shining Tor	Construction	Toton
60084	Cross Fell	Construction	Immingham
60085	Axe Edge	Construction	Immingham
60086	Shiehallion	Coal	Stewarts Lane
60087	Slioch	Coal	Toton
60088	Buachaille Etive Mor	Coal	Toton

Running number	Original name	Original livery	Allocated depot
60089	Arcuil	Coal	Cardiff Canton
60090	Quinag	Coal	Toton
60091	An Teallach	Coal	Toton
60092	Reginald Munns	Coal	Toton
60093	Jack Stirk	Coal	Stewarts Lane
60094	Tryfan	Construction	Immingham
60095	Crib Goch	Construction	Immingham
60096	Ben Macdui	Construction	Immingham
60097	Pillar	Construction	Immingham
60098	Charles Francis Brush	Construction	Immingham
60099	Ben More Assynt	Construction	Toton
60100	Boar of Badenoch	Construction	Toton
60500*	Rail Magazine	Construction	Stewarts Lane

A close-up view of 60001 *Steadfast*'s nameplate, 3 August 2014.
EDWARD GLEED

The *Pumlumon/Plynlimon* nameplate of 60010 at Leicester. The sun highlights the drops of rain on the side of the locomotive, affording varying shades of colour. 10 October 1990. JOHN STRETTON

The nameplate affixed to 60086 *Schiehallion*. British Rail issued strict guidelines for the positioning of nameplates, so the top edge of the nameplate had to be at the top edge of the light grey. JOHN STRETTON

Depots	Depot code	Location	Region
St Blazey	**BZ**	Par	Western
Cardiff Canton	**CE**	Cardiff	Western
Stewarts Lane	**SL**	London	Southern
Immingham	**IM**	Immingham	Eastern

Renumbered from 60016 during 1997

Depots	Depot code	Location	Region
Thornaby Tees	**TE**	Thornaby	Eastern
Hither Green	**HG**	London	Southern
Westbury	**WY**	Westbury	Western
Leicester	**LR**	Leicester	Midland

Original Name Details[11]

Steadfast	Name indicates power and efficiency. It was the winning entry in a Railfreight staff competition, the winner being Mr Raymond Wynn of the Regional Signal & Telecommunications Engineers at York
Capability Brown	(1716–1783) b. Lancelot Brown. Landscaper/gardener
Christopher Wren	(1632–1732) Astronomer and architect. Also appointed architect for the magnificent St Paul's Cathedral in London, and more than fifty other churches following the Great Fire of London. Knighted in 1673
Lochnagar	Mountain, Grampians of Scotland
Skiddaw	Mountain (Lake District National Park)
Great Gable	Mountain (Lake District National Park)
Robert Adam	(1728–1792) Scottish Neoclassical architect. Interior/exterior designer
Moel Fammau	Welsh mountain on the border between Denbighshire/Flintshire
Carnedd Dafydd	Welsh mountain (Snowdonia National Park)
Pumlumon/Plyinlymon	Mountain range in mid-Wales
Cader Idris	Mountain range in mid-Wales
Glydr Fawr	Welsh mountain (Snowdonia National Park)
Robert Boyle	(1627–1691) Seventeenth-century natural philosopher, chemist, physicist and inventor
Alexander Fleming	(1881–1955) Scottish bacteriologist who discovered penicillin, and botanist
Bow Fell	Mountain range (Lake District National Park)
Langdale Pikes	Mountain range (Lake District National Park)
Arenig Fawr	Mountain range (Snowdonia National Park)
Moel Siabod	Welsh mountain (Snowdonia National Park)
Wild Boar Fell	Fell (Cumbria)
Great Whernside	Fell (Yorkshire Dales)
Pen-y-Ghent	Fell (Yorkshire Three Peaks)
Ingleborough	Mountain (Yorkshire Dales)
The Cheviot	The summit of the main hill of the Cheviot range, north-east England
Elizabeth Fry	(1780–1872) English Quaker and prison reformer

Joseph Lister	(1827–1912) British surgeon and pioneer of antiseptic surgery who saw the introduction in 1860 of the antiseptic system, which modernized modern surgery
William Caxton	(c.1422–c.1491) English merchant/diplomat writer and printer
Joseph Banks	(1744–1820) English naturalist, botanist and patron of the natural sciences
John Flamsteed	(1646–1719) First Astronomer Royal
Ben Nevis	Scottish mountain (Grampian mountains)
Cir Mhor	Scottish mountain (Arran)
Ben Lui	Scottish mountain (Highlands)
William Booth	(1829–1912) British Methodist preacher (founder and general of the Salvation Army)
Anthony Ashley Cooper	(1621–1683) First Earl of Shaftesbury and Lord Chancellor. Legal reformer and statesman
Carnedd Llewelyn	Welsh mountain (Snowdonia)
Florence Nightingale	(1820–1910) Crimean War nurse (celebrated English reformer and statistician)
Sgurr Na Ciche	Scottish mountain (Knoydart region)
Helvellyn	English mountain (Lake District National Park)
Bidean Nam Bian	Scottish mountain (Highland region)
Glastonbury Tor	Hill (Glastonbury, Somerset)
Brecon Beacons	Mountain range (South Wales)
High Willhays	Highest point on Dartmoor
Dunkery Beacon	Highest point on Exmoor
Yes Tor	Second highest point on Dartmoor
Ailsa Craig	Scottish Island/Firth of Clyde
Josephine Butler	(1828–1906) Victorian English feminist
William Wilberforce	(1759–1833) English politician, philanthropist, and slavery abolitionist
Robert Owen	(1771–1858) Welsh social reformer who developed the New Lanark cotton mills
Saddleback	Mountain in the Lake District National Park
Scafell	Highest peak in England at 3,210ft (Lake District National Park)
Roseberry Topping	Hill, North Yorkshire, and unitary authority Redcar Cleveland
Mary Somerville	(1780–1821) Scottish science writer and polymath
Goat Fell	Highest point on the Isle of Arran
John Reith	(1889–1971) Scottish broadcasting executive
Charles Babbage	(1792–1871) English mathematician, inventor and mechanical engineer
Thomas Barnardo	(1845–1905) Philanthropist, founder and director of homes for destitute children
William Beveridge	(1879–1963) British economist who also worked on social insurance

Adam Smith	(1723–1790) Economist and philosopher
John Howard	(1726–1790) Philanthropist and first English prison reformer
Samuel Plimsoll	(1824–1790) Social reformer; known as the sailor's friend. Created the Plimsoll line on ships to show loading level under certain types of water
James Watt	(1736–1819) Engineer and designer of the first efficient steam engine
Alexander Graham Bell	(1847–1922) Inventor of the telephone, engineer and innovator
Samuel Johnson	(1709–1784) Poet, critic and dictionary writer
James Murray	(1837–1915) Philologist and lexicographer; editor of the *New English Dictionary*, finished after his death in 1928 as *Oxford English Dictionary*
Back Tor	Hill (Peak National Park)
Kinder Low	Hill (Peak National Park)
John Logie Baird	(1888–1946) Scottish engineer; inventor of world's first practical television
James Clerk-Maxwell	(1831–1879) Scottish theoretical physicist who worked on electromagnetic radiation and kinetic theory of gases
Charles Darwin	(1809–1882) English naturalist
Humphry Davy	(1778–1829) English chemist and inventor of the Davy safety lamp; also discovered the metals potassium, sodium, barium, strontium, calcium and magnesium
John Loudon McAdam	(1756–1836) Scottish engineer and road builder
Dorothy Garrod	(1892–1968) British archaeologist who became the first woman professor at Cambridge in 1939
Cairn Toul	Fourth highest mountain in Scotland
Cairn Gorm	Mountain range, Eastern Highlands of Scotland
Braeriach	Third highest mountain in Britain; Cairngorms
Liathach	Torridon hills, north-west highlands of Scotland
Suilven	One of the most distinctive mountains in Scotland, lying in a remote area of west Sutherland
Canisp	Mountain in Highland region near Lochinver
Stac Pollaidh	Mountain, north-west highlands of Scotland
Foinaven	Mountain, north-west highlands of Scotland
Kinder Scout	Moorland plateau and National Nature Reserve (Peak District)
Bleaklow Hill	Peat-covered gritstone hill near Glossop (Peak National Park)
Mam Tor	Hill, High Peak (Peak National Park)
Shining Tor	Mountain 1,833ft (Peak National Park)
Cross Fell	Highest point in the Pennine Hills, Cumbria
Axe Edge	Moorland, Peak District
Schiehallion	Mountain, Perth and Kinross
Slioch	Mountain (Scottish Highlands)

Buachaille Etive Mor	Mountain in Glen Coe (Scottish Highlands)
Arcuil	Mountain in Highland region
An Teallach	Scottish mountain
Reginald Munns	Liaison officer between BR, the National Coal Board and Central Electricity Generating Board. He was one of the architects of the 'Merry-Go-Round' system
Jack Stirk	BR's National Coal Manager between 1969 and 1982. His work led to the major development of MGR operation and many contracts to move coal by rail
Tryfan	Welsh mountain (Snowdonia)
Crib Goch	Welsh mountain (Snowdonia)
Ben Macdui	Scottish mountain, second highest in the UK
Pillar	Peak in Lake District north-west of Great Gable; an outcrop of rock much favoured by climbers
Charles Francis Brush	(1849–1929) An inventor who, among other things, invented a system of generating electricity and arc lighting; the UK company of 1879 was set up to exploit his patents in Britain
Ben More Assynt	Scottish mountain in Highland region near Loch Assynt
Boar of Badenoch	Scottish mountain in Grampian range near Dalwhinnie

Additional Names [5, 11]

60001	The Railway Observer	Railway Correspondence & Travel Society (RCTS); the naming formed an inspection of the loco supplier
60002	High Peak	Geographical location in the High Peak (Derbyshire)
60003	Freight Transport Association	The name commemorates the work of the FTA
60005	BP Gas Avonmouth	Applied to mark ten years of delivery of gas oil to Avonmouth
60007	Spirit of Tom Kendell	DB Schenker engineer who tragically lost his life during a road accident
60008	Gypsum Queen ii	Name after Gypsum Queen Packet Co. ship, which was torpedoed in the Atlantic Ocean on 10 September 1941
60008	Sir William McAlpine	Name to mark the twenty-first anniversary of the Railway Heritage Trust of which Sir William McAlpine is Chairman
60006	Scunthorpe Ironmaster	Twinning of EWS with British Steel Corporation
60017	Shotton Works Centenary 1996	Name to mark the centenary of BSC Shotton Works
60019	Pathfinder Tours 30 Years of Railtouring 1973–2003	Twinning of Pathfinder Railtours with EWS to mark the thirtieth year of operating tours. Years of railtouring 1973–2003
60019	Port of Grimsby & Immingham	Twinning of EWS with ABP Grimsby and Immingham: the last duty of the port director before retirement
60021	Star of the East	Twinning of loco fleet with Immingham depot
60025	Caledonian Paper	Twinning of EWS with UPM Caledonian Paper to mark a new ten-year supply contract
60029	Clitheroe Castle/Castle Cement	Twinning between EWS and Castle Cement

60031	*ABP Connect*	Twinning of EWS with customer (Hams Hall)
60033	*Tees Steel Express*	Twinning of EWS with British Steel Corporation
60036	*GEFCO*	Twinning of EWS with GEFCO
60037	*Aberddawan/Aberthaw*	Twinning of EWS with Aberthaw
60038	*AvestaPolarit*	Unveiled at the launch of the Steel Bridge project
60039	*Dove Holes*	Unveiled on 27 April 2015 at Dove Holes quarry to celebrate the despatching of 2 million tonnes of aggregate from the quarry in 2014 by DB Schenker Rail UK and CEMEX
60040	*The Territorial Army Centenary*	Name to commemorate the centenary of the Territorial Army. The naming was undertaken by HRH Duke of York during a ceremony held at York National Railway Museum on 14 June 2008
60042	*The Hundred of Hoo*	Unveiled to mark staff open day held at Hoo Junction in recognition of the centenary of freight operations from Hoo Junction
60045	*The Permanent Way Institution*	Twinning of railway with institution
60048	*Eastern*	Named to mark the partnership between Clydeport, Easter Group and EWS. Unveiled to coincide with the reopening of Hunterston Terminal
60052	*Glofa Twr/Tower Colliery the last deep mine in Wales*	Twinning between EWS and customer – Tower Colliery
60053	*Nordic Terminal*	Twinning between EWS and Nordic terminal
60059	*Swinden Dalesman*	Cementing business relations between Loadhaul and one of their largest customers, 'TILCON'
60062	*Stainless Pioneer*	Marking the celebration of 100 years of stainless steel in the City of Sheffield
60065	*Spirit of Jaguar*	Opening of new facility and railhead in Castle Bromwich
60071	*Ribblehead Viaduct*	Unveiled to mark the tenth anniversary of saving the S&C line from closure
60074	*Teenage Spirit*	Name in support of the Teenage Cancer Trust
60080	*Cloudside Junior School Sandiacre EWS Rail Safety Competition Winners 2001'*	Annual naming of Class 60 locomotive (school safety award)
60080	*Little Eaton Primary School, Little Eaton EWS Rail Safety Competition Winners 2002'*	Annual naming of Class 60 locomotive (school safety award)
60080	*Stanley Common C of E Primary School, Ilkeston EWS Rail Safety Competition Winners 2003'*	Annual naming of Class 60 locomotive (school safety award)
60080	*Bispham Drive Junior School, Toton EWS Rail Safety Competition Winners 2004'*	Annual naming of Class 60 locomotive (school safety award)
60081	*Isambard Kingdom Brunel*	Unveiled at the Old Oak Common open day 2 August 2000 as EWS's contribution to the event
60082	*Hillhead '93*	Temporarily renamed to mark the world's biggest quarry exhibition (15–17 June 1993), which consisted of stick-on nameplates that covered the Mam Tor nameplates. These were removed following the event

60083	Mountsorrel	Reapplication of name to continue the close relationship between EWS and Redland
60085	Mini-Pride of Oxford	Named to mark the contract between EWS and BMW to transport the new Mini from Cowley to Purfleet
60087	Barry Needham	Named after the EWS controller who was killed in the Great Heck accident (plates were later transferred to 60091)
60087	CLIC Sargent WWW. CLICSARGENT.ORG.UK	Named at Long Marston on 18 June 2014. Naming took place at the 'Rail Live 2014'
60089	The Railway Horse	Named at Severn Valley Railway's 'Heavy Horse Power' weekend to note the association of the use of the horse in rail-shunting
60091	Barry Needham	Named after the EWS controller who was killed in the Great Heck accident. Plates transferred from 60087 during June 2014.
60093	Adrian Harrington 1955-2003 Royal Navy/Burgess Salmon	Named after a Bristol-based solicitor (Burgess/Salmon) who died in 2003. Burgess/Salmon specialize in railway work
60094	Rugby Flyer	Twinning between EWS and Rugby Cement to mark business relationship to transport PFA from West Burton power station to Heathrow Terminal 5 construction site
60100	Pride of Acton	Twinning of EWS fleet with depot and staff
60500	Rail Magazine	Named to commemorate 500th issue publication

Original Name		Further Names[5]
60001	Steadfast	The Railway Observer
60002	Capability Brown	High Peak
60003	Christopher Wren	Freight Transport Association
60004	Lochnagar	
60005	Skiddaw	BP Gas Avonmouth
60006	Great Gable	Scunthorpe Ironmaster
60007	Robert Adam	Spirit of Tom Kendell
60008	Moel Fammau	Gypsum Queen ii, and then Sir William McAlpine
60009	Carnedd Dafydd	
60010	Pumlumon/Plynlimon	
60011	Cader Idris	
60012	Glydr Fawr	
60013	Robert Boyle	
60014	Alexander Fleming	
60015	Bow Fell	
60016	Langdale Pikes*	Rail Magazine (then renumbered 60500 to commemorate the publication's 500th issue)
60017	Arenig Fawr	Shotton Works Centenary 1996

Original Name	Further Names[5]
60018 *Moel Siabod*	
60019 *Wild Boar Fell*	*Pathfinder Tours 30 Years of Railtouring 1973–2003* then *Port of Grimsby & Immingham*
60020 *Great Whernside*	
60021 *Pen-y-Ghent*	*Star of the East* (additional application of a miniature 'Metals' branding while wearing EWS livery)
60022 *Ingleborough*	
60023 *The Cheviot*	
60024 *Elizabeth Fry*	*Clitheroe Castle* (transferred from 60029)
60025 *Joseph Lister*	*Caledonian Paper*
60026 *William Caxton*	
60027 *Joseph Banks*	
60028 *John Flamsteed*	
60029 *Ben Nevis*	*Clitheroe Castle* (transferred to 60024)
60030 *Cir Mhor*	
60031 *Ben Lui*	*ABP Connect*
60032 *William Booth*	
60033 *Anthony Ashley Cooper*	*Tees Steel Express*
60034 *Carnedd Llewellyn*	
60035 *Florence Nightingale*	
60036 *Sgurr Na Ciche*	*GEFCO*
60037 *Helvellyn*	*Aberddawan/Aberthaw*
60038 *Bidean Nam Bian*	*AvestaPolarit*
60039 *Glastonbury Tor*	*Dove Holes*
60040 *Brecon Beacons*	*The Territorial Army Centenary*
60041 *High Willhays*	
60042 *Dunkery Beacon*	*The Hundred of Hoo*
60043 *Yes Tor*	
60044 *Ailsa Craig*	
60045 *Josephine Butler*	*The Permanent Way Institution*
60046 *William Wilberforce*	
60047 *Robert Owen*	
60048 *Saddleback*	*Eastern*

Original Name	Further Names[5]
60049 *Scafell*	
60050 *Roseberry Topping*	
60051 *Mary Somerville*	
60052 *Goat fell*	*Glofa Twr/Tower Colliery* The last deep mine in Wales
60053 *John Reith*	*Nordic Terminal*
60054 *Charles Babbage*	
60055 *Thomas Barnardo*	
60056 *William Beveridge*	
60057 *Adam Smith*	
60058 *John Howard*	
60059 *Samuel Plimsoll*	*Swinden Dalesman*
60060 *James Watt*	
60061 *Alexander Graham Bell*	
60062 *Samuel Johnson*	*Stainless Pioneer*
60063 *James Murray*	
60064 *Back Tor*	
60065 *Kinder Low*	*Spirit of Jaguar*
60066 *John Logie Baird*	
60067 *James Clerk-Maxwell*	
60068 *Charles Darwin*	
60069 *Humphry Davy*	*Slioch* (name transferred from 60087 during 2004)
60070 *John Loudon McAdam*	
60071 *Dorothy Garrod*	*Ribblehead Viaduct*
60072 *Cairn Toul*	
60073 *Cairn Gorm*	
60074 *Braeriach*	*Teenage Spirit*
60075 *Liathach*	
60076 *Suilven*	
60077 *Canisp*	
60078 *Stac Pollaidh*	
60079 *Foinaven*	
60080 *Kinder Scout*	*Stanley Common EWS Rail Safety Competition Winners 2003*

Original Name		Further Names[5]
60081	Bleaklow Hill	Isambard Kingdom Brunel
60082	Mam Tor	Temporarily named Hillhead '93 with Mam Tor plates re-affixed
60083	Shining Tor	Mountsorrel
60084	Cross Fell	
60085	Axe Edge	MINI-Pride of Oxford
60086	Shiehallion	
60087	Slioch	Barry Needham
60088	Buachaille Etive Mor	
60089	Arcuil	The Railway Horse
60090	Quinag	
60091	An Teallach	Barry Needham – EWS COAL TRAIN CONTROLLER TRAGICALLY KILLED AT GREAT HECK 26TH FEBRUARY 2001. A TRUE RAILWAYMAN ADMIRED FOR HIS HIGH REGARD FOR SAFETY, HIS INTEGRITY AND HIS GOOD HUMOUR. (Name transferred from 60087, which became a member of the Colas fleet)
60092	Reginald Munns	
60093	Jack Stirk	Adrian Harrington 1955–2003 Royal Navy/Burgess Salmon
60094	Tryfan	Rugby Flyer
60095	Crib Goch	
60096	Ben Macdui	
60097	Pillar	ABP Port of Grimsby & Immingham
60098	Charles Francis Brush	
60099	Ben More Assynt	
60100	Boar of Badenoch	Pride of Acton

Differing styles of nameplate and background colour are seen on the nameplate on EWS-liveried 60019 PATHFINDER TOURS – 30 YEARS OF RAILTOURING 1973–2003.
JOHN STRETTON

A pristine 60038 gleams in the sun with AvestaPolarit nameplate and logo on 19 March 2002. RICHARD TUPLIN

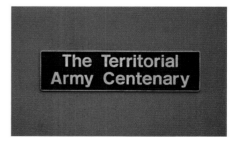

Following a repaint into DBS colours, 60040 retains its name The Territorial Army Centenary depicting the usual black background colour on the plate. 29 May 2014.
EDWARD GLEED

The silver livery of the nameplate affixed to 60044 *Ailsa Craig* at Leicester, 6 April 1996. Although the typeface is standard, the silver contrasts well with the blue, which has also been applied to the plate perimeter. JOHN STRETTON

A completely different style of plate is seen on 60065 *Spirit of Jaguar* at Bristol Temple Meads. 23 September 2008. EDWARD GLEED

A rather grubby 60074 *Teenage Spirit* is seen at Westerleigh. Its nameplate follows the standard typeface. 30 January 2014. EDWARD GLEED

Naming Ceremonies

The naming of the first Class 60 had been planned well in advance and it is quite fitting that the first Class 60 naming ceremony is detailed below.

Naming Ceremony of No. 60001 *Steadfast*

Class 60 No. 60001 *Steadfast* was the first member of the class to be constructed that was released wearing the Trainload Construction livery. The actual handover ceremony was undertaken at the Brush Falcon Works on 30 June 1989 by Mr W.M.M. Petrie, Managing Director for Brush Electrical Machines, which coincided with the actual naming of the locomotive. The naming of 60001 was undertaken by Mr Colin Driver, Director of Freight for British Rail. The naming ceremony was similar to other ceremonies in that the locomotive was placed in a pre-arranged point with the nameplate concealed behind a curtain.[11]

The naming ceremony of 60006 *Scunthorpe Ironmaster* and 60033 *Tees Steel Express* at the Frodingham platform inside BSC Scunthorpe in July 1997. The gentleman standing nearest to the rostrum is Mr Ed Burkhardt, Chairman of EWS. RICHARD TUPLIN

The naming of 60097 *Port of Grimsby & Immingham*, a ceremony that was held in the DFDS Logistics Centre at Immingham Dock on 11 March 2003.
RICHARD TUPLIN

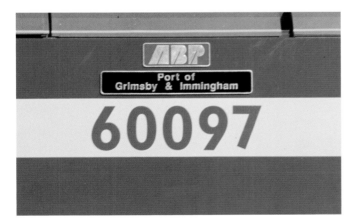

Detail of the nameplate showing the ABP logo on 60097 at Warrington Bank Quay in 2002. EDWARD GLEED

In the case of the Class 60, many nameplates were fitted at Brush Traction without ceremony, whilst other members of the Class 60 locomotives received their names under high profile ceremonies. Sometimes locomotives had their name-plates fitted without ceremony either at the point of manu-facture or on depot, or at other locations such as stations or companies that have connections with the railway industry. 60006 *Scunthorpe Ironmaster* and 60033 *Tees Steel Express* received their names at the same time as their British Steel Corporation livery was unveiled.

A further naming ceremony saw 60097 receiving its name-plates at DFDS Nordic Terminal; it was named *APB Port of Grimsby & Immingham* and staff members were invited to attend.

Some very high profile and influential figures in railway preservation have been invited to unveil names. During one naming ceremony, Sir William McAlpine unveiled the name on 60008, which bore his name.

A further naming was 60087 *CLIC Sargent/www.clicsargent. co.uk* at the 2014 Rail Live event, held at Long Marston. Employees of Colas Rail and Network Rail held the name-plate and a fundraising cheque for £15,000.

During the construction of the Class 60s, the various Trainload sectors were invited to put forward possible names. Some names for the Class 60 that had been put forward and were subsequently rejected are listed below:

Railway Heritage Trust Chairman Sir William McAlpine unveils his name on the side of EWS Class 60 No. 60008 at King's Cross on 11 April 2006, marking the twenty-first anniversary of the Trust.
BRIAN MORRISON

The naming ceremony of 60087 *CLIC Sargent WWW. CLICSARGENT.ORG.UK* at the 2014 Rail Live event held at Long Marston on 18 June 2014. COLAS RAIL UK

Nameplate detail of 60087. The nameplate carries both upper and lower case, together with the CLIC Sargent website address (www.clicsargent.org.uk). 21 July 2014.
EDWARD GLEED

Hay Tor	
Dovestone Tor	
Elidr Fwr	
Tremadog	
Pen-y-Fan	
Bleaklow Head	
Snowdon (Yr Wyddfa)	Name carried by A.C. Electric Class 86 Locomotive 86043, then applied to 86257 'Snowdon'
Blencathra	
Cross Fell	Name previously carried by Class 44 locomotive 44005
Whittenham Clumps	
Devils Dyke	Requested to be affixed to 60100
The Old Man of Coniston	Listed for 60100 but then not allocated

Black Tor	Corrected to read Back Tor, the 'l' being removed (situated in the High Peak, Derbyshire, and not to be confused with Black Tor, which is situated in the Dartmoor National Park)
Humphrey Davy	Corrected to Humphry Davy, the 'e' being removed
William Bramwell Booth	Altered to read William Booth. In selecting William Bramwell Booth a mistake was made. This was not realized until the locomotive was about to be fitted with its plates when a Salvationist at Brush pointed out that Bramwell was the founder's son and that William Booth was the founder. The nameplates were cast incorrectly as Willlam Booth – painters blacked out part of the offending l with paint to produce a square dot.
Pumlumon/Plynlimon	The original plates were incorrect reading as Pumlomon/Plynlimon. They were corrected to read Pumlumon/Plynlimon
Buachaille Etive Mor	Wrongly cast to read Buachaille Etive More, the 'e' being removed.
Bow Fell	The name was correct, however it was affixed to 60009 between 1 December 1989 and 9 January 1990 due to confusion within BR as to which Class 60 should receive the name. The Bow Fell plates were affixed to 60015 while 60009 received the name Carnedd Dafyd
Charles Francis Brush	Correct nameplate, although the statement on the smaller plate is incorrect. It is the nominal No. 1000 in the locomotive register credited as being built by Brush

Two further names put forward for consideration were *Sir Sam Fay* and *Sir Edward Watkin*.

Ironically, both of these names have been applied to GBRf Class 66/7 locomotives, the former 66707 and the latter 66722, both of which wear the 'Metroland' livery.

Several mis-spellings and wrong names had also been noted, though these were corrected before being affixed.[5, 6, 11]

Orders for the nameplates were placed with Newton Replicas through the Public Affairs department. When the nameplates had been cast, they were delivered to Brush to be fitted before the locomotive was released from the factory. A full list of names had been agreed, and it was to be determined which subsector received which names, though it had not been intended to allocate all 100 names all at once.

The Class 60s have undergone a variety of livery changes and number codes over the years. In the next chapter I shall be exploring how certain members of the Class 60s fleet have undergone a major refurbishment.

CHAPTER SIX

THE CLASS 60 REFURBISHMENT PROGRAMME

Since their construction, the Class 60s have had a very chequered career. The first examples underwent numerous modifications. Indeed, it is understood that deliveries were halted so that the Class 60s that had already been constructed could have the necessary modifications carried out, and subsequent builds could have them included.[11] Eventually reliability within the class improved, enabling vast tonnages to be hauled throughout the length and breadth of the country, which is what the Class 60s were designed to do.

In addition to their normal duties, many members of the class have attended diesel galas as well as undertaking charter work, sometimes taking passengers to some very remote locations that would normally be out of the public view. During the early to mid-2000s, up until the current on-going 'Super 60' refurbishment programme, the number of Class 60s in traffic has fluctuated over the years, dipping to a low point of only four in late 2009, but then increasing as overhauls commenced. Some class members have been returned to traffic, whilst others have not been so fortunate. The first Class 60 to be withdrawn was 60098 *Charles Francis Brush* during 2004 at only eleven years old, and along with many other class members was put into store. Thankfully, to date not one Class 60 has been scrapped, although it is understood that some Class 60s have been 'cannibalized' to some extent in order to provide spares for other class members.

It is thought that there have not been any occasions where a Class 60 has not been in traffic, though it has come very close to it. From the original batch of 100 locomotives, only four were on active main-line service on 7 December 2009: 60011, 60065, 60085 and 60096.

In late 1996, the former Loadhaul, Transrail Freight and Mainline Freight companies amalgamated, and EW&S Railway Company assumed custodianship of their assets. The new EW&S Railway (the parent of whom was Wisconsin in the USA) was soon to assert its influence on the railway industry

A low point of the Class 60s' operation was during late 2009 with just four left in traffic. Here at Bishton, unrefurbished 60011 soldiers on with 6B13 Robeston–Westerleigh tanks, on 6 November 2009. EDWARD GLEED

in the UK, and its chairman, Mr Ed Burkhardt, severely criticized the freight rolling stock that had been placed before his company. In Canada and indeed in the USA only a small number of wheel diameters is allotted to vehicles, whereas in the UK there is a myriad of wheel sizes, which are very costly to maintain. In fairness to Mr Burkhardt, his idea was to standardize his entire fleet; after all, the railway is a business, and the business must be cost effective, so why use seven different sizes of wheel when only two or three would suffice?

It is believed that Mr Burkhardt thought that much of the UK's traction fleet was in an utterly deplorable state. His first sight of UK traction was of postal-allocated Class 47s at Crewe diesel depot; this influenced his view, and their dishevelled appearance contributed to his poor opinion of them. Again, similar to the freight rolling stock, the motive power available to EWS was to all intents and purposes not fit for purpose and was subject to much ridicule – and unfortunately this included the Class 60, the final members of which had only been constructed a mere five years earlier. However, Mr Burkhardt was keen to eradicate most of what was on offer.

To an extent his thoughts bore some weight. Trains in the USA, amongst others, were grossing 20,000 tonnes and were being regularly transported throughout their networks, while in the UK certain trains grossing a mere 4,000 tonnes were considered to be staggering by UK standards, and were most certainly the exception rather than the rule. However, it must be remembered that the loading gauge for the UK is rather conservative as compared to the generous loading gauges present in other countries. Nevertheless it was clear that the traction on offer was woefully inadequate and a solution was needed quickly. Indeed the only locomotive that did meet with favour with Ed Burkhardt was the humble and most versatile Class 08 diesel electric shunting locomotive. It might be small but it is extremely powerful, and this is one reason why it is still in use today. The Class 08s are operated by a number of train-operating companies throughout the length and breadth of the UK. It has often been said that the Class 08s are the 'Morris Minor' of locomotives: rudimentary, but above all, reliable.

During 1996 EW&S announced that an order had been placed for 250 diesel electric locomotives that could develop 3,300hp at 904rpm. The Electro-Motive Division Class 66s were to be classified under the BR TOPS system as Class 66. It is worth a brief mention here that although the Class 66 locomotive looks very similar to the Class 59 in overall

shape, in reality it is totally different. Above all, the Class 59's 16-cylinder 645 two-stroke engine was superseded by the 12-cylinder 710 model with electronic fuel injection. One feature of the Class 66 that the Class 60s do not have is radial steering bogies, where the outer axles on each bogie are allowed to turn under the control of cams, though the centre axle is fixed; this is designed to reduce and minimize flange squeal and track wear on corners.

During 1997, EW&S Railway authorized extensive repairs on a number of Class 60s at Brush in Loughborough. During the late 2000s the general decline of Class 60s registering high hours and high mileage, and which had not been overhauled, was becoming increasingly obvious both in the operations department of EWS and to front-line operational staff. Some high profile failures were starting to appear, namely major engine failures – in one case of 60081 *Isambard Kingdom Brunel*, which it is thought led to many Class 60s being put into store at high engine hours (around 20,000 hours). However, it must be understood that during the first fourteen years of full fleet usage there was not one single major engine failure. Even in 2015, the infamous line-up of Class 60s can still be seen in sidings adjacent to the main line at Toton.[2]

EWS's Keith Heller issued the 'sweat the assets' directive, ordering the leased Class 66s to be used to the maximum, even if they were pushed to their operational limit. In other words, 'If the wheels do not turn, the wheels do not earn'. EWS maintained the few overhauled Class 60s by swapping engines and bogies around between locomotives to conserve the fleet. But when DB Schenker Rail UK took over they evaluated how good the Class 60s really were, and developed plans for overhaul – which the Recession delayed.

During 2008, all EWS's assets came under the auspices of DB Schenker Rail UK. DB Schenker of Germany has rail operations in several European countries including Belgium, the Netherlands and Switzerland, while DB Schenker Rail UK is responsible for operations in the United Kingdom.

The Class 59s were reserved mainly for heavy stone trains, which could possibly dispense with the Class 60s, which EWS had wanted. Clearly EWS had thought of doing away with the Class 60 for some time, and to that end had undertaken trials of pairs of 66s on heavy services, notably the very heavy oil workings that had hitherto been hauled by the Class 60.

Internal correspondence was sent out to signalmen and other operational railway staff advising the trial of two Class 66 locomotives instead of a single Class 60. This information

The infamous line-up of Class 60s at Toton with 60081 *Isambard Kingdom Brunel* nearest to the camera. It is open to conjecture as to whether this stored locomotive will ever run again. 22 July 2013. EDWARD GLEED

was important for signalmen as it involved two major factors: first, adding a second locomotive would obviously lengthen the train; and second, this in turn had a bearing on whether the longer train could be recessed in loops for regulation purposes. From a commercial point of view there were power implications as well. Two locomotives are better than one, as they will restart a train from a stand more quickly than one single unit, but the drawbacks were the cost of fuel and inevitably the higher maintenance costs of an additional locomotive.

The trials got underway and, as mentioned earlier, the 6A11 and 6B13 diagrams went over to Class 59 and Class 66 operation. The 6A11 diagram runs between Robeston and Theale and is booked to run through the Severn Tunnel: this had been a strong Class 60 diagram and it would not pose any problems for that class of locomotive, but a single Class 66 would almost certainly be an issue. From the depths of the Severn Tunnel to Patchway Junction there is an unrelenting climb of 1 in 100 that would test even the most able Class 60, but a Class 66 would probably be over the permitted weight limit for that diagram. The only viable option for the Class 66 would be to shorten the train from the usual twenty-nine 100-tonne bogie tanks to perhaps twenty-two. But this situation might be an issue for the customer, as an additional train might be needed at some stage to cover the shortfall of a shorter train, thereby incurring more expense.

60081 devoid of its *Isambard Kingdom Brunel* nameplates along with brass running numbers. The red bar on the driver's cab door prevents unauthorized access. 22 July 2013. EDWARD GLEED

DB Schenker's Class 66s, 66095 and 66165, are seen on trial with the heavy 6B13 Robeston–Westerleigh tanks, here leaving the gloom of Wickwar tunnel on 31 October 2013. EDWARD GLEED

Clearly the costly pairing of Class 66s could not be allowed to continue, and during early 2010 changes were afoot with the Class 60s. Despite the announcement made by DBS indicating their intention to overhaul a number of Class 60s, nothing further had been forthcoming regarding the overhaul programme. As 2010 progressed, a few more Class 60s that had hitherto been stored were returned to traffic, which in turn could release the Class 66s back to other traffic.

Having spoken to many drivers over the years, there is quite rightly a trend towards efficient driving techniques. At certain locations around the rail network 'coasting boards' have been erected to advise drivers when they can shut off power to conserve fuel. One very important feature of the Class 60s is that they are roughly 10 per cent better on fuel economy than even the newest Class 66 locomotive.

During 2010, DB Schenker Rail UK had offered twenty Class 60s for sale. Many 60s had suffered various failures, some of them as a result of significant engine defects. The trials continued right through 2009 and into 2010, and it is understood that DBS were clearly struggling with this very costly exercise as it meant their strength was effectively reduced by one Class 66, which could have been used on other diagrams. This was particularly felt during the autumn period, when Network Rail undertakes its annual national programme of running a rail-head treatment train (RHTT) in an attempt to arrest the issues surrounding leaf-fall contamination. Although other TOCs operate this train, DBS's requirement for Class 66s would possibly have fallen short, so as an alternative, some Class 60s were brought back into use to cover the shortfall on the oil diagrams. For many months after the RHTT season finished, pairs of Class 66s continued to be employed on certain oil diagrams. On a few occasions Class 59s were used, and certainly one working reportedly had a Class 59 hauling a Class 60.

DBS were aware of these issues, and it is understood that correspondence was sent to Network Rail Infrastructure Limited informing them that they wished to run trials of a single Class 66 on a fully loaded service train, namely 6A11, the heavy Robeston–Theale tanks. The trials required the train to move from a standing start from the base of the Severn Tunnel, which was a tough criterion and which unsurprisingly had embarrassing results. On one of the trials, the Class 66 was unable to complete the task, and the driver of that particular working declared the locomotive a failure. The Class 66s are equipped with the 'Super Series' control system designed to control wheelslip, but the 500KN of tractive effort of a Class 60 with wheel-creep control from zero speed always outclasses the 420KN of the Class 66, whose 'Super Series' control commences at 4mph

(6.5km/h). A Class 66 is unable to pull hard enough, and cannot correct for poor adhesion as effectively.[11]

From an operational point of view the Class 60 was quite the opposite on this diagram. They regularly haul this working up to four times a week without adhesion problems. I have had the pleasure of speaking to drivers with first-hand knowledge of the Class 60's traction ability, and all have said the Class 60 is 'the loco of choice'. Questioned further, some of these drivers revealed that although they considered the Class 66s to be reliable, they felt 'cheap', lacked build and ride quality, and were very noisy. Furthermore after only a few years of service the 66s showed signs of becoming unkempt, whilst the Class 60 was – and still is – a highly regarded machine, able to haul tremendous tonnages and with an excellent build quality.

The 'Super 60' Programme

Initial plans to overhaul certain members of the Class 60 were discussed in 2007, but because of the economic climate at that time these plans had not come to fruition.

However, during mid-January 2011, developments had started to progress. On the 14th of that month, the first Class 60 to be outshopped in the company's house colours was 60011. This raised interest among rail enthusiasts because it looked as though DBS were beginning to start the overhauls that had been announced in 2010. However, it transpired that although 60011 had been called to Toton for a repaint, it would not be given the pending complete 'Super 60' programme, although some of the first modifications were implemented.

Nevertheless, on 18 January 2011, DBS announced that they were investing £3 million to upgrade seven Class 60s, with a view to overhauling more at a later date. It was initially planned to overhaul these seven during the first half of 2011. This investment was in order to improve the reliability of the class, and also to extend the operational lifespan of the locomotives by fifteen years. It was also proposed to overhaul a further fourteen locomotives, thus creating a fleet of twenty-one.

The extensive overhaul programme was branded 'Super 60', and required the locomotives to be out of traffic for about six weeks. The Toton overhaul team was awarded the

The first Class 60 to be repainted into the DBS corporate livery was 60011. At this time it was given an electrical upgrade, but not the full Super 60 refurbishment programme. This is Westerleigh on 14 January 2011. EDWARD GLEED

'Award for Excellence', along with the Freight Association award. At the time of writing, twenty-one DBS Class 60s have been put through the Super 60 refurbishment programme, fulfilling the requirements set out by DBS. Whether DBS and latterly Colas Rail decide to overhaul more Class 60s is open to conjecture, as such a decision will no doubt be dictated by the state of the economy.

As of June 2015, roughly thirty-one Class 60s remain operational, and of these, twenty-nine have been put through the Super 60 programme. Two Class 60s acted as test beds for the Super 60 programme: 60011, which received an electrical upgrade, and 60099, which was given a mechanical upgrade. The Super 60 programme is most extensive and is divided into three phases: in phase one the locomotive is stripped down; in phase two it is rebuilt; and in phase three it is tested.[11]

The first Class 60 to undergo the Super 60 programme was 60007; it was released back into traffic during September 2011. However, at the time of writing, this locomotive has now been equipped with a Napier turbocharger and awaits testing. During their careers the Class 60s underwent major examinations, but none were called into works for major refurbishment of this nature. (It is worth noting that a Class 56 of this age would have been through works five times!)

Prior to the Super 60 programme, rumours had circulated that members of the class could undergo refurbishment with the possibility of also being re-engined. Although the refurbishment programme is now well underway, it has been decided not to replace the engine, as technological advance has meant that even the most severe cases of failure can be repaired. DBS's view is that the Mirrlees engine is 'good' and does not need replacing at this stage.

When to Refurbish?

There are many factors that have to be considered before a locomotive is called into works for the Super 60 refurbishment programme. One of the most important of these is how many 'engine hours' it has accumulated.[11] A locomotive with 20,000 hours is deemed 'out of life' and will therefore require an overhaul. It would not make economic sense to put a locomotive through this kind of work if the engine hours are still within limits, so a locomotive called into works for a repaint will not necessarily be overhauled during that time. This was the case for 60011, which, as we have seen, was the first member of the class to be repainted during January 2011.

60032 stands in the yard at Toton: the 'Group 2' category label can be seen on the cab door window, indicating that it requires only minor attention. 15 July 2014. EDWARD GLEED

From a mechanical point of view, according to DBS, it is easier to carry out work on a locomotive that has been out of traffic for a few days rather than several months or even longer. Further to this, DBS have four categories for locomotives that are out of traffic, grouped as follows:

Group 1: Locomotives that are serviceable
Group 2: Locomotives requiring only minor attention
Group 3: Locomotives requiring more serious repairs
Group 4: Locomotives for disposal. To date, no Class 60s have been put into Group 4[11]

**The collection of stored Class 60s basking in the early morning sun at Toton as they await a decision on their future.
15 July 2014.** EDWARD GLEED

There are several long rows of Class 60s at Toton depot, many with 'group' status affixed to the cab door windows, many of which are in Group 2. The number of Class 60s that will be considered for the Super 60 programme, which is the most expensive, will to an extent depend on the economic climate. It would not make commercial sense to overhaul the entire Class 60 fleet if only a quarter will actually see service.

The Refurbishment Programme

The details of the refurbishment programme are very extensive, making the locomotives better than new, due to the extra modifications. Most of this work has been undertaken at Toton depot, with a fleet of dedicated engineers assigned to the job, with specialist contractors supplying parts and services.

The bogies have been completely stripped down and upon detailed inspection, nothing was found to be amiss. The overhaul of the bogies takes about three weeks, though when the bogies are removed from a particular locomotive it does not necessarily mean that the same bogies will be refitted upon completion of the overhaul. Were this to be the case, it could hinder the lengthy overhaul process. The reasoning behind this is because if the bogies of a particular locomotive were removed for overhaul and possible subsequent repair, it could possibly delay the locomotive's return to traffic. Therefore a locomotive that may also be undergoing the same work might be out of traffic for a longer period and in this instance the use of its bogies would enable the first locomotive to be returned to traffic.

In the course of refurbishment the engine would be completely stripped down, and new pistons fitted along with new cylinder liners, the block skimmed and the crank reconditioned. One component that would not be repaired at Toton is the alternator.

Extensive work would also be undertaken in the driving cab; this would include new driving seats, also installed on the Class 66 fleet.

The bodywork would be subjected to a detailed examination, and should any corrosion be found, it would be replaced before the surface was primed and painted.

It is understood that to date, twenty-nine engines have been extensively overhauled, three by an external contractor and twenty-six by Toton. (Due to commercial

sensitivity, the external company cannot be identified.) The overhaul required the crankshaft to be removed for modification, as well as all internal components, including pistons, rods, cylinder heads, liners and big-end blocks. Indeed, such has been the success of the Super 60 refurbishment programme that Colas Rail UK have purchased a growing fleet of Class 60s and they have been put through exactly the same refurbishment programme as the DBS Class 60s. An agreement was signed on 14 March 2014 between DBS and Colas Rail UK to overhaul the Class 60s in the same manner as the Super 60 programme that was applied to a number of refurbished DBS Class 60s. The first Colas Class 60 to be put through the programme was 60087, the overhaul work commencing on 22 March 2014.[10]

The 'Super 60' programme is made up of twenty-six requirements, and to effect this work a total of forty-one DBS team members was involved in the overhaul at Toton. There is a total of six project areas, which are as follows:

60066 stands inside Toton depot immediately prior to undergoing the Super 60 refurbishment programme. This locomotive was released in the Drax silver livery during December 2013.
DB SCHENKER RAIL UK

Six Class 60s inside Toton during various stages of the Super 60 overhaul. The Class 60 nearest to the camera shows the vast space that would be taken up by the engine. DB SCHENKER RAIL UK

Two Class 60s inside Toton depot during the Super 60 refurbishment. The Class 60 on the right is in the process of being prepared before painting. DB SCHENKER RAIL UK

Modification team, electrical and mechanical
Strip and build team, electrical and mechanical
Welding (for corrosion damage)
Bogie team
Power unit team
Spray painters

Certain aspects of the overhaul and modifications were undertaken by the following sub-contractors: various engine sub-contractors, KBRS braking (Knorr-Bremse Rail Services, Melksham), KBRS wheelsets (Knorr-Bremse Rail Services, Springburn) and Brush Control Gear.[10]

The twenty-six requirements of the refurbishment project are as follows:[10]

Modification to the GSM-R
Strip down the locomotive body
Strip down the cab
Remove the engine and cooler
Clean the radiator room
Clean the engine room
Clean the clean-air compartment
Lift the locomotive
Clean the underbody
Strip down the bogies
Strip down the underframe
Build the underframe
Fit the accommodation bogies if required
Effect corrosion repairs
Clean and paint parts

A general view of Toton Traction Maintenance Depot, where the vast majority of the Super 60 work is undertaken, on 15 July 2014. EDWARD GLEED

A view of 60024 in the final stages of overhaul at Toton. The rich tones of the DBS livery are clearly seen. August 2013. DB SCHENKER RAIL UK

A close-up photograph of 60024 viewed from the No. 1 cab, side A. The exceptionally high standard of the paint finish is a credit to the highly skilled painters at Toton. August 2013. DB SCHENKER RAIL UK

Strip down the engine
Build the engine
Build the locomotive
Refit the cabs
Build the bogies
Re-install the bogies and engine
Re-fit the cooler group
Re-fit the alternator
Load test the locomotive
Test run the locomotive
Repaint the locomotive

A great deal of modification work has also been undertaken to increase reliability; the details are as follows:[10]

- Circle plug re-wires: hardwire of the plug to remove issues surrounding the burning of pins, thereby causing locomotive failure (radiator fan circuit)
- MCBs for chokes; the fuses were removed as failures could not be rectified in the field by the driver. Now that this modification has been carried out, drivers can reset the MCBs so the locomotive can remain in traffic
- MCB upgrade for radiator fan motor circuit breakers and wiring, because the older-style MCBs were repeatedly failing. This more robust MCB has proved to be more reliable
- MCBs for main alternator chokes, replace 3 × fuses
- MCB for auxiliary chokes, replace 3 × 50 amp fuses with more robust MCB

A general view inside Toton depot showing three Class 60s at varying stages of overhaul in August 2013. DB SCHENKER RAIL UK

- New-style AC scavenger pump fitted, replacing the DC type. The MCB DC style had a fuse, which resulted in reliability issues
- Re-positioning of the radiator fan temperature box sensing unit. The box has been removed from the engine room where the temperature affected the PCB causing overheating and resulting in false readings. This box has now been positioned in the clean-air compartment, which has eradicated failures caused by overheating
- The traction motor field chokes have had new upgraded fuses fitted to afford better reliability
- Resilient mounts for the main electronics, input and output racks; this eliminates vibration issues and failures
- Governor LVDT upgraded, and the governor overhauled to a revised specification. The harness has also been rewired due to insulation properties/problems of the existing cabling
- Modified traction motor seals have been fitted, to prevent ingress of Motak from the gear case into the armature, which had previously caused traction motor bearing problems. The gear cases are now filled with gear oil instead of Motak
- The windscreen wiper motor, arm and blade have been upgraded to a Class 66 type that has proved more reliable

- The camshafts have had new ceramic rollers fitted to the cam followers because the old-style steel rollers suffered damage
- A top carbon cutting ring has been fitted to the new piston liners: this cleans the top of the piston, so the engine runs more efficiently
- The driver's seat has been replaced by a Class 66 seat, to afford a more comfortable driving experience

Super 60 Programme

Situation as at 14 December 2013:

Test bed locos: 60 011 electrical upgrade – DBS red; 60 099 mechanical upgrade – Tata Steel silver

No.	Date to traffic	livery	Notes
60007	05.09.2011	DBS red	*The Spirit of Tom Kendell*
60054	21.10.2011	DBS red	
60091	28.11.2011	DBS red	*Barry Needham*
60074	06.01.2012	DBS blue	*Teenage Spirit*

The finished product of the Super 60 refurbishment programme: 60017 is another Class 60 to have been overhauled, seen here on 15 July 2014 at Kingsbury before its return to Lindsey. EDWARD GLEED

No.	Date to traffic	livery	Notes
60079	02.02.2012	DBS red	
60063	07.03.2012	DBS red	
60059	05.04.2012	DBS red	*Swinden Dalesman*
60015	23.05.2012	DBS red	
60040	21.06.2012	DBS red	*The Territorial Army Centenary*
60019	20.07.2012	DBS red	*Port of Grimsby & Immingham*
60017	03.09.2012	DBS red	
60010	07.10.2012	DBS red	Released, but returned to Toton same day, fault. Rtt by 18.11.2012
60092	14.11.2012	DBS red	Rtt not repainted. Released repainted 22.12.2012
60020	c09.01.2013	DBS red	Out on test c.20.12.2012 (red c.04.01.2013)
60039	18.05.2013	DBS red	*Dove Holes*
60062	c.15.06.2013	DBS red	*Stainless Pioneer*

No.	Date to traffic	livery	Notes
60024	03.08.2013	DBS red	*Clitheroe Castle*
60001	04.09.2013	DBS red	
60100	01.10.2013	DBS red	
60044	c.10.11.2013	DBS red	
60066	07.12.2013	Drax silver	(No DB Schenker legend on sides)
60007	Napier turbo fitted, undergoing examination and evaluation		
60099	Mechanical upgrade partly undertaken		
60011	Electrical upgrade partly undertaken		

* Candidates for 2014's Super 60 refurbishment may include 60 011/035/045/049/065/070 or 071/099

Two further photographs depict the Super 60s at work. The final image is worthy of inclusion as it depicts 60079 at the helm of the diverted 6E41 Westerleigh–Lindsey tanks, which is seen at Yate Middle siding, a small section of line that at one time saw traffic working to Tytherington, though at present does not see any traffic.[11]

Designed for haulage of the heavier freight trains throughout the UK, refurbished 60020 wheels 6B25 Westerleigh–Robeston tanks through Wickwar on Good Friday, 23 March 2013. EDWARD GLEED

60079 leads the diverted 6E41 to Lindsey oil refinery, seen departing Yate Middle, with sister 60099 attached to the rear of the working on 29 September 2012.
EDWARD GLEED

CHAPTER 7

THE COLAS CLASS 60s

To date, the entire Class 60 fleet had been owned either by British Rail (Trainload Freight), then Mainline Freight, Transrail Freight, Loadhaul, also EWS and then latterly DBS. During 2010, several members of the class had been offered for sale by DBS, but no buyers were forthcoming offering the right price. It is understood that DBS had indicated that their 'reserve price' had not been met.

Further to the twenty-one Class 60s in use by DBS, in April 2014 an announcement had been made through various railway periodicals to the effect that Colas Rail UK had purchased up to twenty Class 60 locomotives that had previously been offered for sale by DBS in 2010. This purchase was a surprise to many rail enthusiasts, as Colas Rail had recently purchased a fleet of ten brand new Class 70 diesel electric locomotives, manufactured by General Electric in Erie Pennsylvania, all of which had been out-shopped in the company's house colour of yellow, black and orange. It is understood that the purchase was made with

a view to complementing the existing fleet of locomotives currently under the auspices of Colas Rail UK, though it is thought that in the fullness of time the Class 60s would possibly be utilized on infrastructure duties.

Hitherto the Colas Class 60s had undergone the same detailed Super 60 refurbishment programme as the DBS Class 60s, with work being undertaken at Toton. The staff at both Brush Traction and Toton, along with other organizations involved with the refurbishment of the DBS Class 60s, have clearly demonstrated their ability to put these locomotives back to operational main-line service to a very high standard.

Furthermore, the Toton facility can undertake most of the aforementioned refurbishment work, and any work that cannot be undertaken at Toton will be outsourced to other companies. Following refurbishment, the Colas Class 60s have emerged from the works in the current Colas Rail livery, described in detail in Chapter 5.

An unidentified Class 60 during the advanced stages of its refurbishment at Toton. Various patches of undercoat can be seen as it awaits full repainting in the Colas livery. 23 July 2013.
EDWARD GLEED

60021 undergoes the Super 60 refurbishment programme at Toton. This is the interior of the cab at the No. 2 end of the locomotive. COLAS RAIL UK

60021's cab interior at the No. 1 end showing the hinged driver's desk with all lower covers removed. COLAS RAIL UK

The table opposite details the locomotives that have been purchased as of 15 April 2014. For the time being they have been assigned to the 'COLS' pool, which is the Colas Rail UK's 'stored' pool.[9]

Exterior of 60021 at Toton showing the absence of the cab roof, revealing the missile plate and protruding horn apparatus. Note the painted window surrounds and windscreen wipers.
(Image courtesy of Colos Rail UK)

Loco	Pool	Origin	Last Location
60002	COLS	CREWE	CREWE
60021	COLS	TOTON	TOTON
60026	COLS	TOTON	TOTON
60047	COLS	CREWE	CREWE
60056	COLS	CREWE	CREWE
60076	COLS	CREWE	CREWE
60085	COLS	TOTON	TOTON
60087	COLS	TOTON	TOTON*
60095	COLS	CREWE	CREWE
60096	COLS	ST BLAZEY	ST BLAZEY

First loco for Colas Rail to be released to traffic

As mentioned in Chapter 6, the first batch of Colas Class 60s to enter revenue-earning service were 60087, 60021, 60076, 60085 and 60002. These Class 60s are listed in the correct order of release to traffic following refurbishment.

60095, 60096 and 60047 are locomotives from the second batch of Class 60s that have undergone refurbishment and are now in traffic.

The remaining Colas Class 60s awaiting refurbishment and subsequent release into traffic are 60026 and 60056.

Details of the Colas Class 60 refurbishment are given in Chapter 6.

On 20 May 2014, 60087 was the first member of the Colas Class 60 fleet to be tested on the main line following refurbishment. It was trialled between Toton and Leicester, hauling a DBS Class 60.

As briefly mentioned in Chapter 5, the first revenue-earning main-line run for 60087 took place on Monday 2 June 2014. The working ran from Toton to Barrow Hill to collect Class 86/7, 86701 *Orion*, and the duo then continued from Barrow Hill to Washwood Heath. Following on from this run, the locomotive attended the 'Rail Live 2014' event hosted by Network Rail at Long Marston; during this event,

This pristine locomotive is 60087, the first Class 60 to be refurbished at Toton by DB Schenker Rail UK for Colas Rail UK in 2014. COLAS RAIL UK

60087, having completed the Super 60 refurbishment programme. It is viewed from the B side at the No. 2 end of the locomotive during 2014. COLAS RAIL UK

60026 during the early stages of the Super 60 refurbishment inside Toton. It is in the second batch of five locomotives to undergo the work. COLAS RAIL UK

60087 with 70804 pass Wimbledon West Junction with 6Z70 08:50 Rugby–Eastleigh West Yard, with 70801 attached to the rear on 4 July 2014. MARK V. PIKE

60087 was named *CLIC Sargent*. Since then, 60087 has spent much of its time working between Eastleigh Yard and Hoo Junction, though accessing the Southern Region was done by a working from Rugby depot to Eastleigh Yard.

During the latter half of 2014, the Colas Class 60s have been kept for much of the time at Westbury whilst being employed on engineering trips, and this is where 60087 arrived on the weekend of 19/20 July 2014. On Monday 21 July 2014, the locomotive ran 'light' engine from Westbury

On a very dull and overcast morning in the London suburb of Gospel Oak, 60021 is at the helm of 6V62, the 11:30 Tilbury–Llanwern steel on 26 November 2014.
EDWARD GLEED

Yard to Cardiff Canton, where it is understood it was required at the depot for train crew familiarization. During August and September 2014 the same locomotive was employed on the 6L63 Llanwern–Tilbury Riverside steel working; the return working was 6V62, 11:20 Tilbury Riverside–Llanwern. This was one of the first of the Colas diagrams to go over to Class 60 haulage. As more Colas Class 60s have been released into traffic, others have been assigned to this diagram.

In June 2015 eight Colas Class 60s were in revenue-earning service, with the remaining two Class 60s in various stages of refurbishment. As more Colas Class 60s were put through the Super 60 refurbishment programme, their sphere of operation widened. To date, many workings for which Colas Rail UK had hitherto used their fleet of Class 56, Class 66 or Class 70 locomotives, now include the Class 60, namely oil (including bitumen) and certain infrastructure diagrams including Rail-Vac duties, which invariably require two locomotives working in 'top and tail' mode.

In addition to these diagrams, Class 60 operations now include the timber workings that operate between the paper mill at Chirk to destinations such as Teigngrace, Baglan Bay and latterly Ribblehead, ousting the Class 56s, 66s and 70s on these diagrams. On 1 May 2015, 60076 became the first Class 60 to work the timber traffic, namely 6V54 Chirk–Baglan Bay. It was also allocated to work the empty timber train from Chirk to Teigngrace using the 6V54 headcode from the previous day. Whether any of the Colas Class 60s will undertake charter work and diesel galas is open to conjecture.

A very long 6V62, the Tilbury–Llanwern steel, exits the 4,444yd Chipping Sodbury tunnel hauled by 60085 on a warm 18 March 2015. The village of Old Sodbury can be seen in the distance. EDWARD GLEED

The first Class 60 to work the 6V54 Chirk–Teigngrace log train was 60076. It is seen passing through the Bristol suburb of Parson Street on a cloudy 6 May 2015. EDWARD GLEED

The Future for the Class 60

What does the future hold for the Class 60 fleet? At this point in time it is a difficult question to answer. Although at the time of writing there are over a quarter of the original 100 Class 60 locomotives in service, it is not clear how many more will be returned to the main line. This book has discussed some of the problems that have beset the Class 60, but there have been several highlights. In particular DB Schenker Rail UK has returned overhauled Class 60s to the main line, and Colas Rail UK has purchased a number of Class 60s. Also there has been a rise in freight workings following the return of refurbished Class 60s to revenue-earning service.

A Class 60 preservation group website (www.cl60pg.co.uk) has been set up inviting enthusiasts to join the group and/or to make a donation with a view to hopefully purchasing a Class 60 when the Class 60s are no longer required by the TOCs. One thing that is for certain is that the Class 60s have always been hugely popular with train crews and enthusiasts alike, and to this day the latter will still travel many miles to look at this highly acclaimed form of motive power.

A sullen morning of drenching rain gives way to a sunny afternoon. Here at Narroways Junction, 60002 positively storms its way through atop 6M51 Exeter–Chirk logs on 3 July 2015. EDWARD GLEED

It is a credit to DB Schenker Rail UK that they have virtually saved the Class 60 from extinction from the main line, and further credit is due to the expertise and skill of the maintenance staff at Toton depot, who have undertaken most of the refurbishment work and who keep the fleet serviceable. Full credit is also due to the highly skilled staff at Brush Traction (now a part of the Wabtec Rail Group) in Loughborough, both for their painstaking work in eradicating the faults that proved so troublesome during the early years of the Class 60 and for continuing to support the locomotives.

What the rail industry has now is a locomotive that is even better than it was when new, and it is hoped that the Class 60 will continue operating, and will continue to be seen and enjoyed, for many years to come.

60076 leaving the No. 1 loco spur at Bristol Temple Meads whilst en route to East depot to collect timber wagons for 6M51 to Chirk on 19 June 2015. EDWARD GLEED

Oil-seed rape fields spread as far as the eye can see as **DB Schenker Class 60 No. 60059** *Swinden Dalesman* approaches **Westerleigh Junction on 21 April 2015.** EDWARD GLEED

A disgraceful act of vandalism perpetrated on former **Petroleum Subsector 60014** as it awaits a decision on its future amidst the weeds at **Toton on 15 July 2014.** EDWARD GLEED

The lights are on at the Westerleigh oil terminal as 60044 prepares to shunt 6B47 to Robeston at dusk on 28 October 2014. The Bristol suburb of Mangotsfield and Downend is seen in the distance. EDWARD GLEED

A portrait view of DB Schenker Class 60 No. 60039 whilst on shunting duties at Tees Yard on 17 June 2014.
EDWARD GLEED

On a glorious summer afternoon the sixth Colas 60 to be overhauled, 60096, is at the head of 6V62 Tilbury–Llanwern steel at Acton Turville, near Badminton, on 6 June 2015. EDWARD GLEED

Following the failure of 60007 at Gloucester while working 6B13 Robeston–Westerleigh tanks, 60079 was sent to assist, and the duo are seen at Wickwar running some three hours late on 4 April 2012. EDWARD GLEED

The last remnants of autumn at Thornwell as EWS-liveried Class 60 works 6V05 Round Oak–Margam steel on 28 November 2013. Chepstow is just visible in the distance. EDWARD GLEED

The spire belonging to the parish church of St Mary Redcliffe dominates the skyline as 60017 and 60063 power 'The Taffy Tug' railtour past Bristol Barton Hill depot on 25 August 2013. EDWARD GLEED

In the popular location of Peak Forest 60039 *Dove Holes* is on full power as it lifts the heavy 6F05, 15:10 Tunstead–Lostock aggregate working away from Peak Forest on 16 June 2015. EDWARD GLEED

Cows chew the fat of the land at Purton as DBS 60063 wheels 6B47 Westerleigh–Robeston on a beautiful summer's evening. The Cotswold hills are seen in the distance on 6 June 2013. EDWARD GLEED

COMPONENTS, EQUIPMENT AND TOPS SCHEDULES

Engine: Mirrlees 8MB275RT

Major Components

Item	Design life
Crankcase/cylinder block	Indefinite
Sub/bedplate	Indefinite
Crank shaft (bare)	Indefinite
Cylinder liner	Indefinite
Cylinder liner	20 years
Cylinder head	Indefinite
Connecting rod (no bearings)	Indefinite
Large-end bearings (pair) (A)	5/10 years
Main bearings (pair (A)	10/20 years
Piston	Indefinite
Rings (set for one piston)	5 years
Air inlet valve	5/10 years
Exhaust valve	5/10 years
Fuel pump c/w follower	Recon at 10 years
Fuel injector	Recon at 10 years
Fuel nozzle	5/10 years
Turbocharger	Recon at 5 years
Governor	Recon at 5 years
Crankshaft damper	Serviced at 10 years
Cylinder head stud bolt	Indefinite
Engine complete (each)	40 years
Cooler group complete (less motors)	20 years
Cooling element	20 years
Fan	20 years
Breakdown of control components	12 years

Electrical Machines

Item	Design life
Main alternator (complete)	40 years
Auxiliary alternator (complete)	
Traction motor (complete)	40 years
Traction motor carcass	40 years
Traction motor armature	40 years
Traction motor brush gear	20 years
Traction motor gear case	40 years
Traction motor suspension tube	40 years
Traction motor pinion	20 years
Traction motor gearwheel	20 years

Item	Design life
Traction motor blower	20 years
Fuel lift pump motor	180,000hr rec at 60,000
Lubricating oil priming pump motor	180,000hr rec at 60,000
Compressor motor	180,000hr rec at 60,000
Starter motor	180,000hr rec at 60,000
Radiator fan motor	40 years
Transformer (typical)	40 years
Choke (typical)	40 years

Control Equipment

Item	Design life
Main rectifier	40 years
Battery charger	40 years
Converter unit	25 years
Battery	5 years
Master controller	16 years
Control cubicle (complete)	40 years
EP contactors	12 years
Diagnostic fault panel (complete)	25 years
General control resistors	25 years
EM contactors (general)	12 years
Clapper relay	25 years
Control relays (general)	12 years
General control resistors	25 years
EP valves for armature contactors	20 years
Pressure switch (203386/03)	25 years
Main ammeter (2037990)	20 years
Battery charge ammeter (2018841)	20 years
Main speedometer	20 years
Slow-speed speedometer	20 years
Circuit breaker (2031895/01)	20 years
Circuit breakers (general)	20 years
Lighting inverter	12 years
3210 battery isolating switch	25 years
Rotary switches (general)	12 years
3230 door interlock switch (2039794)	25 years
Toggle switches (general)	12 years
3267 DSD pedal switch (2044191)	12 years
5100 DC supply transformer (2038161)	25 years
5105 field phase reference transformer	25 years
Current transformers (general)	25 years
Chokes (general)	25 years
Current transducers (general)	25 years

Control Electronics (Complete) 40 Years

Comprising:
DC supply control module
Main alternator control module
Auxiliary alternator control module
Quad firing module
Three-phase reference filter module
Voltage buffer module
Armature current buffer module
Input interface module
Output interface module
Main microprocessor module
Analogue interface module
Digital interface module
Quad timer module
Axle probe/radar driver module
Temperature monitor module
Meter driver module
Microprocessor monitor module
LVDT module
Waveform generator No. 1 module
Waveform generator N.o 2 module
Auxiliary current buffer module
CT test module
Speed microprocessor module
Power supply input module
Communications module
Power supply monitor module
5V power supply
15V power supply
30V power supply
Rack 2 motherboard
Rack 3 upper and lower motherboard
Rack 4 upper motherboard
Rack 4 lower motherboard
Rack 5 micro motherboard
Rack 5 motherboard
Rack 6 micro motherboard
Rack 6 motherboard
Rack 6 upper and lower motherboard

Bogie

Item	Design life
Bogie frame (fab, frame and fully m/cd)	40 years
Axle box	40 years
Axle-box bearing	40 years
Primary rolling rubber unit guidance system	40 years
Axle	40 years
Wheel	5 years
Axle end transducer	may not be fitted
Primary spring	40 years with 50% rec
Primary rolling rubber unit	10 years
Secondary spring unit	10 years
Brake unit	40 years
Parking brake unit	40 years
Sand ejector	40 years
Primary damper	15 years
Secondary lateral damper	15 years
Damper end mount (sec only)	5 years
Traction centre housing	40 years

Item	Design life
Traction centre spigot	40 years
Traction centre spring	10 years
Traction motor nose rubbers/bearings/links	10 years
Body/bogie safety loops	40 years
Complete bogie (less traction motors)	40 years
Ventilator fan or fans and motor	50,000 hours
Electrical heater element	7.5 years
Thermostats	7.5 years
Air filters	1 month
Ram air ventilation unit	10 years
Structure	40 years
Silencer	15 years
Westinghouse brake equipment	40 years

List of Main Spares[4]

Diesel engine	£271,369.00
Electric traction motor	£22,477.50
Brake equipment frame/module	£16,883.75
Bogie (less traction motors) and AWS receiver	£87,221.94
Wheelset L & T	£7,676.82
centre	£8,457.07
Main alternator (complete)	£50,336.00
Cooler group (complete)	£29,922.00
Cab (complete)	not applicable: cab is integral with structure
Electric control cubicle	£74,487.10
Diesel engine (complete with alternator)	£333,455.00
Turbocharger	£39,982.58
Main rectifier	£11,004.48
Converter unit	£12,136.51
Battery charger	£3,184.33
Silencer (c/w elbow and bellows)	£6,918.00
Air compressor (c/w motor)	£8,970.00
Bogie (C/W traction motors) (but less AWS receiver)	£155,127.50

TOPS Lists[9]

The following tables in this Appendix look at some of the actual workings in detail of the Class 60s operation schedule. Reproduced with kind permission of Network Rail Infrastructure Limited.

DBS Class 60 TOPS Status Log for 3 June 2013

Loco	Pool	Origin	Last Location	Destination	Next WTT	Exam
60 001	WCBI	TOTON UP	TOTON UP	6Z18		5D
60 011	WCAI	FIDLERSFY	6F38	LPOOLBKTM		8D
60 015	WCBI	MARGAM TC	MARGAM TC	6H35		3D
60 017	WCBK	MIDDBRODW	MIDDBRODW	10D		
60 019	WCAI	TOTON UP	TOTON TMD	1D		
60 020	WCBI	COLBROOK	COLNBROOK	6E38		6D
60 035	WCAI	THORNE JN	GOOLE UGL	8D		
60 039	WCAK	SANDAR BS	SANDAR BS	11D		
60 040	WCAI	IMINGORET	6T22	SANTON		3D

60 049	WCAK	ELEGHYDRP	EASTLGHYD	6D		
60 054	WCBI	DEE MARSH	6V75	MARGAM TC		6D
60 063	WCAI	ROBESTON	6B13	WESTRLEGH	6B47	7D
60 065	WCAK	OAKLEGHSG	6H03	TUNSTDBLI		3D
60 074	WCAI	LPOOLBKTM	6F81	FIDLERSFY		8D
60 079	WCAI	FIDLERSFY	FIDLERSFY	6D		
60 091	WCBK	PENDLTON	6H43	TUNSTDBLI		8D
60 092	WCBI	PRESTNDKS	6E32	LINDSEYOR		11D
60 099	WCAI	JARROWTML	JARROWTML	6D43		2D
LOCOS:	TOTAL 18		OUT OF SERVICE 0		AVAILABLE 18	

DBS Class 60 TOPS Status Log for 21 December 2013

Loco	Pool	Origin	Last Location	Destination	Next WTT	Exam
60 001	WCAI	JARROWTML	6D43	LINDSEYOR		4D
60 007	WCBK	HOPE STSL	HOPE STSL			9D
60 010	WCBI	FIDLERSFY	FIDLERSFY			3D
60 015	WCBI	TOTON UP	TOTON TMD			11D
60 017	WCBI	KNGSBYCHN	6E54	HUMBER OR		5D
60 019	WCAK	TOTON TMD	TOTON TMD			9D
60 020	WCBI	RECTORY J	6E28	LINDSEY OR		9D
60 024	WCAK	FIDLERSFY	FIDLERSFY			4D
60 035	WCAK	DONCS TMD	DONCS TMD			1D
60 039	WCAI	MARGAM TC	MARGAM TC			4D
60 040	WCAI	MARGAM TC	6B33	ROBESTON		9D
60 044	WCAI	DON UP DCY	DONCS TMD			8D
60 045	WCAK	EASTLGHYD	EASTLGHYD			3D
60 049	WCAK	BESCOT DS	BESCOT DS	6D44		3D
60 054	WCBI	BESCOT DS	BESCOT DS	6B07		4D
60 059	WCBI	IMINGORET	IMINGORET	6D		
60 062	WCAI	ROBESTON	6B13	WESTERLEGH		11D
60 063	WCAI	LINDSEY OR	6M57	KNGSBYCHN		3D
60 065	WCAI	LLANWEXSD	6E66	SC ENT C		9D
60 066	WCAI	THEALE OS	THEALE OS	6D		
60 071	WCBK	LACKENBY	6D05	SC ENT C		4D
60 074	WCAK	TEES YARD	6J72	ALDWKE NS		10D
60 079	WCAK	TUNSTDBLI	6F05	OAKLEGHSG		7D
60 091	WCBI	DONCS TMD	DONCS TMD	0M67		1D
60 092	WCBI	DONCS TMD	DONCS TMD	6T51		5D
60 099	WCAI	MARGAM TC	MARGAM TC			10D
60 100	WCAK	TUNSTDBLI	TUNSTDBLI			1D
LOCOS:	TOTAL 27		OUT OF SVC 0		AVAILABLE 27 (100%)	

DBS Class 60 TOPS STATUS Log for 25 September 2014

Loco	Pool	Origin	Last Location	Destination	Next WTT	Exam
60 001	WCAT	WALSALL FT	WALSALL FT			5D
60 007	WCBT	MARGAM TC	6E30	HARTLPLSW		5D
60 010	WCBT	LINDSEY OR	6M24	KNGSBYCHN		4D
60 011	WCAT	IMING TMD	IMING TMD			5D
60 015	WCBT	HOPE STSL	6H60	PK FOR SL		7D
60 017	WCBT	TOTON TMD	TOTON TMD			2D
60 019	WCAT	HUMBER OR	6M00	KNGSBYCHN		11D
60 020	WCBT	MARGAMLIP	0M03	ROBESTON		10D
60 024	WCAT	KNGSBYCHN	6E59	LINDSEY OR	0D59	12D
60 035	WCAT	TOTON TMD	TOTON TMD		0Z33	7D
60 039	WCAT	MARGAM TC	6B13	WESTRLEGH		2D
60 040	WCAT	WESTRLEGH	6E41	LINDSEY OR	0D41	8D
60 044	WCAT	KLONDKSDG	6D08	DON UPDCY		11D
60 045	WCAT	TUNSTDBLI	PK FOREST			6D
60 049	WCAT	TOTON UP	TOTON TMD			7D
60 054	WCBT	TINSLEY	6M12	SEAFTH CT	6E14	11D
60 059	WCBT	TOTON UP	TOTON UP			9D

60 062	WCAT	FIDLERSFY	FIDLERSFY			11D
60 063	WCAT	IMINGORET	IMINGORET			5D
60 065	WCAT	LPOOL BKTM	6F84	FIDLERSFY		3D
60 071	WCBT	TOTON TMD	TOTONN YD		CL08	10D
60 074	WCAT	TUNSTDBLI	6F05	LOSTOKWKS	6H06	4D
60 079	WCAT	MARGAM TC	6E30	HARTLPLSW		5D
60 091	WCBT	EASTLHLWR	EASTLIGHYD		CL08	4D
60 092	WCBT	IMIMG TMD	IMING TMD			11D
60 099	WCAT	BRIGGSSDG	6H23	TUNSTDBLI		5D
60 100	WCAT	THEALE	6B33	ROBESTON		6D
LOCOS:	TOTAL 27		OUT OF SVC 3		AVAILABLE 24 (89%)	

DBS Class 60 TOPS Status Log for 15 JANUARY 2015

Loco	Pool	Origin	Last Location	Destination	Next WTT	Exam
60 001	WCAT	PKFORSTUS	PK FOR SL			3D
60 010	WCBT	TOTON TMD	TOTON TMD			9D
60 011	WCAT	TEES YARD	6N73	LACKENBY		11D
60 015	WCBT	LINDSEY OR	6V98	WESTRLEGH	6E41	4D
60 017	WCBT	TOTON TMD	TOTON TMD			0D
60 019	WCAT	LINDSEY OR	6M24	KNGSBYCHN	6E46	5D
60 020	WCBT	FIDLERSFY	6F88	LPOOLBKTM		3D
60 024	WCAT	WARRTNARP	6Z35	LPOOLBKTM		3D
60 039	WCAT	TOTON YD	6T34	TAPTON JN	6T34	11D
60 040	WCAT	MARGAM TC	MARGAM TC			1D
60 044	WCAT	PK FOR SL	PK FOR SL			6D
60 049	WCAT	DON UPDCY	DONWOODYD			3D
60 054	WCBT	WESTRLEGH	6B47	ROBESTON	6B13	2D
60 059	WCBT	TUNSTDBLI	6J43	PENDLTON		12D
60 062	WCAT	IMNG NOR	IMING TMD		0M35	9D
60 063	WCAT	WARRTNARP	WARRTNLHS			12D
60 074	WCAT	IM DK T F	6T01	LINDSEY OR		5D
60 079	WCAT	IMINGORET	6T31	SANTONOBP		7D
60 091	WCBT	IMMHM SS	6M99	WOLVES ST		6D
60 092	WCBT	LINDSEY OR	LINDSEY OR		0D59	6D
60 099	WCAT	TOTON TMD	TOTON TMD			2D
60 100	WCAT	LPOOLBKTM	6F77	FIDLERSFY		6D
LOCOS:	TOTAL 22		OUT OF SVC 3		AVAILABLE 19	

It will be noticed that certain locations within the TOPS lists are abbreviated. This is because the TOPS system is only able to accommodate locations of no more than nine characters, consisting of numbers, letters and numbers. Locations that fit within that criterion are shown in full. For example, LUDLOW is shown as LUDLOW, but locations that are clearly too long for the mainframe, for example KING EDWARD BRIDGE SOUTH JUNCTION (Newcastle), is shown on TOPS as KEBGSTHJN. A list is provided below affording full names for easier identification.

BRIGGS ICI SDGS	BRIGGS IMPERIAL CHEMICAL INDUSTRIES SIDINGS
BRISTLEDE	BRISTOL EAST DEPOT
COLNBRKCR	COLNBROOK COLAS RAIL
DERBY LIT	DERBY LITCHURCH LANE
DONWOODYD	DONCASTER WOOD YARD
DON UPDCY	DONCASTER UP DECOY YARD
FIDLERSFY	FIDDLER'S FERRY POWER STATION
HOPE STSL	HOPE STREET PEAK STONE SIDINGS
IM DK T F	IMMINGHAM STORAGE WEST TERMINAL

IM DK T Q	IMMINGHAM TRANIST QUAY
IMING NOR	IMMINGHAM DOCK NORDIC
IMINGORET	IMMINGHAM BSC ORE TERMINAL
IMMHM SS	IMMINGHAM SORTING SIDINGS
KEBGSTHJN	KING EDWARD BRIDGE SOUTH JUNCTION (NEWCASTLE)
KLONDKSG	YORK ENGINEER'S SIDING
LLANWEXSD	LLANWERN EXCHNGE SIDINGS
LNDSYORCR	LINDSEY OIL REFNERY COLAS
LPOOLBKTML	LIVERPOOL BULK HANDLING TERMINAL
MARGAM TC	MARGAM TRAIN CREW
MIDDBRODW	MIDDLESBOROUGH DAWSON AYRTON
OAKLEGHSG	OAKLEIGH SIDINGS
PKFORSTUS	PEAK FOREST UP SIDINGS
PK FOR SL	PEAK FOREST CEMEX SIDINGS
PRESTNDKS	PRESTON DOCKS LAFINA
RHAM ST	MASBOROUGH
RHAMMAS JN	MASBOROUGH SOUTH JUNCTION
SANADAR BS	STAPLEFORD & SCCE SIDING
SCTRENTYD	SUNTHORPE TRENT TC
SCUNTHPRS	SCUNTHORPE REDBOURNE SIDINGS
TUNSTEAD BLI	TUNSTEAD BUXTON LIME INDUSTRIES
WALSALL FT	WALSALL FREIGHT TERMINAL
WALSALL MY	WALSALL BUXTON LIME INDUSTRIES CEMENT
WOLVES ST	WOLVERHAMPTON STEEL TERMINAL
WARRTNHLS	WARRINGTON FUELING APRON
WASHWDHAC	WASHWOOD HEATH METRO-CAMMELL
WHERE THE INITIALS BSC ARE USED, THIS REFERS TO THE FORMER BRITISH STEEL CORPORATION	

Colas Class 60 TOPS Status Log for 13 April 2014

Loco	Pool	Origin	Last Location	Destination	Next WTT	Exam
60 002	COLS	TOTON TMD	TOTON TMD			11D
60 021	COLS	TOTON TMD	TOTON			4D
60 026	COLS	TOTON TMD	TOTON			4D
60 047	COLS	TOTON TMD	TOTON TMD			4D
60 056	COLS	TOTON TMD	TOTON TMD			6D
60 076	COLS	TOTON TMD	TOTON TMD			6D
60 085	COLS	TOTON TMD	TOTON			1D
60 087	COLS	TOTON	TOTON TMD**			–4D
60 095	COLS	TOTON TMD	TOTON TMD			10D
60 096	COLS	ST BLAZEY	ST BLAZEY			3D
60 087	COLO is allocated to this pool code as from June 2014**					

The first revenue main-line run for **60087** took place on Monday 2 June 2014. The working ran from Toton to Barrow Hill to collect Class 86/7, No. 86701 *Orion*, and the duo worked from Barrow Hill to Washwood Heath in Birmingham. The details of the working are shown below.

In the second working **60 087** worked from Rugby to Eastleigh. This was routed via the WCML, Mitre Bridge and Wimbledon; the details are set out in the following tables.

Colas Class 60 TOPS Status Log for 19 September 2014

Loco	Pool	Origin	Last Location	Destination	Next WTT	Exam
60 002	COLS	TOTON TMD	TOTON TMD			11D
60 021	COLS*	RATCLIFFE	6F58	LPOOLBKTML		5D
60 026	COLS	TOTON TMD	TOTON			4D
60 047	COLS	TOTON TMD	TOTON TMD			4D
60 056	COLS	TOTON TMD	TOTON TMD			6D
60 076	COLS	TOTON TMD	TOTON TMD			6D
60 085	COLS	TOTON TMD	TOTON			1D
60 087	COLO	CANTON SDG	CANTON SDG			—
60 095	COLS	TOTON TMD	TOTON TMD			10D
60 096	COLS	ST BLAZEY	ST BLAZEY**			3D

*Allocated to the COLO POOL during late September and ran without 'Colas Freight' branding. The branding was applied a week later at Toton.
**Note: 60096 was moved from St Blazey to Bodmin as a static exhibit for the Bodmin Diesel Gala. On 30 September 2014, the Class 56 No. 56302 hauled 60096 as 0Z53 from Bodmin to Toton for refurbishment work to be undertaken.

Colas Class 60 TOPS Status Log for 19 June 2015

Loco	Pool	Origin	Last Location	Destination	Next WTT	Exam
60002	COLO	TOTON UP	TOTON TMD			2D
60021	COLO	LNDSYORCR	6V70	COLNBRKCR		9D
60026	COLS	TOTON TMD				4D
60047	COLO	BOSTONDKS	6M08	WASHWDHAC		6D
60056	COLS	TOTON TMD				6D
60076	COLO	BRISTLEDE	BRISTLEDE			7D
60085	COLO	IM DK T Q	IM DK T Q			12D
60087	COLO	CHIRKCOLS	6C37	CSLE YD		12D
60095	COLO	IM DK T Q	OZ63	LNDSYORCR		6D
60096	COLO	CANTONTMD	CANTONTMD			8D

Schedule details for 0Z42 Barrow Hill–Washwood Heath Metro-Cammell. 2 June 2014

Location	Booked	Miles	
BARROW HILL	12:50	0	ORIGINATING POINT
BARROW HILL SOUTH JUNCTION	12:54–12:58	0	CALLING POINT
BARROW HILL NORTH JUNCTION	13:02–13:06	1	CALLING POINT
BARROW HILL SOUTH JUNCTION	13:09	2	
TAPTON JUNCTION	13:12	5	
CHESTERFIELD	13:13	5	
CHESTERFIELD SOUTH JUNCTION	13:14	6	
CLAY CROSS NORTH JUNCTION	13:16	8	
AMBERGATE JUNCTION	13:27	19	
ST MARY'S JUNCTION	13:36	28	
DERBY	13:39	29	
DERBY LONDON & NORTH WESTERN JN	13:45–13:57	31	CALLING POINT
STENSON JUNCTION	14:04	34	
NORTH STAFFORD JUNCTION	14:05	35	
CLAY MILLS JUNCTION	14:08	38	
BURTON ON TRENT	14:11	41	
WICHNOR JUNCTION	14:17	46	
TAMWORTH HIGH LEVEL	14:28	53	
KINGSBURY JUNCTION	14:37	59	
WATER ORTON	14:41	63	
CASTLE BROMWICH	14:44	65	
WASHWOOD HEATH WEST JUNCTION	14:54–15:00	68	CALLING POINT
WASHWOOD HEATH METRO-CAMMELL	15:02	69	TERMINATING POINT

Schedule details for 6Z42 Rugby Depot–Eastleigh Yard. 4 July 2014

Location	Booked	Miles	
RUGBY ACCESS DEPOT LINE	08:50	0	ORIGINATING POINT
RUGBY	08:56–09:04	1	CALLING POINT
HILMORTON JUNCTION	09:07	2	
DAVENTRY NORTH JUNCTION	09:11	5	
LONG BUCKBY	09:18	10	
NORTHAMPTON	09:30	20	
HANSLOPE JUNCTION	09:42	29	
MILTON KEYNES	09:52	36	
BLETCHLEY	09:57	39	
LEDBURN JUNCTION	10:07	48	
TRING	10:14	54	
BOURNE END	10:22	60	
WATFORD JUNCTION	10:31	68	
HARROW & WEALDSTONE	10:37	74	
WEMBLEY CENTRAL	10:43	78	
SUDBURY JUNCTION	10:45	79	
WEMBLEY YARD SOUTH JUNCTION	10:46	79	
WILLESDEN No 7	10:49	80	
WILLESDEN WEST LONDON JUNCTION	10:53	81	
MITRE BRIDGE JUNCTION	10:57	81	
NORTH POLE JUNCTION	10:58	81	
KENSINGTON OLYMPIA	11:03	83	
LATCHMERE JUNCTION	11:11	86	
CLAPHAM JUNCTION	11:17	87	
BLAHAM	11:22	89	
STREATHAM NORTH JUNCTION	11:24	90	
STREATHAM SOUTH JUNCTION	11:25	90	
WIMBLEDON	11:37	93	
WIMBLEDON WEST JUNCTION	11:39	94	
RAYNES PARK	11:42	95	
NEW MALDEN	11:44	96	
SURBITON	11:49	99	
HAMPTON COURT JUNCTION	11:51	100	
WOKING	12:15	111	
WOKING JUNCTION	12:17	111	
PIRBRIGHT JUNCTION	12:22	116	
FARNBROUGH	12:26	119	
BASINGSTOKE	12:42	134	
WORTING JUNCTION	12:46	137	
WALLERS ASH LOOP	12:58–13:08	147	CALLING POINT
WINCHESTER	13:14	153	
SHAWFORD JUNCTION	13:28	155	
ALLBROOK JUNCTION	13:34	159	
EASTLEIGH EAST YARD	13:37	159	TERMINATING POINT

Schedule details for 6Y14 Eastleigh Yard–Hoo Junction. 14 July 2014

Location	Booked	Miles	
EASTLEIGH EAST YARD	09:02	0	ORIGINATING POINT
ALLBROOK JUNCTION	09:05	0	
SHAWFORD	09:09	3	
WINCHESTER	09:13	6	
WORTING JUNCTION	09:29	23	
BASINGSTOKE	09:34	25	
FLEET	09:46	36	
FARNBROUGH	09:50	40	
PIRBRIGHT JUNCTION	09:55	43	
WOKING JUNCTION	10:01	48	
WOKING	10:06	48	
BYFLEET & NEW HAW	10:14	52	

Location	Booked	Miles	
ADDLESTON JUNCTION	10:16	53	
VIRGINIA WATER	10:27–10:37	58	CALLING POINT
STAINES	10:48	62	
FELTHAM	10:54	66	
FELTHAM JUNCTION	10:57	68	
WHITTON JUNCTION	10:58	68	
TWICKENHAM JUNCTION	11:02	69	
TWICKENHAM	11:03	70	
ST MARGRETS	11:04	70	
RICHMOND	11:08	71	
BARNES	11:16	74	
CLAPHAM JUNCTION	11:25	77	
LONGHEDGE JUNCTION	11:28	78	
FACTORY JUNCTION	11:30	78	
VOLTAIRE ROAD JUNCTION	11:31	79	
DENMARK HILL	11:36	81	
CROFTON ROAD	11:38	81	
NUNHEAD	11:41	83	
LEWISHAM VALE JUNCTION	11:45	84	
LEWISHAM	11:47	84	
PARKSBRIDGE JUNCTION	11:49	85	
HITHERGREEN	11:51	86	
LEE	11:53	87	
SIDCUP	12:00	91	
CRAYFORD	12:08	94	
CRAYFORD SPUR	12:17	95	
DARTFORD JUNCTION	12:28	96	
DARTFORD	12:30	96	
SPRINGHEAD JUNCTION CTRL	12:48	101	
GRAVESEND	12:51	103	
HOO JUNCTION UP YARD	12:57	106	TERMINATING POINT

Schedule details for 6V62 11:20 Tilbury Riverside–Llanwern Exchange Sidings. 30 August 2014

Location	Booked	Miles	
TILBURY RIVERSIDE (COLAS)	11:20	0	ORIGINATING POINT
TILBURY WEST JUNCTION	11:25	0	
TILBURY TOWN	11:27	1	
GRAYS	11:30	3	
WEST THURROCK JUNCTION	11:31	3	
PURFLEET	11:35	6	
RAINHAM	11:39	10	
DAGENHAM DOCK	11:41	12	
RIPPLE LANE RENWICK ROAD JUNCTION	11:43	13	
BARKING	11:53	15	
BARKING STATION JUNCTION	11:54	15	
WOODGRANGE PARK	11:56	17	
LEYTON MIDLAND ROAD	12:06	19	
SOUTH TOTTENHAM	12:14	23	
HARRINGAY PARK JUNCTION	12:19	24	
UPPER HOLLOWAY	12:22	26	
JUNCTION ROAD JUNCTION	12:23	26	
GOSPEL OAK	12:26	27	
KENSAL GREEN JUNCTION	12:39	31	
WILLESDEN JUNCTION HIGH LEVEL	12:40	31	
ACTON WELLS	12:44	32	
ACTON MAINLINE	12:48–13:08	32	CALLING POINT
ACTON WEST	13:12	33	
WEST EALING	13:16	34	
HANWELL	13:18	35	
SOUTHALL	13:23	37	
AIRPORT JUNCTION	13:28	38	
DOLPHIN JUNCTION	13:36	44	

Location	Booked	Miles	
SLOUGH	13:38	45	
MAIDENHEAD	13:45	51	
TWYFORD	13:54	58	
KENNET BRIDGE JUNCTION	14:00	61	
READING	14:02	63	
READING WEST JUNCTION	14:04	64	
DIDCOT EAST JUNCTION	14:29	80	
DIDCOT PARKWAY	14:13–14:33	80	CALLING POINT
FOXHALL JUNCTION	14:34	81	
MILTON JUNCTION	14:37	82	
STEVENTON	14:40–14:45	83	
WANTAGE ROAD	14:50	87	
CHALLOW	14:55	92	
UFFINGTON	14:57	94	
SWINDON	15:10	105	
WOTTON BASSETT JUNCTION	15:17	110	
HULLAVINGTON	15:41–16:18	122	CALLING POINT
WESTERLEIGH JUNCTION	16:33	135	
BRISTOL PARKWAY	16:39–16:41	139	
PATCHWAY	16:43	141	
PILNING	16:47	144	
SEVERN TUNNEL EAST JUNCTION	16:55	145	
SEVERN TUNNEL WEST JUNCTION	17:00	150	
SEVERN TUNNEL JUNCTION	17:02	152	
LLANWERN RECEPTION	17:10	156	
LLANWERN EXCHANGE SIDINGS	17:20	157	TERMINATING POINT

Schedule details for 6E08 Wolverhampton Steel Terminal–Immingham. 25 June 2014

Location	Booked	Miles	
WOLVERHAMPTON STEEL TERMINAL	11:04	0	ORIGINATING POINT
MONMORE GREEN	11:07	—	
DUDLEY PORT	11:12	5	
GALTON JUNCTION	11:16	8	
SOHO NORTH JUNCTION	11:19	10	
SOHO SOUTH JUNCTION	11:23	10	
PERRY BARR WEST JUNCTION	11:26	12	
PERRY BARR NORTH	11:26	12	
NEWTON JUNCTION	11:33	16	
BESCOT UP/DOWN GOODS LOOP	11:38–14:31	17	CALLING POINT
BESCOT JUNCTION	14:34	17	
PLECK JUNCTION	14:36	18	
WALSALL	14:39	19	
RYCROFT JUNCTION	14:41	20	
PARK LANE	15:08	31	
WATER ORTON WEST JUNCTION	15:10	32	
WATER ORTON	15:15	33	
KINGSBURY JUNCTION	15:20	37	
TAMWORTH HIGH LEVEL	15:27	42	
WICHNOR JUNCTION	15:34	50	
BURTON ON TRENT	15:40	55	
CLAY MILLS JUNCTION	15:42	57	
NORTH STAFFORD JUNCTION	15:46	61	
STENSON JUNCTION	15:47	61	
DERBY	15:56	66	
BROADHOLME	16:11	75	
AMBERGATE JUNCTION	16:14–16:43	76	CALLING POINT
CLAY CROSS NORTH JUNCTION	16:56	86	
CHESTERFIELD SOUTH JUNCTION	16:58	89	
CHESTERFIELD	16:59	90	
TAPTON JUNCTION	17:00	90	
BARROW HILL NORTH JUNCTION	17:07	93	
BEIGHTON JUNCTION	17:14	99	
TREETON JUNCTION	17:17	102	

Location	Booked	Miles	
MASBOROUGH SOUTH JUNCTION	17:22	104	
MASBOROUGH	17:26–18:28	104	CALLING POINT
MASBOROUGH SOUTH JUNCTION	18:34–18:44	104	CALLING POINT
MASBOROUGH JUNCTION	18:48	106	
ALDWARKE JUNCTION	18:51	108	
THRYBERG JUNCTION	18:53	109	
MEXBOROUGH	18:58–19:08	111	
HEXTHORPE JUNCTION	18:22	116	
BENTLEY JUNCTION	19:29	120	
KIRK SANDALL	19:33	122	
HATFIELD & STAINFORTH	19:38	126	
THORNE JUNCTION	19:43	127	
CROWLE	19:53	134	
GUNHOUSE LOOP	20:06–20:20	139	CALLING POINT
SCUNTHORPE	20:29	142	
APPLEBY LC	20:41	146	
ELSHAM	20:46	150	
WRAWBY JUNCTION	20:53	152	
BARNETBY	20:56–21:15	153	CALLING POINT
BROCKLESBY JUNCTION	21:22	157	
ULCEBY	21:24	158	
HUMBER ROAD JUNCTION	21:43	162	
IMMINGHAM SORTING SIDINGS	21:49	163	TERMINATING POINT

Schedule details for 6V70 Lindsey Oil Refinery–Colnbrook. 4 February 2013

Location	Booked	Miles	
LINDSEY OIL REFINERY	22:20	0	ORIGINATING POINT
ULCEBY	22:42	4	
BROCKLESBY JUNCTION	22:44	5	
BARNETBY	22:52	10	
WRAWBY JUNCTON	22:53	10	
HOLTON-LE-MOOR S.B	23:08	18	
WICKENBY	23:23	28	
LANGWORTH	23:34	33	
PELHAM STREET	23:45	39	
LINCOLN	23:48	39	
WEST HOLMES JUNCTION	23:50	40	
BOULTHAM JUNCTION	23:51	40	
NEWARK CROSSING EAST JUNCTION	00:16	54	
NEWARK CROSSING	00:17	54	
NEWARK CASTLE	00:20	55	
STAYTHORPE CROSSING	00:27	57	
FISKERTON	00:29	59	
LOWDHAM	00:36	64	
NETHERFIELD	00:42	69	
NOTTINGHAM	00:48–00:50	72	CALLING POINT
MANSFIELD JUNCTION	00:54	73	
TRENT EAST JUNCTION	01:05	79	
TRENT SOUUTH JUNCTION	01:07	79	
LOUGHBROUGH	01:19	87	
SILEBY JUNCTION	01:33	91	
SYSTON SOUTH JUNCTION	01:38	95	
LEICESTER	01:44	99	
WIGSTON NORTH JUNCTION	01:52	102	
MARKET HARBOROUGH	02:11	115	
KETTERING	02:28	127	
HARROWDEN JUNCTION	02:35	132	
WELLINGBOROUGH	02:38	134	
SHARNBROOK JUNCTION	02:54	142	
BEDFORD NORTH JUNCTION	03:05–03:19	148	CALLING POINT
BEDFORD	03:22	149	
BEDFORD SOUTH JUNCTION	03:24	150	
FLITWICK	03:38	158	

Location	Booked	Miles	
LEAGRAVE JUNCTION	03:49	165	
LUTON	03:52–04:21	168	CALLING POINT
HARPENDON JUNCTION	04:27	174	
ST ALBANS CITY	04:35	178	
RADLET JUNCTION	04:43	184	
SILKSTREAM JUNCTION	04:54	190	
HENDON	05:00	191	
BRENT CURVE JUNCTION	05:07	192	
DUDDING HILL JUNCTION	05:10	193	
ACTON CANAL WARF	05:16	196	
ACTON WELLS JUNCTION	05:18	196	
ACTON MAIN LINE	05:21–05:23	197	CALLING POINT
ACTON WEST	05:30	197	
SOUTHALL	05:39	201	
AIRPORT JUNCTION	05:44	203	
WEST DRAYTON	05:52–05:54	205	CALLING POINT
COLNBROOK	06:15	208	TERMINATING POINT

Location	Booked	Miles	
NEWARK CASTLE	20:12	154	
NEWARK CROSSING	20:13	154	
NEWARK CROSSING EAST JUNCTION	20:14	154	
BOULTHAM JUNCTION	20:35	168	
WEST HOMES JUNCTION	20:36	169	
EAST HOLMES	20:40–20:54	169	CALLING POINT
LINCOLN	20:57	170	
PELHAM STREET	20:58	170	
LANGWORTH	21:07	176	
WICKENBY	21:13	181	
HOLTON-LE-MOOR	21:24	190	
WRAWBY JUNCTION	21:38	199	
BARNETBY	21:40	199	
BROCKLESBY JUNCTION	21:46	204	
ULCEBY	21:48	205	
LINDSEY OIL REFINERY	21:58	209	

Schedule details for 6E38 Colnbrook–Lindsey Oil Refinery. 5 February 2013

Location	Booked	Miles	
COLNBROOK	13:54	0	ORIGINATING POINT
WEST DRAYTON	14:24–14:29	3	
AIRPORT JUNCTION	14:36	5	
SOUTHALL	14:40	7	
WEST EALING	14:45	9	
ACTON WEST	14:50	11	
ACTON MAINLINE	14:54–15:11	11	CALLING POINT
ACTON WELS JUNCTION	15:15	12	
ACTON CANAL WHARF	15:17	12	
DUDDING HILL JUNCTION	15:23	15	
BRENT CURVE JUNCTION	15:27	16	
HENDON	15:31	17	
SILKSTREAM JUNCTION	15:36	18	
RADLETT JUNCTION	15:44	24	
ST ALBANS CITY	15:53	30	
HARPENDEN JUNCTION	16:00	34	
LUTON	16:07	40	
LEAGRAVE JUNCTION	16:15	43	
FLITWICK	16:25	50	
BEDFORD SOUTH JUNCTION	16:39	58	
BEDFORD	16:42	59	
BEDFORD NORTH JUNCTION	16:44	60	
SHARNBROOK JUNCTION	16:53	66	
WELLINGBOROUGH	17:06	74	
HARROWDEN JUNCTION	17:13	76	
KETTERING	17:21	81	
MARKET HARBOROUGH	17:32	92	
KILBY BRIDGE JUNCTION	17:43	103	
WIGSTON NORTH JUNCTION	17:50–18:34	106	CALLING POINT
LEICESTER SOUTH JUNCTION	18:40	108	
LEICESTER	18:41	109	
LEICESTER 421 SIGNAL	18:42–18:48	109	CALLING POINT
SYSTON SOUTH JUNCTION	18:58	114	
SILEBY JUNCTION	19:02	117	
LOUGHBOROUGH	19:08	121	
RATCLIFFE JUNCTION	19:18	128	
TRENT SOUTH JUNCTION	19:25	129	
TRENT EAST JUNCTION	19:27	130	
MANSFIELD JUNCTION	19:37	135	
NOTTINGHAM	19:40–19:42	136	CALLING POINT
NETHERFIELD JUNCTION	19:47	139	
LOWDHAM	19:54	144	
FISKERTON	20:00	149	
STAYTHORPE LC	20:02	151	

Schedule details for 6V98 Lindsey Oil Refinery–Westerleigh. 7 February 2013

Location	Booked	Miles	
LINDSEY OIL REFINERY	22:32	0	ORIGINATING POINT
ULCEBY	22:47	4	
BROCKLESBY JUNCTION	22:49	5	
BARNETBY	23:05	10	
WRAWBY JUNCTION	23:09	10	
HOLTON-LE-MOOR SB	23:24	18	
WICKENBY	23:44	28	
LANGWORTH	23:51	33	
PELHAM STREET	00:04	39	
LINCOLN	00:05	39	
WEST HOLMES JUNCTION	00:07	40	
BOULTHAM JUNCTION	00:08	40	
NEWARK CROSSING EAST JUNCTION	00:33	54	
NEWARK CROSSING	00:34	54	
NEWARK CASTLE	00:36	55	
STAYTHORPE CROSSING	00:43	57	
FISKERTON	00:46	59	
LOWDHAM	00:53	64	
NETHERFIELD	01:00	69	
NOTTINGHAM	01:06–01:10	72	CALLING POINT
MANSFIELD JUNCTION	01:15	73	
TRENT EAST JUNCTION	01:26	79	
SHEET STORES JUNCTION	01:28	79	
CASTLE DONNINGTON	01:35	83	
STENSON JUNCTION	01:50	92	
NORTH STAFFORD JUNCTION	01:51	92	
CLAY MILLS JUNCTION	01:57	96	
BURTON	02:00	98	
WICHNOR JUNCTION	02:07	104	
TAMWORTH HIGH LEVEL	02:19	111	
KINGSBURY JUNCTION	02:28	117	
WATER ORTON	02:34	121	
WASHWOOD HEATH WEST JUNCTION	02:42	126	
DUDDESTON JUNCTION	02:44	126	
LANDORE STREET JUNCTION	02:48–02:48	127	CALLING POINT
ST ANDREWS JUNCTION	02:51	127	
BORDESLEY JUNCTION	02:53	128	
LIFFORD EAST JUNCTION	03:03	132	
KINGS NORTON	03:05	133	
LONGBRIDGE	03:17	135	
BARNT GREEN	03:23	138	
BROMSGROVE	03:28	141	

Location	Booked	Miles	
STOKE WORKS JUNCTION	03:31	143	
ABBOTSWOOD JUNCTION	03:44	155	
ASHCHURCH	03:56	165	
CHELTENHAM	04:06	173	
GLOUCESTER BARNWOOD JUNCTION	04:14	178	
GLOUCESTER YARD JUNCTION	04:15	179	
STANDISH JUNCTION	04:23	185	
CHARFIELD	04:39	198	
YATE	04:52	205	
WESTERLEIGH OIL TERMINAL	05:05	208	TERMINATING POINT

Schedule details for 6E41 Westerleigh–Lindsey Oil Refinery. 5 February 2013

Location	Booked	Miles	
WESTERLEIGH OIL TERMINAL	11:35	0	ORIGINATING POINT
YATE GPL 607	11:44–11:49	0	CALLING POINT
YATE	11:51	3	
CHARFIELD	11:59	9	
STANDISH JUNCTION	12:12	22	
GLOUCESTER YARD JUNCTION	12:19	28	
GLOUCESTER BARNWOOD JUNCTION	12:20	29	
CHELTENHAM	12:29	35	
ALSTON LEVEL CROSSING	12:33–13:15	36	CALLING POINT
ASHCHURCH	13:25	43	
ABBOTSWOOD JUNCTION	13:35	53	
STOKE WORKS JUNCTION	13:46	65	
BROMSGROVE	13:49	67	
BARNT GREEN	13:55	70	
LONGBRIDGE	13:58	73	
KINGS NORTON	14:03	75	
LIFFORD EAST JUNCTION	14:05	76	
BORDESLEY JUNCTION	14:12	80	
ST ANDREWS JUNCTION	14:14	81	
LANDOR STREET JUNCTION	14:17–14:27	81	CALLING POINT
WASHWOOD HEATH WEST JUNCTION	14:31	82	
CASTLE BROMWICH JUNCTION	14:41	86	
WATER ORTON WEST JUNCTION	14:43	87	
WATER ORTON	14:45	87	
KINGSBURY JUNCTION	14:49	91	
TAMWORTH HIGH LEVEL	14:55	97	
WICHNOR JUNCTION	15:04	104	
BURTON ON TRENT	15:10	110	
CLAY MILLS JUNCTION	15:12	112	
NORTH STAFFORD JUNCTION	15:18	116	
STENSON JUNCTION	15:19	116	
CASTLE DONNINGTON	15:31	125	
SHEET STORES JUNCTION	15:39–15:45	129	CALLING POINT
TRENT EAST JUNCTION	15:48	130	
BEESTON SOUTH JUNCTION	15:53	133	
MANSFIELD JUNCTION	16:05–16:34	135	CALLING POINT
NOTTINGHAM	16:37–16:39	136	CALLING POINT
NETHERFIELD JUNCTION	16:44	139	
LOWDHAM	16:49	144	
FISKERTON	16:55	149	
STAYTHORP	16:57	151	
NEWARK CASTLE	17:02	154	
NEWARK CROSSING	17:03	154	
NEWARK CROSSING EAST JUNCTION	17:04	154	
BOULTHAM JUNCTION	17:28	168	
WEST HOLMES JUNCTION	17:31	169	
PELHAM STREET	17:34	170	

Location	Booked	Miles	
LANGWORTH	17:43	176	
WICKENBY	17:49	180	
HOLTON-LE-MOOR	18:00	190	
WRAWBY JUNCTION	18:13	198	
BARNETBY	18:15	199	
BROCKLESBY JUCNTION	18:23	203	
ULCEBY	18:25	204	
LINDSEY OIL REFINERY	18:35	208	TERMINATING POINT

Schedule details for 6M57 Lindsey Oil Refinery–Kingsbury. 4 February 2014

Location	Booked	Miles	
LINDSEY OIL REFINERY	07:15	0	ORIGINATING POINT
ULCEBY	07:32	4	
BROCKLESBY JUNCTION	07:35	5	
BARNETBY	07:48–07:50	10	CALLING POINT
WRAWBY JUNCTION	07:54	10	
HOLTON-LE-MOOR S.B	08:09	18	
WICKENBY	08:29	28	
LANGWORTH	08:37	33	
PELHAM STREET	08:49	39	
LINCOLN	08:50	39	
WEST HOLMES JUNCTION	08:52	40	
BOULTHAM JUNCTION	08:53	40	
NEWARK CROSSING EAST JUNCTION	09:20	54	
NEWARK CROSSING	09:21	54	
NEWARK CASTLE	09:23	55	
STAYTHORPE CROSSING	09:30	57	
FISKERTON	09:33	59	
LOWDHAM	09:40	64	
NETHERFIELD	09:46	69	
NOTTINGHAM	09:52–09:54	72	CALLING POINT
MANSFIELD JUNCTION	09:58	73	
BEESTON SOUTH JUNCTION	10:03	75	
TRENT EAST JUNCTION	10:10	79	
SHEET STORES JUNCTION	10:12	79	
CASTLE DONNINGTON	10:19	83	
STENSON JUCNTION	10:36–11:00	92	CALLING POINT
NORTH STAFFORD JUNCTION	11:03	93	
CLAY MILLS JUNCTION	11:07	96	
BURTON	11:10	98	
WICHNOR JUNCTION	11:17	104	
ELFORD LOOP	11:25–12:09	107	CALLING POINT
TAMWORTH HIGH LEVEL	12:19	111	
KINGSBURY JUNCTION	12:30–12:31	116	CALLING POINT
KINGSBURY	12:38–12:41	116	CALLING POINT
KINGSBURY OIL SIDINGS	13:11	116	TERMINATING POINT

Schedule details for 6N03 Lindsey Oil Refinery–Jarrow. 6 December 2013

Location	Booked	Miles	
LINDSEY OIL REFINERY	01:13	00	ORIGINATING POINT
ULCEBY	01:26		
BROCKLESBY JUNCTION	01:30		
BARNETBY	01:42		
WRAWBY JUNCTION	01:45		
ELSHAM	01:49		
APPLEBY LEVEL CROSSING	01:57		
SCUNTHORPE	02:10		
CROWLE	02:22		
THORNE JUNCTION	02:33		
HATFIELD & STAINFORTH	02:40		

Location	Booked	Miles	
APPLEHIRST JUNCTION	02:51		
JOAN CROFT JUNCTION	02:53		
TEMPLEHIRST JUNCTION	03:07		
HAMBLETON JUNCTION	03:14		
COLTON JUNCTION	03:25		CALLING POINT
SKELTON JUNCTION	03:44		
TOLLERTON	03:58		
THIRSK	04:18		
LONGLANDS JUNCTION	04:44		
NORTHALLERTON	04:46		
DARLINGTON	05:06		
FERRYHILL SOUTH JUNCTION	05:28		
TURSDALE JUNCTION	05:33		
DURHAM	05:46		
BIRTLEY	06:11		
TYNE YARD (SIGNAL 193)	06:16		CALLING POINT
LOW FELL JUNCTION	06:29		
KING EDWARD BRIDGE SOUTH JCN	06:35		
KING EDWARD BRIDGE EAST JCN	06:36		
GREENSFIELD JUNCTION	06:37		
PARK LANE JUNCTION GATESHEAD	06:40		
PELAW	06:48		
JARROW TERMINAL	07:03		TERMINATING POINT

Schedule details for 6B13 Robeston–Westerleigh. 7 July 2014

Location	Booked	Miles	
ROBESTON	05:00	0	ORIGINATING POINT
HEBRANDSTON JUNCTION	05:10	2	
JOHNSTON	05:19	5	
HAVERFORDWEST	05:30–05:40	10	CALLING POINT
CLARBESTON ROAD	05:57	15	
WHITLAND	06:14	27	
CARMARTHEN JUNCTION	06:33	41	
FERRYSIDE	06:43	47	
KIDWELLY	06:49	51	
PEMBURY & BURYPORT	06:57	57	
LLANELLI	07:03	60	
LLANDIELLO JUNCTION	07:06	62	
MORLIAS JUNCTION	07:16	66	
FELINFRAN	07:45	74	
DYNEVOR JUNCTION	07:53	77	
BRITON FERRY	08:02–08:17	79	CALLING POINT
PORT TALBOT PARKWAY	08:31	82	
MARGAM MOORS JUNCTION	08:29	86	
STORMY	08:42	90	
BRIDGEND	08:48	94	
PONTYCLUN	09:03	104	
MISKIN LOOPS	09:07–09:21	106	
CARDIFF CENTRAL	09:39	115	
MARSHFIELD	09:51	121	
EBBW JUNCTION	09:59	125	
NEWPORT	10:02	126	
MAINDEE WEST JUNCTION	10:03	127	
LLANWERN JUNCTION	10:08	129	
SEVERN TUNNEL JUNCTION	10:29	136	
CHEPSTOW	10:39	143	
LYDNEY	10:51	151	
AWRE JUNCTION	10:57	157	
GLOUCESTER	11:16	171	
HORTON ROAD JUNCTION	11:19	172	
GLOUCESTER YARD JUNCTION	11:21	172	
HARESFIELD LOOP	11:30–11:37	178	CALLING POINT

Location	Booked	Miles	
STANDISH JUNCTION	11:42	179	
CHARFIELD	11:58	192	
YATE	12:09	199	
WESTERLEIGH OIL TERMINAL	12:21	202	TERMINATING POINT

Schedule details for 6B47 Westerleigh–Robeston. 7 July 2014

Location	Booked	Miles	
WESTERLEIGH OIL TERMINAL	18:20	0	ORIGINATING POINT
YATE	18:30	3	
CHARFIELD	18:37	9	
STANDISH JUNCTION	18:50	22	
HARESFIELD LOOP	18:53	23	
GLOUCESTER YARD JUNCTION	19:13	29	
HORTON ROAD JUNCTION	19:14	30	
GLOUCESTER	19:16	30	
AWRE JUNCTION	19:32	45	
LYDNEY	19:37	50	
CHEPSTOW	19:46	58	
SEVERN TUNNEL JUNCTION	19:58	65	
LLANWERN JUNCTION	20:09	72	
MAINDEE EAST JUNCTION	20:15	75	
NEWPORT	20:18	75	
EBBW JUNCTION	20:24	76	
MARSHFIELD	20:32	80	
CARDIFF CENTRAL	20:42	87	
PONTYCLUN	20:55	98	
BRIDGEND	21:06	107	
STORMY	21:12	111	
MARGAM MOORS JUNCTION	21:19	115	
MARGAM TC	21:24–00:03	116	CALLING POINT
MARGAM YARD JUNCTION	00:06	116	
PORT TALBOT PARKWAY	00:08	118	
COURT SART JUNCTION	00:13	123	
DYNEVOR JUNCTION	00:15	124	
FELINFRAN	00:21	127	
MORLAIS JUNCTION	00:40	135	
LLANDEILLO JUNCTION	00:48	139	
LLANELLI	00:50	141	
PEMBURY & BURYPORT	00:54	144	
KIDWELLY	00:59	150	
FERRYSIDE	01:04	154	
CARMARTHEN JUNCTION	01:14	160	
WHITLAND	01:31	174	
CLARBESTON ROAD	01:45	186	
HAVERFORDWEST	01:52–01:54	191	
JOHNSTONE	02:04	196	
HEBRANDSTON JUNCTION	02:09	198	
ROBESTON	02:19	201	

Schedule details for 6V51 Warrington–Portbury. 22 March 2013

Location	Booked	Miles	
WARRINGTON ARPLEY	03:05	0	ORIGINATING POINT
WALTON OLD JUNCTION	03:08	1	
ACTON GRANGE JUNCTION	03:10	2	
WEAVER JUNCTION	03:17	7	
ACTON BRIDGE	03:19	10	
HARTFORD JUNCTION	03:21	12	
WINSFORD	03:28	17	
CREWE COAL YARD	03:38	23	
CREWE SALOP GOODS JUNCTION	03:43	24	
GRESTY LANE	03:47	25	
NANTWICH	03:54	28	
WRENBURY	04:02	33	

Location	Booked	Miles	
PREES	04:13	43	
WEM	04:16	46	
HARLESCOT CROSSING	04:25	54	
SHREWSBURY	04:28	56	
ENGLISH BRIDGE JUNCTION	04:30	57	
SUTTON BRIDGE JUNCTION	04:32	57	
DORRINGTON	04:40	63	
MARSHBROOK LEVEL CROSSING	04:53	72	
CRAVEN ARMS	04:58	76	
BROMFIELD	05:03	81	
WOOFERTON	05:10	88	
LEOMINSTER	05:17	95	
MORETON-ON-LUGG	05:26	103	
SHELWICK JUNCTION	05:34	106	
HEREFORD	05:37–05:39	107	CALLING POINT
TRAM INN	05:49	114	
PONTRIALLIS	05:55	120	
ABERGAVENNY	06:09	131	
LITTLE MILL JUNCTION	06:18	139	
MAINDEE NORTH JUNCTION	06:34	150	
MAINDEE WEST JUNCTION	06:36	150	
NEWPORT	06:38	151	
ALEXANDRA DOCK JUNCTION	06:41–07:45	152	CALLING POINT
NEWPORT	07:51	153	
MAINDEE WEST JUNCTION	07:53	153	
LLANWERN JUNCTION	07:57	155	
SEVERN TUNNEL JUNCTION	08:08	162	
SEVERN TUNNEL WEST JUNCTION	08:09	164	
SEVERN TUNNEL EAST JUNCTION	08:14	169	
PILNING	08:16	170	
PATCHWAY	08:21	173	
FILTON ABBEY WOOD	08:33	175	
NARROWAYS HILL JUNCTION	08:37	177	
DR DAYS JCN	08:42	179	
BRISTOL EAST JUNCTION	08:42	179	
BRISTOL TEMPLE MEADS	08:45–08:48	179	CALLING POINT
BRISTOL WEST JUNCTION	08:50	180	
PARSON STREET	08:53	181	
ASHTON JUNCTION	08:56–09:01	182	CALLING POINT
PORTBURY DOCK STOP BOARD	09:17–09:22	187	
PORTBURY AUTOMOTIVE	09:32	188	TERMINATING POINT

Schedule details for 6V05 Round Oak–Margam. 20 February 2013

Location	Booked	Miles	
ROUND OAK	10:01	0	ORIGINATING POINT
KINGSWINFORD JUNCTION	10:16–10:18	2	CALLING POINT
STOURBRIDGE JUNCTION	10:29	4	
BLAKEDOWN	10:33	8	
KIDDERMINSTER	10:36	11	
HARTLEBURY	10:42	15	
DROITWICH	10:53	20	
DROITWICH SIGNAL 68	10:56	23	
WORCESTER TUNNEL JCN	11:02	25	
WORCESTER YARD	11:07–11:23	26	CALLING POINT
WORCESTER SIGNAL 59	11:26	27	
WORCESTER WYLDS LANE JCN	11:27	27	
NORTON JUNCTION	11:33	30	
ABBOTTSWOOD JUNCTION	11:35	31	
ASCHURCH	11:49–12:07	42	CALLING POINT
CHELTENHAM	12:16	49	
GLOUCESTER BARNWOOD JCN	12:23	54	
HORTON ROAD JUNCTION	12:25–12:29	55	CALLING POINT
GLOUCESTER	12:31	56	
AWRE JUNCTON	12:48	70	

Location	Booked	Miles	
LYDNEY	12:53	75	
CHEPSTOW	13:04	83	
SEVERN TUNNEL JUNCTION	13:16	91	
LLANWERN STEEL WORKS EAST	13:24	95	
LLANWERN EXCHANGE	13:34–14:28	96	CALLING POINT
LLANWERN WEST JUNCTION	14:43	98	
MAINDEE EAST JUNCTION	14:49	100	
NEWPORT	14:51	100	
EBBW JUNCTION	14:54	102	
MARSHFIELD	15:00	105	
CARDIFF CENTRAL	15:18–15:21	112	CALLING POINT
LECKWITH NORTH JUNCTION	15:28	113	
PONTYCLUN	15:39	123	
BRIDGEND	15:55	132	
STORMY	16:01–16:19	136	CALLING POINT
MARGAM MOORS JUNCTION	16:31	140	
MARGAM	16:36	141	TERMINATING POINT

Schedule details for 6B49 Llanwern–Swindon. 21 January 2014

Location	Booked	Miles	
LLANWERN EXCHANGE SIDINGS	08:19	0	ORIGINATING POINT
LLANWERN STEEL WORKS EAST	08:29	1	
SEVERN TUNNEL JUNCTION	08:42	5	
SEVERN TUNNEL WEST JUNCTION	08:41	6	
SEVERN TUNNEL EAST JUNCTION	08:47	11	
PILNING	08:52–09:06	12	CALLING POINT
PATCHWAY	09:17	16	
BRISTOL PARKWAY	09:20	17	
WESTERLEIGH JUNCTION	09:28	22	
CHIPPING SODBURY	09:34–09:46	25	CALLING POINT
HULLAVINGTON	10:03–10:19	35	CALLING POINT
WOOTTON BASSETT JUNCTION	10:39	46	
SWINDON	10:50	52	
SWINDON COCKLEBURY	10:52–10:55	52	CALLING POINT
SWINDON STORES	11:00	53	TERMINATING POINT

Schedule details for 6B50 Swindon–Llanwern. 21 January 2014

Location	Booked	Miles	
SWINDON STORES	15:10	0	ORIGINATING POINT
SWINDON COCKLEBURY	15:15	1	CALLING POINT
SWINDON	15:46	2	
WOOTTON BASSETT JUNCTION	15:53	7	
HULLAVINGTON	16:04	19	
WESTERLEIGH JUNCTION	16:29	31	
BRISTOL PARKWAY	16:35–16:49	36	CALLING POINT
PATCHWAY	16:52	36	
PILNING	16:56	41	
SEVERN TUNNEL EAST JUNCTION	16:57	42	
SEVERN TUNNEL WEST JUNCTION	17:03	47	
SEVERN TUNNEL JUNCTION	17:05	48	
LLANWERN STEEL WORKS EAST	17:13	52	
LLANWERN EXCHANGE	17:23	53	TERMINATING POINT

Schedule details for 6F09 Fiddlers Fy–Liverpool Bk Terminal. 9 February 2013

Location	Booked	Miles	
FIDDLERS FERRY	17:15	0	ORIGINATING POINT
FIDDLERS FERRY SIGNAL BOX	17:19	1	
WARRINGTON ARPLEY JUNCTION	17:27	4	

Location	Booked	Miles	
WARRINGTON LATCHFORD SIDINGS	17:29–17:59	5	CALLING POINT
WARRINGTON ARPLEY JUNCTION	18:02–18:04	6	CALLING POINT
FIDDLERS FERRY SIGNAL BOX	18:14	10	
DITTON EAST JUNCTION	18:23	14	
LIVERPOOL SOUTH PARKWAY	18:31	19	
WAVERTREE JUNCTION	18:39	22	
EDGE HILL SIGNAL BOX	18:41	23	
EDGE HILL DOWN WAPPING	18:45–19:27	23	CALLING POINT
EDGE HILL SIGNAL BOX	19:30	24	
BOOTLE BRANCH JUNCTION	19:31	24	
EDGE LANE JUNCTION	19:33	24	
BOOTLE JUNCTION	19:46	29	
REGENTS ROAD LEVEL CROSSING	19:50–19:52	30	CALLING POINT
LIVERPOOL BULK TERMINAL	20:02	30	TERMINATING POINT

Schedule details for 6V75 09:30 Dee Marsh–Margam TC. 3 June 2013

Location	Booked	Miles	
DEE MARSH	09:30	0	ORIGINATING POINT
DEE MARSH JUNCTION	09:34	1	
PENNYFFORD	09:53	7	
WREXHAM GENERAL	10:06	14	
GOBOWEN	10:20	26	
SHREWSBURY	10:44	44	
ENGLISH BRIDGE JUNCTION	10:45	44	
SUTTON BRIDGE JUNCTION	10:50	45	
DORRINGTON	10:59	50	
MARSHBROOK LEVEL CROSSING	11:15	59	
CRAVEN ARMS	11:20	64	
BROMFIELD	11:26	69	
WOOFERTON	11:33	76	
LEOMINSTER	11:39	83	
MORETON-ON-LUGG	11:50	91	
SHELWICK JUNCTION	11:54	93	
HEREFORD	11:58–12:45	95	CALLING POINT
TRAM INN	12:57	102	
PONTRIALIS	13:03	107	
ABERGAVENNY	13:18	119	
LITTLE MILL JUNCTION	13:27	127	
MAINDEE NORTH JUNCTION	13:48	138	
MAINDEE EAST JUNCTION	13:50	138	
LLANWERN JUNCTION	13:53	140	
LLANWERN EXCHANGE SIDINGS	14:08–15:31	142	CALLING POINT
LLANWERN JUNCTION	15:46	144	
MAINDEE WEST JUNCTION	15:51	146	

Schedule details for 6F96 10:17 Ratcliffe–Warrington Arpley. 19 June 2013

Location	Booked	Miles	
RATCLIFFE	10:17	0	ORIGINATING POINT
TRENT SOUTH JUNCTION	10:20	1	
TRENT EAST JUNCTION	10:22	2	
LONG EATON TOWN LEVEL CROSSING	10:25	2	
TOTON NORTH YARD	10:30–12:14	3	CALLING POINT
LONG EATON TOWN LEVEL CROSSING	12:20	4	
TRENT EAST JUNCTION	12:24	5	
SHEET STORES JUNCTION	12:26	6	
CASTLE DONNINGTON	12:32	10	
STENSON JUNCTION	12:47–13:03	19	CALLING POINT

Location	Booked	Miles	
NORTH STAFFORD JUNCTION	13:05	19	
TUTBURY & HATTON	13:12	25	
UTTOXETER SIGNAL BOX	13:26	33	
CAVERSWALL	13:40	45	
LONGTON	13:44	48	
STOKE JUNCTION	13:50–14:03	49	CALLING POINT
STOKE	14:05–14:07	50	CALLING POINT
KIDSGROVE	14:22	56	
ALSAGER	14:27	59	
BARTHOMLEY JUNCTION	14:32	61	
CREWE SOUTH JN / NORTH STAFFORD	14:38	64	
CREWE	14:43	65	
CREWE COAL YARD	14:46	66	
WINSFORD	14:57	72	
HARTFORD JUNCTION	15:03	77	
ACTON BRIDGE	15:06–15:28	79	
WEAVER JUNCTION	15:33	82	
ACTON GRANGE JUNCTION	15:39	87	
WALTON OLD JUNCTION	15:42	88	
WARRINGTON ARPLEY	15:45	89	TERMINATING POINT

Schedule details for 6H03 10:47 Oakleigh–Tunstead (BLI) Sidings. 18 September 2013

Location	Booked	Miles	
OAKLEIGH SIDINGS	10:47	0	ORIGINATING POINT
HARTFORD EAST JUNCTION	10:57	1	
NORTHWICH	10:59	2	
PLUMLEY WEST SIGNAL BOX	11:02	5	
MOBBERLEY	11:09	11	
HALE	11:13	14	
ALTRINCHAM	11:16	15	
NAVIGATION ROAD	11:18	15	
DEANSGATE JUNCTION	11:19	16	
NORTHENDEN JUNCTION	11:26	20	
HAZEL GROVE HIGH LEVEL JUNCTION	11:40	26	
NEW MILLS SOUTH JUNCTION	11:47	31	
CHINLEY NORTH JUNCTION	11:54	35	
CHINLEY SOUTH JUNCTION	11:56	36	
PEAK FOREST SIGNAL BOX	12:09–12:11	40	CALLING POINT
GREAT ROCKS JUNCTION	12:14	40	
TUNSTEAD BLI SIDINGS	12:20	41	TERMINATING POINT

Schedule details for 6F05 15:19 Tunstead (BLI) Sidings– Oakleigh. 7 January 2013

Location	Booked	Miles	
TUNSTEAD BLI SIDINGS	15:19	0	ORIGINATING POINT
GREAT ROCKS JUNCTION	15:27	1	
PEAK FOREST SIGNAL BOX	15:32–15:34	2	CALLING POINT
CHINLEY SOUTH JUNCTION	15:49	6	
CHINLEY NORTH JUNCTION	15:51	6	
NEW MILLS SOUTH JUNCTION	15:55	10	
HAZEL GROVE HIGH LEVEL JUNCTION	16:03	15	
NORTHENDEN JUNCTION	16:18	22	
DEANSGATE JUNCTION	16:28	26	
NAVIGATION ROAD	16:29	26	
ALTRINCHAM	16:31	26	
HALE	16:32	27	
MOBBERLEY	16:40	31	
PLUMLEY WEST SIGNAL BOX	16:50	37	
NORTHWICH EAST JUNCTION	16:55	39	

Location	Booked	Miles	
NORTHWICH YARD	16:58–19:53	39	CALLING POINT
NORTHWICH	19:56	40	
HARTFORD EAST JUNCTION	20:01	41	
OAKLEIGH SIDINGS	20:08	42	TERMINATING POINT

Schedule details for 1Z58 09:33 Bristol TM–Machen Quarry 'The Taffy Tug'. 25 August 2013

Locaation	Booked
BRISTOL TEMPLE MEADS	09:33
BRISTOL EAST JUNCTION	09:35
DR DAY'S JUNCTION	09:36
NARROWAYS HILL JUNCTION	09:39
FILTON ABBEY WOOD	09:43.5
PATCHWAY	09:45.5
PILNING	09:52–09:53
SEVERN TUNNEL EAST	09:55
SEVERN TUNNEL WEST	10:01
SEVERN TUNNEL JUNCTION	10:02
LLANWERN WEST JUNCTION	10:13
MAINDEE EAST JUNCTION	10:27
MAINDEE WEST JUNCTION	10:29
NEWPORT	10:36
GAER JUNCTION	10:38
PARK JUNCTION	10:41
PARK NORTH JUNCTION	10:43
RISCA SOUTH JUNCTION	10:47
CROSS KEYS	10:53
EBBW VALE PARKWAY	11:13–11:33
CROSS KEYS	11:53
RISCA SOUTH JUNCTION	11:59
PARK NORTH JUNCTION	12:03
PARK JUNCTION	12:05–12:25
MACHEN QUARRY	12:45

Schedule details for 1Z59 13:04 Machen Quarry–Cwmbargoed 'The Taffy Tug'

Location	Booked
MACHEN QUARRY	13:04
PARK JUNCTION	13:24–13:26
EBBW JUNCTION	13:29
MARSHFIELD	13:35
CARDIFF CENTRAL	13:43–13:45
PENARTH CURVE SOUTH JUNCTION	13:49
COGAN JUNCTION	13:55–13:56
PENARTH	14:00–14:19
COGAN JUNCTION	14:25–14:26
PENARTH CURVE SOUTH JUNCTION	14:32
CARDIFF CENTRAL	14:36
CARDIFF QUEEN STREET	14:40
HEATH JUNCTION	14:45
CAERPHILLY	14:55
YSTRAD MYNACH SOUTH	15:09–15:11
CWMBARGOED	15:43–15:45
CWMBARGOED OPENCAST COLLIERY	15:50

Schedule details for 1Z60 16:09 Cwmbargoed–Bristol TM 'The Taffy Tug'

Location	Booked
CWMBARGOED OPEN CAST COLLIERY	16:09
CWMBARGOED	16:19–16:21
YSTRAD MYNACH SOUTH	17:11–17:13

Location	Booked
CAERPHILLY	17:22
HEATH JUNCTION	17:30
CARDIFF QUEEN STREET	17:35
CARDIFF CENTRAL	17:41–17:43
CARDIFF WEST	17:46–18:07
CARDIF CENTRAL	18:10
CARDIFF QUEEN STREET	18:14
HEATH JUNCTION	18:19
CORYTON	18:27–18:47
HEATH JUNCTION	18:55
CARDIFF QUEEN STREET	19:01
CARDIFF CENTRAL	19:05
CARDIFF WEST	19:08–19:27
CARDIFF CENTRAL	19:30–19:32
MARSHFIELD	19:41
EBBW JUNCTION	19:45
NEWPORT	19:49–20:08
MAINDEE WEST JUNCTION	20:10
MAINDEE EAST JUNCTION	20:12
LLANWERN WEST JUNCTION	20:16
SEVERN TUNNEL JUNCTION	20:28
SEVERN TUNNEL UP GOODS LOOP	20:31–20:32
SEVERN TUNNEL WEST	20:34
SEVERN TUNNEL EAST	20:39
PILNING	20:43–20:44
PATCHWAY	20:53
BRISTOL PARKWAY	20:56–21:17
FILTON ABBEY WOOD	21:20
NARROWAYS HILL JUNCTION	21:23
DR DAY'S JUNCTION	21:25
BRISTOL EAST JUNCTION	21:26
BRISTOL TEMPLE MEADS	21:28

Class 60 Pool Codes[9]

COLO   Colas Class 60 locomotives (including Colas Class 66s and 70s)

COLS   Colas Rail-owned Class 60s (stored)

WNTS   General DBS locos. Tactical stored unserviceable

WNWX   General DBS locos. On heavy repair or for heavy repair

WCAI   Industrial Class 60

WCBI   Industrial Class 60. Extended range fuel tanks

WCAK   Construction Class 60

WCBK   Construction Class 60. Extended range fuel tanks fitted

WFMU   DB Schenker-Fleet Management Unit Maintenance Pool CE/TO

Two new Class 60 Pool Codes were created, which were effective from 31 December 2013:

WCAT	DB Schenker Class 60 (TO)	Normal fuel capacity
WCBT	DB Schenker Class 60 (TO)	Extended fuel capacity

Class 60s allocated to WCAT Pool 9 January 2014:

60001 60019 60024 60039 60040 60044 60045 60062 60063 60065 60066 60074 60079 60099 60100

Class 60s allocated to WCBT pool 9 January 2014:

60007 60010 60011 60015 60017 60020 60054 60059 60071 60091 60092

Class 60 pool status on October 2013:9

WCAI	60011 60024 60039 60040 60045 60062 60063 60065 60074 60099
WCAK	60035 60049 60079
WCBI	60007 60010 60015 60017 60054 60059 60091 60092
WCBK	60020 60071
WSSK	60001
WFMU	60019 60100
WNWX	60044 60066
WNTS	60002 60003 60004 60005 60006 60008 60009 60012 60014 60018 60021 60022 60023 60025 60026 60027 60028 60029 60030 60031 60032 60033 60034 60036 60037 60038 60041 60042 60044 60046 60047 60048 60050 60051 60052 60053 60055 60056 60057 60058 60060 60061 60064 60067 60068 60069 60070 60072 60073 60075 60076 60077 60078 60080 60081 60082 60083 60084 60085 60086 60087 60088 60089 60090 60093 60094 60095 60096 60097 60098 60500*

* Re-numbered from 60016

References

The National Archives at Kew pertaining to Class 60 locomotive files under the records of AN 184 series (reproduced with kind permission).

1. AN 184/226 Class 60 locomotive reports
2. AN 184/232 Mirrlees engine
3. AN 184/242 User groups
4. AN 184/247 Contract with Brush
5. AN 184/250 General information
6. AN 184/251 General information
7. AN 184/252 General information
8. www.tugtracker.co.uk Engine and livery data (reproduced with permission)
9. Network Rail TOPS lists (reproduced with permission)
10. Colas Rail UK Super 60 overhaul (reproduced with permission)
11. Former employees of Class 60 technical detail, construction and historical Brush Traction information

Further Reading

Boocock, Colin *Railway Liveries Privatisation 1995–2000* (Ian Allan, ISBN 0-86093-441-1)

Marsden, Colin *25 Years of the Railway Technical Centre* (OPC, ISBN 0-7110-2783-8)

Morrison, Gavin *Power of the Class 60s* (OPC, ISBN 978-0-86093-609-1)

Engineering Consultants – Tendering and Contract

Merz & McLellan
Consulting Engineers
Amberley
Killingworth
Newcastle on Tyne
NE12 0RS

Kennedy Henderson Limited
Consulting Engineers & Economists
Westbrook Mills
Godalming
Surrey GU7 2AJ

Bechtel Limited
Bechtel House
PO Box 739
245 Hammersmith Road
London
W6 8DP

Rendel, Palmer & Tritton
Consulting and Designing Engineers
61 Southwark Street
London SE1 1SA

Index

AC circuit breakers 61
adhesion 16, 44, 45, 107, 160
aggregate workings 103–06
air brake 17, 44, 56, 57, 59, 74
air dryer 57
air reservoir gauge 66
airflow indicator 66
alternator 18, 20, 30, 37, 38, 43,
    45, 52, 55, 58, 61, 162, 165,
    178, 179
ammeter 66, 178
artisan staff training 50
artist impression of the Class
    60 27
'A' Side 32, 61, 76, 134
assets 108, 122, 156, 157
auto brake controller 65
automotive workings 79, 86, 97,
    112, 187
auxiliary engine equipment 57
AVR-controlled three phase
    windings 61
awarding of contract 23
AWS 17, 55, 60, 66, 67, 69, 179,
    181
axle load 53

Bassett Lowke (Class 60 models)
    17, 25, 136
battery box 70, 72
battery chargers 61
Battery Isolation Switch 70, 73
Bechtel Limited 20
bodyshell 12, 30, 31, 34–37, 43,
    70, 113
bodyshell transportation 36
bogie 12, 15, 18, 24, 25, 27, 29,
    30, 32, 38, 39, 42–45, 48, 52,
    57, 59, 61, 66, 74, 75, 85, 88,
    94, 96, 107, 118, 157, 158, 162,
    164, 165, 179
Bonan, B.S. 18
BR (British Rail) 7, 10–23, 25,
    28–30, 32, 35, 39, 40, 42, 43,
    45, 46, 51, 58, 61, 63, 74, 75,
    77–79, 88, 89, 112–17, 132,
    133, 138, 142, 152, 168
brake actuators 74
brake frame 59, 60
Brake Overcharge Button 66
brake pipe 56, 57, 65–67, 74, 129
braking system 31, 56, 45, 56,
    brake type 53
BRB (British Railways Board) 17,
    18, 20, 22, 23, 27, 46, 77
BREL (British Rail Engineering
    Limited) 15, 22, 74
British Steel (60006 & 60033)
    125, 152
British Transport Commission
    21, 63,
Brown Boveri, 18, 19, 57
Brush Electrical Machines Limited
    2, 7, 10, 11, 13–16, 18–25,
    27–43, 45–48, 50, 56, 61, 63,

74, 77, 78, 109, 110, 113, 133,
    136, 142, 146, 151, 152, 155,
    156, 157, 164, 168, 173, 178,
    190
Brush Traction 27, 30, 32, 33, 36,
    37, 39, 41, 61
'B' Side 32, 61, 72, 76
Buchannan, Jim 48
buffers 52, 76, 129
Burkhardt, Ed 152, 157
business specification for the
    Class 60 17

cab design 29, 63
cab heating/ventilation 29
cab instrumentation and controls
    63, 64, 65, 66, 67, 68, 69
cab interior 63, 68, 169
cab mock-up (decorated) 31
cab steps 62, 129
cab switches, 60, 64, 65, 66
cab windows 61, 63, 66, 67, 76,
    129, 132, 137,
camshaft 56, 166
Capelle, Nigel 90, 91, 96, 103
Cardiff Canton 110, 131, 138–42,
    171
cement workings 88
Channon, Paul 17, 23
China clay workings 88, 89, 90
circuit breakers and switches 60,
    61, 165, 178
Class 47s 10, 16, 86, 157
Class 56s 10, 11
Class 58s 11, 12, 15, 23, 63, 139
Class 59s 11, 12, 13, 16, 18, 20,
    23, 63, 85, 104, 157, 159
Class 60 delivery 40
Class 60 design 10–13, 15, 19–25,
    27, 57, 43, 45, 46, 52, 56, 57,
    58, 61, 62, 63, 65, 67, 70, 74,
    75, 78, 111, 112–14, 116, 117,
    119, 121, 132, 143, 145, 156,
    157, 159, 167, 178, 179
Class 60 identification chart 57,
    58
Class 60 in works and on depot
    109
Class 60 official handover
    ceremony brochure 41
Class 60 testing 24, 30, 37–39,
    42, 43, 44, 47, 48, 50, 78, 161
Class 60 timeline 46
Class 66s 13, 70, 79, 86, 87, 94,
    104, 139, 157, 159, 160
Clean Air Compartment 56–60,
    62, 76, 77, 164, 166
coal workings 85, 86, 87
Colas Rail U.K. 62, 84, 102,
    131–32, 153, 154, 169, 170,
    173, 175
Coles, Tony 48
computers for Class 60 testing
    and evaluation 47, 63
connecting rods 127, 178
construction/process 5, 7, 11,
    12, 14, 15, 18, 20–23, 24, 25,

27–34, 36–39, 42–50, 63, 65,
    67, 73, 74, 76, 78, 79, 89, 101,
    110, 133, 138, 153, 156, 190
contract 5, 10, 15, 17, 18, 19–27,
    31, 35, 42, 43, 45, 46, 48–50,
    78, 93, 115, 146–48, 162, 164,
    190
control cubicle 58, 178, 179
converters/choke cubicle 59
coolant 38, 43, 54
cooler group 33, 53, 57, 133, 165,
    178, 179
cooling radiators 76
Cornwell, Martyn 117
Corus Steel (60006 & 60033) 3,
    94, 125
costs (Class 60) 16, 17, 23, 25,
    30, 113
couplings 33, 73, 76
Coxon, Dave 31
'CP' (bogie) 74
crankcase/breather 55, 57, 77,
    178
crankshaft 163, 178
creep control 13, 45, 66, 71, 159

Datacord-6100 (Q-Tron) 65, 68
DB Schenker Rail UK 2, 6, 8, 14,
    51, 79, 81–83, 90, 96–100, 103,
    108, 127–28, 133, 160, 164–67,
    174–77
DC Circuit breakers 60
delivery of the Class 60
    locomotives 5, 18, 19, 21–25,
    27, 28, 35, 39, 40, 42, 43, 45,
    46, 48–50, 78, 117, 146
design (Class 60) 27–30, 32, 34,
    35, 37, 43, 45, 46, 52, 56, 57,
    58, 61–63, 65, 70, 74, 75, 78,
    111, 114, 121, 157, 159, 178,
    179
Deuta Health Monitoring System
    4, 13, 43, 46, 48, 60
development model 28
diagnostic panel 58–60
direct brake 65
door handles 61, 62
Doppler radar 52, 71
Drax (60066) 80, 99, 100,
    130–31
Driver, Colin 20, 42, 48, 152
driver's desk 65, 66, 169
driver's master key 69
driver's seat 63, 64, 69, 166
DSD/vigilance 68, 178
dump blower 58
Dunn, Ken 48

electrical equipment 24, 39, 44,
    61, 52, 178, 179
EMD (Electro Motive Division)
    12, 16, 18, 20, 22, 23, 27, 42,
    77, 157
emergency brake plunger 65
engine (Mirrlees 6MB275RT) 78
engine (Mirrlees 8MB275RT) 20,
    42, 46, 52–56, 58, 77, 78, 178

engine (Mirrlees 8MB275RT)
    measurement diagram 186
engine cross section diagram
    54, 55
engine room 48, 50, 51, 54, 61,
    62, 76, 77, 118, 164, 166
engineers' workings 94, 95, 96
EWS 83–101, 103, 105, 106, 111,
    122–24, 136, 152, 153, 162,
    164, 167, 168, 170, 76
excitation (traction motor/
    wheelslip control) 61, 75
extractor fan 48, 57, 58, 61

fibre optic link, 63
filler/caps 71, 72
fire bell 63
fire protection equipment 20, 61,
    63, 66, 70, 71, 73
firing order of cylinders 54
flexible mount 76
Foster Yeoman 12, 13, 16, 61
Frampton, Mike 48
fuel capacity 52, 189
fuel conservation arm 69
fuel consumption 17
fuel delivery 55
fuel lift pump 57, 178
fuel tank 53–56, 70–72, 138, 189
fuel tank (long range) 53–55,
    70, 138
fuel tank sight glass 72

Garrett, Brian 88, 93, 107, 108
gauges, 64, 157
gear ratio 53
gearboxes 38
GEC Transportation Projects
    Limited 18–23
general details of the Class 60
    52, 53
General Motors 12, 16, 18, 19,
    22, 23, 27, 67, 77, 87, 104
Gleed, Edward 2, 8, 11–14, 16, 37,
    51–53, 58–60, 62–69, 71–77,
    79, 80–82, 84, 86–88, 94,
    96–100, 102, 103, 108, 111,
    119–20, 122–36, 142, 151, 153,
    154, 156, 158, 160–64, 166–68,
    171–77
governor (Woodward) 38, 43,
    52, 55, 56, 57, 166, 178
GPS antennae 76, 77
Great Western Green (60081)
    127, 158
grilles 28, 51, 74, 76, 77, 133
group categories (locomotives
    out of traffic) 161, 162
GRP cab roof/fixings
    arrangements 33, 34
GSM-R equipment 69, 70, 99,
    164
guarantee 19, 26
guide post (suspension) 42, 48,
    74
gypsum/fly ash traffic traffic
    101

handover ceremony 40–42, 46
handrails 61, 76,
Hawker Siddeley 18, 20, 23, 26, 37
hazzard warning 65
Heller, Keith 157
Hill, Dr Stuart 78
Hither Green 44, 119, 138, 139, 143
Hore, Dr 21, 22
hotplate 60, 66, 68
Hutchinson, Roy 35, 107

Immingham 14, 83, 86, 96–99, 110, 138, 139, 140, 141, 142, 146, 149, 153, 180
injector pumps 43, 56
intermodal workings 91, 92, 93
iron ore workings/steel workings 96–100

Jones Garrard 33–35, 114

Kennedy Henderson Limited 20
Knapp, J. 22
Knorr Bremse 164

lamp bracket modifications and differences 35, 36, 37
Leicester 23, 40, 44, 110, 119, 121, 139, 142, 143, 152, 170, 183, 184
Leighton Prado 13, 83
lifting points 61, 70, 71
liquidated damages dispute 26, 45, 46
livery diagram 115
load bank 38
loadhaul 80, 103, 109, 120
loading gauge 39, 157
locomotive contract lessons learned 46
locomotive drawings/diagrams 24, 25, 29, 33, 35, 115
locomotive exterior 70, 71, 72, 73, 74, 75
Lothian, Ian 82, 83, 85, 91, 93, 97, 101, 102, 106, 125, 127
Loughborough, 23, 30, 31, 37, 42, 113, 133, 157, 173, 184
lubricating oil 38, 43, 54, 55, 72, 178
lubricating oil priming pump, 55, 57 178

main rectifier 42, 59, 178, 179
main spares 24, 179
mainline 82, 87–88, 90, 100, 106, 110, 121–22, 156, 163, 164
marker lights 64, 65
McAlpine, Sir William 153, 154
MCBs 165, 166
Merz & Mclellan 18, 20
Metro-Cammell Limited 18, 19, 21, 181

MGR (Merry-Go-Round) 11, 44, 85–87, 121, 125, 146
Mickleover test track 43, 44, 46–48
Mirrlees 18, 20, 21, 31, 37, 42, 46, 52, 53, 58, 77, 78, 161, 178, 190
missile plate 33–35
Mod State (No 17) 78
MOD workings 93
monocoque body 11, 12, 32, 70
Morrison, Brian 34, 40, 90, 93, 104, 105, 120, 154

names (Class 60) 138–80
naming (corrections/proposals) 153, 154
naming ceremonies 152, 154
National Archives 9, 34, 36, 40, 54, 55–57, 115–17, 190
National Radio Network (NRN) 17, 69, 70
National Union of Railwaymen 22
Nederlands Spoorwegen NS 150 (Class 60 cab) 31, 40
NEI Peebles Limited 18
no. 1 end 53, 57, 61, 72, 76, 169
no. 2 end 52, 53, 56, 57, 59–61, 72, 76, 77, 169, 170, 186
numbering (running) 132, 138, 169
official Class 60 brochure 114
oil and derivative workings 80, 81, 82, 83, 84
Old Dalby test track 44, 46, 47
Oliver, B.R. 114
overhaul 9, 13–15, 46, 48, 52, 68, 111, 137, 15–59, 160–66, 172, 175, 190

parking brake, 59, 60, 65, 129, 179
payment 25, 39, 45, 46, 77
pedestal 63, 69
performance 12, 13, 15–22, 24, 30, 42–44, 47, 56, 115, 116
Petrie, W.M.M. 40, 152
Pike, Mark V. 82, 92, 95, 106, 171
pistons 54, 55, 162, 163, 166, 178
pool codes 189–190
power handle 43, 55, 65, 69, 139
priming pump 54, 55, 57, 178
Procor 30, 31, 33–35, 40, 113, 115
proposed Class 60 names and alterations 155

Railtours 107, 108, 109, 110, 146
Railway Technical Centre (RTC) 44, 46, 47, 186
refuse workings 90, 91
Reid, Sir Robert 17–19, 23, 114
Rendel Palmer & Tritton 20
retention tank 32
Roe, Mick 48

rolling rubber ring 42
roof components 76, 77
roof hatches 32, 76, 77
Rotary Isolating Switches 60
Roundel Design Group 25, 28, 29, 58, 112–114
route availability 9, 91
rubber stack secondary suspension 74
Russell, David 48
Ruston (engine) 16, 19

Salem air dryer 57
sanding equipment 38, 66, 69, 74, 75
scavenger fan/pump 61, 77, 166
secondman's seat 63
selector handle 68, 69
Sepex 12, 25, 52, 75
Sephton, Bruce 48
silencer 43, 56, 58, 76, 77, 117, 179
slip rings 52, 61
'slow speed' speedometer 66, 178
snowplough 28, 40, 47, 73, 75, 135, 136, 138, notch, 75
specification 16, 24, 29, 30, 39, 43, 115
Speed Sensor Fitted (SSF) 11, 67
speedometer 45, 64, 66, 67, 178
spillage tank 71
Spin Tube Air Filter (Donaldson) 59, 76, 77
St Blazey 142
steel framework drawings and photographs. 32, 33, 34, 35
Stewarts Lane 138–42
Stretton, John 7, 12, 18, 37–40, 45, 47, 74, 85, 87, 88, 105, 106, 109, 110, 118, 119, 121, 142, 151, 152
sump 54
sunflower indicator 66, 67
'Super 60' refurbishment program 7, 48, 52, 109, 110, 115, 130, 156, 157, 160, 161–72
Super Series Control 16, 75, 159

TATA steel (60099) 83, 111, 126, 135
TDM/socket 12, 28, 73
Teenage Spirit (60074) 104, 107, 129, 134
tenderers 18
tendering process 11, 17, 19, 22, 77
Territorial Army (60040) 94, 130
test points 72
testing and commissioning 41–44
Thornaby, 42, 48, 110, 138, 139, 140, 143
Tidmarsh, John 48
timber traffic 102
Toolan, T. 22

tooling costs 25
TOPS lists 179–89
Toton 12, 14, 42, 46, 48, 100, 109, 110, 124, 125, 127, 129, 134, 138–42, 147, 157, 158, 160–64, 165, 167–171, 173, 174, 179–81, 188
TPWS 67, 68
traction motor 12, 30, 31, 38, 46, 47, 52, 57, 59–61, 69, 75–77, 166, 178, 179, 186
traction motor seals 166
train length button 65
Trainload Coal 85, 89, 102, 107, 108, 109, 109, 112, 118
Trainload Construction 39–40, 44–45, 47, 106, 112, 117, 118
Trainload Distribution, 113
Trainload Freight liveries 116
Trainload General 25, 27–28, 41, 58, 113
Trainload livery plan 115–16
Trainload Metals/Automotive 110, 112, 119
Trainload Petroleum, 47, 93, 105, 112, 119, 135
Transrail 122, 161, 162
Tuffs, J. 90, 94, 95, 109, 121
Tuplin, Richard 7, 92, 94, 97, 104, 126, 151, 152, 153
two-pack paint 113, 114

unbranded (60022) 120
underframe 24, 32, 33, 70, 129, 164

Vaughan, C.J. 19, 23, 24
vestibule 62
vinyl/application 113, 125

Wabtec Rail Group 7, 173
warning horn 8, 27, 29, 35, 64, 65, 76, 127
weight 39, 53, 61, 74
Welsby, J.K. 18, 20, 21, 23
Westbury 13, 94, 101, 105, 110, 111, 143, 171
Westinghouse 31, 53, 56, 179
wheel 15, 39, 44, 46, 52, 74, 107, 118, 121, 157, 179
wheel arrangement 15, 52
wheelslip 15, 16, 45, 66, 71, 75, 159
Whitehouse, J. 87, 89, 100, 101, 106, 121, 122
window blind 63
window demister 63
WIPAC lights/clusters 29
wiring looms 37
Wisconsin 4, 12, 122, 156
wooden mock up 25, 28, 30, 31, 36
Works Variation Order 29
Workshop Overhaul Manual 46